Carmen Boullosa

In Between Brooklyn and Coyoacan

Edited by

María del Mar López-Cabrales

Colorado State University Fort Collins

María R. Matz

University Massachusetts Lowell

Series in Literary Studies

VERNON PRESS

www.vernonpress.com

In the Americas:
Vernon Press
1000 N West Street, Suite 1200
Wilmington, Delaware, 19801
United States

In the rest of the world:
Vernon Press
C/Sancti Espiritu 17,
Malaga, 29006
Spain

Series in Literary Studies

Library of Congress Control Number: 2024933064

ISBN: 979-8-8819-0148-6

Also available: 978-1-64889-907-2 [Hardback]; 979-8-8819-0032-8 [PDF, E-Book]

Cover design by Vernon Press. Image by Antonio Nava / Secretaria de Cultura, CC BY-SA 2.0 https://creativecommons.org/licenses/by-sa/2.0 via Wikimedia Commons

Table of Contents

Acknowledgments

Finalizing this volume was a collaborative effort that was as rewarding for the process as it was for the final product. Ultimately, this project led us to appreciate not only the importance of family and friendship but also the privilege of working with such outstanding authors and colleagues. We would like to express our gratitude to all contributors for their invaluable work and, above all, for their patience with us. We also want to thank the author to whom this volume is dedicated, Carmen Boullosa, for believing in us and graciously sparing time from her busy schedule.

We extend our recognition to those who helped us along the way and whose hard work enriched this project. Our thanks go to Nicolás Kulisheck-López for his diligent efforts in translating a substantial portion of this volume and contributing to the initial proofreading. Additionally, we express our gratitude to Lana Bashir for her assistance in compiling the initial Index.

As we conclude this edited volume, we direct our thoughts to all the authors who have contributed their articles on Carmen Boullosa, acknowledging their essential input to this compilation. Their dedication and erudition have provided valuable perspectives that have significantly enriched our understanding of Boullosa's work and its impact on contemporary literature. To each of them, our sincerest thanks for sharing their knowledge and enhancing this project in such a meaningful way.

Foreword

The idea for this volume emerged from a late evening conversation between two friends who discussed one of Carmen Boullosa's novels. We do not recall the specific novel we discussed, but we concluded that Boullosa's work had not been sufficiently studied in English, hence the reason for our choice of English as the main language throughout this body of work. While there are many interviews with the author, critical works dedicated to her writing are not abundant. This co-edited volume, for the English reader, provides access to a critical analysis of Boullosa's writings. We understand the shortcomings of this volume as we are unable to fully cover all the works done by this prolific writer. An important part of our project was to include Boullosa's voice, who gave us her time for this project in the form of an interview. We are also grateful to one of our contributors, Assia Mohssine, who allowed us to publish an English translation of *"Épica mía/ Mi épica" (My Epic)*, a previously published Spanish essay by Carmen Boullosa[1]. While working on this volume, many things changed; a pandemic deeply impacted our ways of living and, more than ever, history and memory serve as the epicenter of many political discussions.

---

[1] Carmen Boullosa, "Épica mía" was published in Assia Mohssine (coord.) *El heroísmo épico en clave de mujer*. Guadalajara, México, Editorial Universidad de Guadalajara (con el apoyo del CELIS, Cátedra Fernando del Paso y Biblioteca Iberoamericana Octavio Paz), 2019, p. 43-55. This essay was translated from the original text by Abbey Ervin.

Introduction

Born in Mexico City, Carmen Boullosa is one of Latin America's most important contemporary authors. As far back as her editorial debut in 1978 with the poemario *La memoria vacía/Empty Memory*, Boullosa's daily writing has produced an enormous and varied literary corpus that includes narrative, theater, and poetry, in addition to her work in television. In talking about her writings and the many genres that she covers, she explains how "friendship and collaboration led [her] to theater, and motherhood led [her] to the novel" while the act of writing, after the death of her mother, was what helped her "transition from a homeless orphaned girl to a woman of the world" (Bady, "After Before"). As it is almost impossible to constrain her works within a specific literary genre, her writing has a distinctive voice and style that often interweaves history and fiction. Boullosa's corpus needs an involved reader who is at all times aware of the creative process. Her works have been translated into many languages and she has received multiple prestigious awards, including the XIX *Premio Casa de América de Poesía Americana* in 2019 for her collection of poems *La aguja en el pajar*. In 2021, she was awarded the IV *Premio Jorge Ibargüengoitia de Literatura* at the Universidad de Guanajuato, México, for her outstanding work as a novelist. More recently, in 2023 she received the prestigious *José Emilio Pacheco Excellence in Literature Award* that recognizes Mexican writers for their work as a whole. With no doubt, we can affirm that she is an integral figure in Mexican and Latin American literature, providing valuable contributions through her diverse works, unique style, critical acclaim, and broad influence.

Primarily known for her narrative, Boullosa states how she was first a published poet and explained that she "wouldn't have become a novelist if [she] hadn't become a mother." She explains that in her opinion one must be "totally devoted to poetry to be a real poet. You have to give yourself over to poetry" (Bady "The Need"). This statement has not eschewed her from writing a prolific poetical corpus with seventeen collections of poetry. It is interesting to note how her poetry is still lacking an in-depth analysis by the critics in the United States. Lawrence Schimel has translated her collection *Hamartia (o Hacha)* and mentions how some of the poems included share Boullosa's personal history, while others have an almost narrative feeling; also mentioned is the clearly present playfulness with language that is so characteristic in her writing. For Schimel, "Boullosa's poetry spans an eclectic range of aesthetic styles and sociocultural themes, traversing national borders in pursuit of a shared humanity." Her language is, simultaneously, an intimate and collective act as "writing is a corporal act" therefore in her pages, the reader finds "a connection between body, pen, and paper." Her writing forces us to see the connections between the importance of language, interpretation, and personal growth.

With theater as the genre that brought her to novelistic writing, her theatrical production started in 1980 with the play *Vacío/Emptiness*[1]. One that, according to Boullosa, "Fassbinder loved so much that he used one of the scenes in his last film" (Gallo). As Boullosa has expressed on several occasions, theater provided her with a space for a different kind of writing: she has written ten plays, seven of which have been staged. According to Roselyn Constantino, for Boullosa, theater is a "move to discover the multiplicity of unstable identities constituting the *I*." Therefore, in her plays, she creates questions of gender, desire, and sexuality that break down the binary representations that traditionally framed these categories (182). Her involvement with theater includes not only its writing but directing, acting, and collaborations with "well-known artists such as Julio Castillo, Jesusa Rodríguez, Magali Lara and Alejandro Aura" (183).

Regarding her narrative, critics have mentioned that her novels display a different point of view of the Mexican literary tradition, and of the representations of the Mexican experience that, since Octavio Paz, have been seen as an auto-reflexive dialogue. In many of her novels, Boullosa transforms History into fiction as she presents the past while giving a new life to those events that are brought into the present time. Boullosa's prolific writing career has yielded nineteen novels, along with two essay collections, including the co-authored work *A Narco History: How Mexico and the USA Jointly Created the "Mexican Drug War"* (2015) with Mike Wallace. In this last work, both authors examine the intertwined twentieth-century histories of both countries that led to this twenty-first-century problem and suggest how to resolve it. Boullosa's most recent novels are *El libro de Eva/ The Book of Eve* (2020), and *El libro de Ana/Ana's Book* (2016) which she describes as an opium-infused fairy tale. In her writing, it is common to use biographical elements; as for Boullosa, if the artist's personal life and work "are completely separate, in the end, the novel lacks an intimate voice." [2] For instance, the fear of growing up was portrayed in her second novel, *Antes /Before* (1989), both a ghost as well as a coming-of-age story in which the narrator attempts to make sense of her identity, through dreams and memories. Furthermore, according to Jessica Burke, in several of her novels, Boullosa has inserted herself as another character, playing with

---

[1] Alessandra Luiselli analyzes *Vacío in her article "Vacío* de Carmen Boullosa y Sylvia Plath: Performatividad, textualidad y adaptación" within the conceptual framework of salient binaries, including the dichotomies between authorship and adaptation, performance and textuality, as well as the contrasts between repertory and archive productions.
[2] All quotes from Carmen Boullosa are taken from the interview at the end of this volume.

notions of identity and authorship. In this way, "Carmen," "Boullosa" or "la autora" ("the author") are subjected to the "questioning and even ridicule of her own characters and narrators" (113). This cannot take the reader by surprise as "the most intimate space is not reached through one's Voice (capitalized); it is reached through the act of Creation. Voice exists to project oneself, to refer to others. Creation is a different territory." Concurrently, "if an author's personal life becomes too apparent, their voice eats up their own creation" (Boullosa) and, for her, creation is a sacred, fragile thing that needs to be protected.

Her writings invite an in-depth analysis due to their rich complexity and explorations of various themes. [3] In the 1990s, some critics referred to her work as postmodernist, an adjective that brings up not only the pastiche elements present in her writings but the deconstruction of both body and language, creating a fragmented narration full of heteroglossia, intertextuality, metafiction, palimpsest, and parody. Boullosa has never labeled herself as a "model writer," and, using her own words, she describes herself as "untamed." In her eyes, as a writer, she is much more of an animal than an intellectual. Furthermore, she also sees herself as a *grafónoma*, relaying in numerous interviews her daily need to write, which began at the age of fifteen.

By analyzing Boullosa's literary corpus, critics can examine how she reshapes historical narratives and offers thought-provoking perspectives on modern society and its problems. Carmen Boullosa's work has a significant social impact, prompting discussions on the topics of gender, power, history, social inequality, and cultural diversity while encouraging critical thinking and empathy. For example, her novel *Duerme/Sleep* (1994) is a multifaceted narration set in Colonial Mexico. This novel is full of intertextuality and its main character, Claire, is a woman passing as a man who will adopt and abandon several identities to end up eternally sleeping at the border of Mexico City, she ends up with no voice and is unable to be part of History. Boullosa's focus on identity, particularly regarding genre and cultural identity, offers the reader a new perspective on societal norms and power dynamics.

In addition, the use of fragmentation creates a space to reinvent the official truth. Many of her works offer a changing concept of History, shying away from a monolith, unique version of events and instead putting forward a multilayered approach where the reader is presented with different, equally valid voices. As such, the reader must accept all perspectives as equally valid, "thus contesting the grand, totalizing historical narratives of the past" (Burke

---

[3] The Manuscripts and Archives Division of the New York Public Library hold the collection "Carmen Boullosa papers" which includes academic and professional files, correspondence, and publicity materials from 1970-2016. MssCol 2321.

113). This choral approach delivers a new version of the official truth/History upon which each specific work is based. In works such as *Son vacas, somos puercos/They're Cows, We're Pigs* (1991), and *Las paredes hablan/The Walls Speak* (2010), the narrator acts as both the memory of past events as well as the sole surviving participant in them. These historical settings do not serve history itself, as they are neither memoirs nor testimonies. As with many novelists, Boullosa observes the surrounding reality, then subverts it by correcting its flaws and finally reinventing it altogether (Gallo).

Conversely, Boullosa's writings also provide a voice to those whom society has muted. These are concepts that she explores in her included essay, *Épica mía/My Epic*, where she explains how women and their societal roles have been silenced throughout History. Across many novels, Boullosa offers a platform for real and fictional women alike who have been forgotten or mistreated by History, with capital H, empowering them to recount their narratives. In her novels, Boullosa features renowned female protagonists like Cleopatra, Sofonisba de Anguisola, or Ana Karenina -among many others- voices that present the reader with their personal intimate experiences. In *El libro de Eva/The Book of Eve* (2020) for instance, Boullosa provides an account diverging from *Genesis*, granting a new perspective to Eve across this imagined memoir-like narrative. A new version of the story that breaks from the Judeo-Christian patriarchal lens which has echoed for centuries, depicting women merely as a companion and accessory to men. In this novel, with a fictional prologue by Teresa de Avila, according to Boullosa's words, lays Eve's verbal space, her voice (lower-case), telling a story that is retractable by those who hear it because it is not capitalized. Through the pages of this apocryphal manuscript (10 books and 91 passages), the reader realizes that History is only a point of view. Therefore, when marginalized voices find expression, History, which we consider immobile, fractures. From these cracks emerges a very different History than what we were previously able to imagine. By giving voice to these excluded perspectives, Boullosa fractures notions of an ossified historical record and allows alternate histories to develop.

Mostly in Spanish, her artistic production has been the subject of extensive literary criticism due to her innovative narrative techniques and the depth with which she explores complex themes. For the reader who is able to read in Spanish, we would like to point out two compilations of critical essays about her literary corpus: *Acercamientos a Carmen Boullosa* (1999), edited by Barbara Dröscher and Carlos Rincon, and *Pensar en Activo* (2019), coordinated by Assia Mohssine. Across the two volumes, readers can explore multiple critical lenses applied to Boullosa's literary canon. Maria Inés Canto provides in her essay a brief overview of the academic study of Boullosa's writings in the United States. Canto mentions the works of Emily Hind and Assia Mohssine, who describe

Boullosa's postcolonial gaze. Some critics, such as Julio Ortega or Jessica Burke note how the author's complex narrative structures are challenging, and her blending of reality and fantasy is disorienting. Hind explains how "Christopher Dominguez Michael finds [Boullosa's] work both fascinating and irritating, sometimes "within the same book" (32). Yet, these elements are often seen as part of her unique literary voice and contribute significantly to her critical acclaim. Despite the diversity of critical perspectives regarding Boullosa's work, analysis often focuses on her exploration of identity and gender, particularly through strong female characters who challenge traditional norms. Other regularly examined topics are power and history. As such, her works are predominantly analyzed in the context of feminist literary criticism as well as sociopolitical and postcolonial literary criticism. As critics, we need to consider that this focus risks overlooking the full complexity at play across the many layers within her writings.

No literary work is separated from the influences that an author receives. Among these, we have to include the location in which they live. In Boullosa's case, while living in central Brooklyn, New York, which the author uses as a background of one of her novels, *La novela perfecta/The Perfect Novel* (2006), she proudly describes herself as a being from Mexico City and spends extended periods in the neighborhood of Coyoacan. For her, she has "an umbilical cord [with Mexico] that never breaks. […] It is a sense of belonging" (Bady, "The Need")). In her own words, "Mexico [is]: my wound, my strength, my pain, my angst, my origin, my motherland, myself. I live there, I work here (*México: mi herida. Mi fuerza. Mi dolor. Mi ansia. Mi origen. Mi matria. Mi ser. Vivo allá, trabajo acá*)." In several interviews, she has mentioned how she has a romance with both cities, Mexico City and New York City. Brooklyn fascinates her as an almost prototypical city, with people from all over the world living together in proximity. Using Boullosa's words, she does not live in constant motion, but on a constant border. Both cities emerge as a muse in her novels shaping her literary universe. As, for her, in Brooklyn, there is always a border zone between cultures, a border in which all these different cultures coexist. This landscape of diversity shapes her literary imagination and appears in the many perspectives presented in her works, which, as several critics noted, are almost impossible to categorize within a single genre. As Ortega states "cada libro recomienza desde su propio vacío, recortado de cualquier tradición narrativa, recusando su repertorio de pretextos y motivos y volviendo, cada vez, a empezarlo todo de nuevo."[4]

---

[4] Our translation: "Each book restarts from its own void, cut off from any narrative tradition, refusing its repertoire of pretexts and motives and choosing, every time, to start everything anew" (Ortega).

Aligning with Boullosa's view that each work begins from its own creative emptiness, away from any literary tradition or genre constrains and thus manifesting a distinct, one-of-a-kind nature; this volume is structured into three distinct yet interrelated segments. The initial part is composed of six essays that analyze Boullosa's narrative and theatrical works. The first of these essays, by Michael Paul Abeyta, "Voices against Empire: Shifting Borders, Decoloniality, and Deterritorialized Subjects in *La otra mano de Lepanto* and *Texas* by Carmen Boullosa," examines how Carmen Boullosa's *La otra mano de Lepanto/Lepanto's Other Hand* (2005) and *Texas: La Gran Ladronería en el Lejano Norte/Texas: The Great Theft* (2012) depicts the violent expansion of imperial borders in the early formation of both nation-state and empire. In this essay, Abeyta interprets these novels in relation to Walter Mignolo's remapping of knowledge in reference to decoloniality and the decolonial responses implied through resistance. Along the lines of the new Latin American historical novel, following Seymour Menton's characterization (22-23), these novels challenge traditional historiographic mimesis by presenting us with innovative picaresque and collective narrators who undermine traditional imperialist tropes. The use of both historical figures and parodied literary characters, from authors contemporary to the two historical periods, establishes extensive intertextual relations. *La otra mano* reinterprets several works by Cervantes, incorporating both literary and historical figures into its novelistic discourse. The protagonist, María *la bailaora* (Maria, the flamenco dancer), rewrites and undermines the character of Preciosa from the exemplary novel *La gitanilla*. Boullosa deconstructs Cervantes's othering of *Roma* people and transforms the gypsy: she is adopted and trained to fight by Moriscos, she cross-dresses to serve as a sailor and soldier in the Spanish Armada and takes on new names and identities. In the satirical spirit of Mark Twain, *Texas* depicts how the shifting border imposes a reconfiguration and questioning of individual and national identities. The novel pays homage to and reinterprets Twain's anti-imperial and satirical depictions of hypocrisy, racism, and capitalism in the western expansion of the United States during the nineteenth century. Both novels also dialogue with other classic authors from Spain and the United States, such as Quevedo, and Stowe, but Cervantes and Twain are of primary concern in this study.

Emily Hind's essay "Boullosa, Driver's License, and the Energy Gratitude Test" presents an original analysis of Boullosa's work from the perspective of the petroculture (oil culture). The critique of fossil-fuel-reliant infrastructures that Carmen Boullosa launches in her work never actually changes the characters' petro-privileges. Those privileges can be summarized as a "driver's license," or a perspective that Boullosa's narrators tend to operate from even as they deny their comfort with it. To illustrate this point, the chapter incorporates five of Boullosa's fictional works, *Antes /Before* (1989), *Llanto: novelas imposibles/ Crying, Impossible Novels* (1992), *Cielos de la Tierra/Heavens on Earth* (1997), *Treinta años/Leaving Tabasco* (1999), and *El complot de los Románticos/The Plot of the Romantics* (2009), along with the collection of personal essays *Cuando me volví mortal/When I Became Mortal* (2010). Boullosa's narrative tends to channel attention not toward any particular source of energy, but toward an imagined threat to the supreme value of literature, which leads to a kind of intellectual paralysis, or inability to refocus attention from what Joseph Masco calls "the crisis in crisis," a tactic that favors status quo spending over sustainable energy development. The chapter proposes that one method for breaking with this energopolitical complicity and crisis discourse is to reprioritize values like gratitude. In the model of the feminist Bechdel test, the chapter proposes a heuristic for energy attitudes. The *energo-tude* test would range from a crisis of obliviousness toward the fueling source, an *energency* that wastes power, to energetic *gratitude*—the desired *energo-tude*.

Our third essay, "The Decolonial Option in Carmen Boullosa's *Llanto: novelas imposibles*" by Assia Mohssine was originally published in Spanish as "La opción descolonial en *Llanto. Novelas imposibles* de Carmen Boullosa" in *Cuadernos Americanos* 166, México, 2018/4, 133-153. In this essay, Mohssine focuses on Boullosa's novel *Llanto. Novelas imposibles* (1992), where the author undertakes an exercise of rethinking the figure of the Aztec emperor Moctezuma II, based on the epistemic proposal of Walter Mignolo who argues in his essay "Capitalism and geopolitics of knowledge" that the decolonial alternative can only be affirmed in diversity, as critical border thinking. Indeed, the novel privileges local histories in the geopolitics of historical knowledge and incidentally imposes the decolonization of the Indian imagination by inserting, from the outside, its word, even if it is imaginatively recreated. In other words, Boullosa uses the figure of Moctezuma, which the colonial discourse has tried to make negative, to make room for a relegated and subaltern knowledge, and to open a gap in the epistemic hegemony of modernity.

Focusing on Boullosa's theater, Ericka H. Parra Téllez's, "Symbolic Violence: Virgins, Witches, and Cooks in Carmen Boullosa's Dramaturgy," discusses how the desire for material goods and sexual desire is performed in the binary virgin-witch representations. Carmen Boullosa's characters problematize their material and sexual desires within their traditional women's roles; the witches create a man from the traditional role of cooking, while virgins denounce representations of women in media and advertising. Parra Téllez analyzes how Boullosa's theater dismantles the virgin-witch dichotomy by incorporating the perspective of men (the cook), thereby subverting, and expanding restrictive archetypes of womanhood centered around virginity and witchcraft and re-signifying women's role in cultural production. According to Parra Téllez, Carmen Boullosa applies experimental theater techniques to illustrate the connections among media, fantasy, legends, and myths while she recreates stories in which the narrative techniques: parody, irony, the juxtaposition of times, and fragmented structure voice women's concerns in different plays. The parodies were taken from reality to open a discussion regarding women's socially constructed roles. For example, what could have been Virgin Maria's reaction when she learned she would be a mother without experiencing a sexual relationship? Or how do characters deconstruct women's traditional roles when experiencing symbolic domestic acts in media advertising? The ludic representation intertwines reality and desire to subvert Oedipal narratives. The plural voices of the witch, virgin, and cook seek to recount their stories or their desires with postmodern aesthetics. The performance and reading of her works allow viewers and listeners to rethink ways of ending passive and active violence toward women by discussing and inquiring critically about women's roles today.

Maria R. Matz's essay, "*Las paredes hablan*: a Crossroad between Time and Memory," focuses on the novel *Las paredes hablan/The Walls Speak*. This non-chronological narration is located in the neighborhood of San Ángel in Mexico City and is inspired by Elena Garro's novel *Recuerdos del Porvenir/The Memories of the Future* (1963). In a loop of three centuries (1810, 1910, and 2010), Boullosa narrates the History of Mexico while presenting an impossible love-story between the two main characters, Javier and María. In this novel, history, passion, hate, corruption, and the repetition of past errors are what keep memories alive, and the remembrances of the past become the present of the novel. Using the History of Mexico as a fictional element in the story, its narrator is a house, *Casa Espíritu* (*Spirit House*), and its voice is located in a perpetual present, offering the reader an account of how Mexico became an independent country. Matz's essay illustrates how memory comprises a three-dimensional puzzle, with *Casa Espíritu* standing as a metaphor for modern Mexico manifested through the convergence of its multi-layered recollections. More than a mere background setting, the sentient *Casa Espíritu* transcends physical form, its walls embedded with the fragmented memories of a nation. It bears witness to the struggles of Mexico's independence, the complexities of the Mexican Revolution, and the modern violence and corruption that exist in the country. *Casa Espíritu*'s attempt to integrate its memories mirrors Mexico's efforts to synthesize its past into a fluid yet cohesive understanding of itself.

María Inés Canto's essay, "The scar of writing pleasure in *El libro de Ana*," focuses on Ana Karenina's creative writing depicted in *El libro de Ana/Ana's Book* (2016), one of Boullosa's most recent novels. Her analysis explores two thematic axes: Women's writing and pleasure. Canto notes how intellectual and sensual pleasures function as small cracks in a social and economic structure sustained by silence, women's labor, and domestic exploitation. These thematic nuclei have in common the negation gestated in the literary myth of the women who ended up dead or lost their "paradise" when their agency challenged the patriarchal structure. She uses *La ética del placer/The Ethics of Pleasure* (2003) by Mexican philosopher Graciela Hierro, who elaborates a series of principles for women to live and reflect on enjoyment, as a methodological framework. Canto also incorporates the concepts of family and evil developed by Kate Millet in *Sexual Politics* (1970), as well as the critical essay by Audre Lorde, "Uses of the Erotic. The erotic as Power" (1978). Thus, writing and pleasure are revolutionary acts that sustain the intriguing structure of Boullosa's book.

These critical essays are followed by an interview with the author "Una mirada caleidoscópica al mundo de Carmen Boullosa. Entrevista con la autora/A Kaleidoscopic Look at the World of Carmen Boullosa" by María del Mar López-Cabrales and María R. Matz.[5] For Boullosa, Spanish is the language of her childhood, and, for her, each Spanish word is filled not only with emotions, but with memories; this is true even for those words that she is presented with for the first time. For this reason, we decided to also include the Spanish version of this interview for those able to read it. In the English translation, as cherry blossoms allow the reader to appreciate the original words presented in Spanish, Boullosa's voice emerges. Through our conversation, a reflection on the act of writing, her writing style, and her themes, among other topics were discussed. In this interview, while she peels the nuances of her writing, the reader is presented with an intimate reflection on her literary work. Boullosa elucidates how her literary voice has evolved through the years, invoking the metaphor of her use of four differently colored fountain pens to represent changes in her language that is "always simultaneously intimate and collective, [and] has also been touched and altered by time." This multi-pen metaphor emphasizes that her stylistic evolution has arisen not from arbitrary self-reinvention, but through attentively listening to the diverse voices emerging from within.

Boullosa's essay, *Épica mía/My Epic* concludes this volume. We extend an open invitation for self-reflection on whose voices most readily shape our accepted understandings of history. Boullosa's kaleidoscopic works continuously push feminine voices into the forefront. In these pages, the author brings to light these voices, at once intimate and epic, to braid a radical counter-history from the margins. Even more, she reflects on the meaning of the epic narration and presents the reader with a different type of epic: one that

---

[5] This in interview was conducted in Spanish and translated into English.

emerges from a female voice. As she states in this essay, the epic that Boullosa would like for herself "would consist of narrating the frenetic plot of our authoresses, their works and lives, going from one generation to the next – perhaps skipping a few – going from the very well-known, like Teresa of Ávila and Juana of Asbaje, to unknown but great authoresses. [Boullosa] would write, having them as heroines, a founding epic, History, and legend, or perhaps more legend than History, as an epic should be." Hence, "to resize these authoresses would be to change the historical and literary body –the literary canon –, not just the proportions" (135). Boullosa's epic is a narration that puts forth the stories of past silenced heroines/women writers who fought their own battles against marginalization not with the sword, but with their pens. Their often-forgotten words create separate spaces for impressive and heroic events that, otherwise, would have been forgotten.

Works Cited

Bady, Aaron. After Before: El Libro de Carmen Boullosa. *Full Stop. Reviews. Interviews. Marginalia*, 31 December 2016. https://www.fullstop.net/2016/12/31/features/essays/aaronbady/after-before-el-libro-de-carmen-boullosa/
—. "The Need of the Forgotten." *The Nation*, 8 April 2016. https://www.thenation.com/article/archive/the-need-of-the-forgotten/
Boullosa, Carmen. *La aguja en el pajar.* Visor libros. 2019.
—. *Antes*. 1989. Suma de letras, 2001.
—. Carmen Boullosa papers, *Manuscripts and Archives Division*, MssCol 23211 The New York Public Library.
—. *Cielos de la Tierra*. Alfaguara, 1997.
—. *Duerme*. Alfaguara, 1994.
—. *El complot de los Románticos*. Siruela, 2009.
—. *Cuando me volví mortal*. Cal y Arena, 2010.
—. *Hamartia (o Hacha)* Ediciones Hiperión, 2015.
—. *Llanto: Novelas imposibles*. Era, 1992.
—. *El libro de Ana*. Alfaguara, *2016*.
—. *El libro de Eva*. Alfaguara, *2020*.
—. *La memoria vacía. Taller Martin Pescador, 1978.*
—. *La Milagrosa*. Era, 1993.
—. "Mis cadáveres." *Debate Feminista*, vol. 28, pp. 23-50., JSTOR, 2003, https://www.jstor.org/stable/42624768.
—. *La novela perfecta*. Alfaguara, 2006.
—. *La otra mano de Lepanto*. Fondo de Cultura Económica, 2005.
—. *Las paredes hablan. Siruela,* 2010.
—. *Son vacas, somos puercos*. Era, 1991.
—. *Treinta años*. Alfaguara, 1999.
—. *Texas. La Gran Ladronería en el Lejano Norte*. Alfaguara, 2012.

—. "Vacío." *Teatro para la escena*, edited by José Ramón Enríquez. Ediciones El Milagro, 1996, pp. 327-61.

Boullosa, Carmen and Mike Wallace. *A Narco History: How Mexico and the USA Jointly Created the "Mexican Drug War."* OR Books, 2015.

Burke, Jessica. "The Reader and the Text in Carmen Boullosa's Fragmented Narratives." *Teaching the Narrative of Mexicana and Chicana Writers* edited by Elizabeth Coonrod Martínez. MLA Teaching Series, 2020 PP. 112-119.

Dröscher, Barbara and Rincón, Carlos (eds.) *Acercamientos a Carmen Boullosa: Actas Del Simposio "Conjugarse En Infinito - La Escritora Carmen Boullosa."* Verlag Walter Frey, 1999.

Gallo, Rubén. "Carmen Boullosa." *Bomb*, 1 January 2001, https://bombmag azine.org/articles/carmen-boullosa/

Garro, Elena. *Los recuerdos del porvenir. 1963.* Planeta Publishing, 2007.

Cervantes Saavedra, Miguel de. *La gitanilla* in *Obras completas*. Aguilar, 1960.

Constantino, Roselyn. "Carmen Boullosa's Obligingly Heretic Art: New Challenges for Criticism" Latin *American women dramatists: theater, texts, and theories* edited by Catherine Larson and Margarita Vargas, Indiana UP, 1998, pp. 181-201.

Hierro, Graciela. *La ética del placer*. Universidad Nacional Autónoma de México, 2003.

Menton, Seymour. *Latin America's New Historical Novel*. U of Texas P, 1993.

Mignolo, Walter. "Capitalismo y geopolítica del conocimiento," *Modernidades coloniales: otros pasados, historias presentes* edited by Saurabh Dube, Ishita Banerjee-Dube, El Colegio de México-Centro de Estudios de Asia y África, 2004.

Millett, Kate. *Sexual Politics*. E-book, Booksurge, 2000. Kindle Edition.

Mohssine, Assia (coord.) *Pensar en activo. Carmen Boullosa, entre memoria e imaginación*. Universidad Autónoma de Nuevo León, 2019.

Lorde, Audre. "Uses of the Erotic. The Erotic as Power." *Sister Outsider: Essays and Speeches*. Crossing Press, 2012, pp. 53-59.

Luiselli, Alessandra. "*Vacío* de Carmen Boullosa y Sylvia Plath: Performatividad, textualidad y adaptación." *Latin American Theatre Review*, vol. 48 no. 2, 2015, p. 55-70.

Ortega, Julio. *La identidad literaria de Carmen Boullosa*. https://cdigital.uv.mx/bitstream/handle/123456789/7868/2002v10p139.pdf?sequence=1&isAllowed=y

Schimel, Laurence. "Translation Tuesday: Three Poems by Carmen Boullosa." *Asymptote*, 27 October 2020. https://www.asymptotejournal.com/blog/by/lawrence-schimel

Chapter 1

Voices against Empire: Shifting Borders, Decoloniality, and Deterritorialized Subjects in *La otra mano de Lepanto* and *Texas* by Carmen Boullosa

Michael Paul Abeyta

University of Colorado Denver

Abstract: Carmen Boullosa's *La otra mano de Lepanto* (2005) and *Texas: La Gran Ladronería en el Lejano Norte* (2012) depict the violent expansion of imperial borders in the early formation of both nation-states and empires. Each novel highlights the displacement and destruction of local communities, and how these, in turn, resist imperial incursion. In this essay, Abeyta interprets these novels in relation to Walter Mignolo's remapping of knowledge in decoloniality and the decolonial responses implied in the resistance: Boullosa portrays the regional diversity in each novel through multiple narrative voices and perspectives that subvert, burlesque, and deconstruct historical representations that glorify imperial designs or affirm the racial and cultural superiority of any one group. Both novels also dialogue with other classic authors from Spain and the United States, such as Quevedo and Stowe, but Cervantes and Twain are of primary concern in this study.

Keywords: *La otra mano de Lepanto*, *Texas: La Gran Ladronería en el Lejano Norte*, Walter Mignolo, Cervantes, Mark Twain, decolonial, *La gitanilla*, *Exemplary novels*, moriscos

***

Carmen Boullosa's *La otra mano de Lepanto* (2005) and *Texas: La Gran Ladronería en el Lejano Norte* (2012) depict the violent expansion of imperial borders in the early formation of both nation-state and empire. *La otra mano* recounts the displacement of the Moriscos from post-conquest Granada during the consolidation of the Spanish nation in the sixteenth century, while *Texas* focuses on the Cortina Revolts that took place on the Texas-Mexico border eleven years after the conclusion of the Mexican-American war (1846-

48). Each novel highlights the displacement and destruction of local communities, and how these, in turn, resist imperial incursion. In this essay, I interpret these novels in relation to Walter Mignolo's remapping of knowledge in decoloniality and the decolonial responses implied in the resistance: Boullosa portrays the regional diversity in each novel through multiple narrative voices and perspectives that subvert, burlesque and deconstruct historical representations that glorify imperial designs or affirm the racial and cultural superiority of any one group.[1]

Along the lines of the new Latin American historical novel, following Seymour Menton's characterization (22-23), Boullosa's novels challenge traditional historiographic mimesis by presenting us with innovative picaresque and collective narrators who undermine traditional imperialist tropes. The use of both historical figures and parodied literary characters from authors contemporary to the two historical periods establishes extensive intertextual relations. *La otra mano,* for instance, reinterprets several works by Miguel de Cervantes Saavedra, incorporating both literary and historical figures into its novelistic discourse. The protagonist, María *la bailaora* rewrites and undermines the character Preciosa from the exemplary novel *La gitanilla;* Cervantes's portrayal of a young, beautiful, and charming gypsy girl was an imposture as she turns out to be a Christian of "clean blood." In this way, Boullosa deconstructs Cervantes's othering of Roma people and transforms the gypsy girl in different directions: she is trained and is adopted by Moriscos, cross-dresses to serve as a sailor and soldier in the Spanish Armada, and takes on new names and identities. *Texas* includes a well-known historical figure, the rebel Juan Nepomuceno Cortina, as a protagonist, and Mark Twain's character Jim Smiley. This novel pays homage to and parodies Twain's anti-imperial and satirical depictions of hypocrisy, racism, and capitalism in the western expansion of the United States during the nineteenth century. Both novels also dialogue with other classic authors from Spain and the United States, such as Francisco de Quevedo and Harriet Beecher Stowe, but Cervantes and Twain are of primary concern in this study.

The protagonists María *la bailaora* and Nepomuceno are forced to uproot and rebel; in this sense, they become deterritorialized subjects as a direct result of imperial expansion. Elizabeth Montes Garcés interprets the character María as a nomad, pointing out that as she begins to negotiate "las fronteras entre lo árabe y lo cristiano, lo masculino y lo femenino, la oralidad y la escritura, y el oriente y el occidente (the borders between both the Muslim and Christian

---

[1] We will discuss further Walter Mignolo's epistemological argument for decoloniality as laid out in *The Darker Side of Modernity* and its relevance for Boullosa's novels at the end of the introduction to this article.

worlds, the masculine and the feminine, orality and writing, and the East and the West)," she reconstructs herself little by little as a "nomadic subject." Following this concept in Rosi Braidotti's *Sujetos nómadas (Nomadic Subjects)*, Montes Garcés argues that María subverts accepted norms of behavior and retakes power and ownership of her body through the manipulation of her body image (no pag.).[2] María witnesses first-hand the repression and expulsion of the Moriscos and gypsies, as well as their defenses against the imposition of Christianity and the Spanish monarchy. Forced to flee after her father Gerardo is arrested, she is trained to fight by a morisco family and entrusted with a mission to take an apocryphal silver book to Cyprus in a ploy to legitimize the presence of the Moriscos in Spain; this effort reflects the historical failure of the "Libros plúmbeos of Sacromonte (*Lead Books of Sacromonte)*," which were likely created in a futile effort to legitimize the Moriscos' presence in the Catholic history of Spain (Pohl 181, *La otra mano* 132). María never completes the quest, and the novel follows several deviations that lead her to captivity in Algiers, from there to Naples, Italy, and then to the Battle of Lepanto, where she temporarily switches sides in the conflict between two empires, the Spanish and the Ottoman, and their respective religions, Christianity and Islam. When she travels to Naples, she falls for Jerónimo de Aguilar and dresses as a male sailor to follow him as he joins the armada that sets out to destroy the Ottoman fleet. Thus, she joins a vast naval war machine that takes her closer to Cyprus but that also shifts her allegiance. She loses sight of her goal, only to be killed by a former ally at the precise moment she remembers to take up her quest once more.

In the case of Nepomuceno in *Texas*, his nomadism largely takes place after the events that Boullosa depicts in the novel, and he does not appear to have any fixed allegiance to either Mexico or the United States. In a paratext, "Nota del autor (author's note)," Boullosa lists some well-known historical deeds: his several imprisonments and escapes from prison, his raising a small army to fight the Confederacy in the U.S. Civil War, and his allegiance with Benito Juárez. In terms of this study, Nepomuceno and María are interesting as deterritorialized subjects in two ways: they are both uprooted and forced to flee through imperial expansion and settler capitalism (their lands and wealth are taken by force) and along with the shifting borders, they both have indeterminate or wavering allegiances to different groups and causes due to the fluidity of their identities or how they are perceived by others. Nepomuceno's revolt, for example, is suppressed on both sides of the border; he is arrested by the Mexican government. Each character faces permanent exile: ultimately, their missions fail in part because there is no longer a home to

---

[2] See also Braidotti 33.

go back to for either of them. The geopolitical histories of each locality, of Granada and the border region of Texas between the Nueces River and the Río Bravo, tell of immense and violent displacement and dispossession, of deliberate imperial efforts to permanently transform these regions. In both novels, there are layered representations of expulsions, namely, of Jews, Moriscos, early Christians, indigenous Iberians in Granada, and several indigenous groups of Texas and Northern Mexico, as well as African slaves. The novels' treatment of these historical purges can be described, following Mary Louise Pratt's formulation, as a decolonizing operation; each story of failed rebellion encompasses not only resistance against imperial expansion but also the distortion of identity that provokes the characters to "define themselves in opposition to the constructs of otherness thrust upon them by imperialist forces" (465, 475).

Several critics have commented on the postcolonial standpoint in Boullosa's novels in general, but I propose that her novels, *La otra mano* and *Texas*, are better described within the theoretical frame of coloniality/decoloniality precisely because they deal explicitly with imperial expansion as well as imperial and colonial difference. Moreover, as Pratt points out, the prefix "post" in 'postcolonial' suggests to some degree that "colonialism and Euro-imperialism are behind us, no longer important determinants of the contemporary world" (460). Indeed, Boullosa's writing accomplishes a reappraisal of history that exposes and contests Latin America's permanent state of *coloniality*, a condition that best defines the transhistorical expansion and the perpetuation of colonialism's effects in contemporary times (Estrada 146, Moraña et al, 2). To understand the two-fold decolonial responses present in Boullosa's novels, how they pertain to the earlier imperial expansions, and how these are still relevant to contemporary Latin America, it behooves us to examine Mignolo's epistemological argument for the notion of decoloniality in *The Darker Side of Modernity*.[3] As Mignolo has pointed out previously, modernity is inseparable from coloniality, a concept he borrows from Aníbal Quijano's discussion of the relationship between "la estructura colonial de poder (colonial power structure)" and the production of knowledge, which created forms of social discrimination that were codified in terms of race, ethnicity, and nation, but also in terms of gender and sexuality.[4] Guided by this general idea, Mignolo elaborates on the coloniality/modernity complex in the production of knowledge as a zero point epistemology (borrowing from the

---

[3] For a discussion of Boullosa's novel *Duerme* along similar lines in relation to Mignolo's rereading of modernity in the New World, see Juli A. Kroll, 106-107.

[4] For the parallel relationship between colonialism and the complex of rationality /modernity, see Quijano, 437-443.

Colombian philosopher Santiago Castro-Gómez), a kind of hubris of knowledge that is the "ultimate grounding of knowledge, which paradoxically is ungrounded, or grounded in neither geo-historical location nor in biographical configurations of the body" (80). The pretension of universality in European epistemology hides "its own local knowledge," but also casts back in time as undeveloped or inferior every "way of knowing and sensing" that does not conform to western epistemology: "the zero point is the site of observation from which the epistemic colonial differences and the epistemic imperial differences are mapped out" (80). For Mignolo, "the first step in decolonial thinking is to accept the interconnection between geohistory and epistemology, and between biography and epistemology that has been kept hidden by linear global thinking and the hubris of the zero-point in their making of colonial and imperial differences" (91). A further step is to "de-link" from western epistemological assumptions about "truth" and "objectivity" by placing parentheses around enunciated facts and to place more emphasis on the who and where of enunciation. Mignolo gives a particularly interesting example of de-linking when he discusses Descartes's maxim "I think, therefore I am" as an example of zero-point epistemology. In its place, he proposes "I am where I think," which evolves to "I am where I do." This spatializes and grounds knowledge and experience in concrete and specific contexts that legitimize the "geo-historical locations and bio-graphic stories that were delegitimized" (xxiii). With respect to decoloniality, being where one thinks has become "a fundamental concern of those who have been mapped out by the colonial and imperial differences and, therefore relegated to a second or third place in the global epistemic order" (80).

These differences are crucial in that they describe well the exclusions and prejudices that Boullosa explores in the two novels: in *La otra mano* the imperial differences have to do with the struggle between the Christian Spanish empire and the Muslim Ottoman empire, and the allegiances characters and communities have to each other; in *Texas*, imperial and colonial differences are propagated in the territorial expansion of the United States through its settlers and the imposition of new laws, as well as through the delegitimation of the Mexican and First Peoples of the region, their laws, cultural practices, and their relation to the land. The imperial and colonial differences impose a hierarchy with real-world consequences, and these appear in the racial prejudices that drive much of the violence in the novel.

Decolonial Responses in *La otra mano de Lepanto*

To frame the discussion of imperial differences and the decolonial gestures made by both the characters and the author, I will examine each novel with respect to such decolonial operations of delinking and of the self-appellation of deterritorialized subject positions following the maxims "I think where I am" and "I think where I do." In the first part of *La otra mano,* when we are introduced to María la Bailaora, Boullosa presents us with the story of her father Gerardo's arrest and expulsion. In both cases, María and Gerardo are described with regard to what they do, but it is his arrest that puts into stark relief the immense cruelty of the expulsions of people who became classified as outsiders even though they were native to Granada. Gerardo is arrested, then subsequently mutilated and converted into a galley slave because he disobeyed "las ordenanzas reales concernientes a 'los egipcianos y caldereros extranjeros' (the royal ordinances concerning 'foreign Egyptian and coppersmith gypsies')." The narrator includes his spoken response and thought process that question this *othering* classification as an outsider, as a foreigner:

> ("¿pues yo por qué he de obedecérselas?"), replicó cuando le vinieron a echar en las narices el bando público antes de tomarlo preso, "si yo no sé qué es eso de ser extranjero; a mucho orgullo soy gitano de Granada, mucho lo tomo en precio, ésta es mi tierra, aquí nacieron mis padres y aquí también mis abuelos, que si camino repetido fuera de esta ciudad, es para salir a mercar caballos, pero siempre vuelvo; yo me muevo cuando a bien me venga en gana; nadie me dice a mí ni te vas ni te quedas, que yo soy gitano y soy de Granada (33-34).[5]

The reiterated self-appellation expressing pride in being a gypsy from Granada can be interpreted as a two-fold decolonial response. On one level, the character resists his classification as an outsider, rejecting the imperial difference imposed upon him; by being called an Egyptian he is associated with eastern religion despite being a Christian –he is orientalized. Even though he is nicknamed "el duque del pequeño Egipto (the Duke of Little Egypt)" for his prowess as a horse trader and association with the Moriscos, he insists on his identity as a Granadan. He rejects the imperial difference even after his ears are cut off: "El padre de María la bailaora no gritó, no salió una queja de su boca, se tragó su dolor, sabiendo lo podría estar viendo su hija, e insistía: ¡No me llamen egipciano! Soy gitano de Granada, aquí nací, soy cristiano, mis padres eran lo mismo, me bautizaron al nacer, pago mi diezmo como lo pagaron ellos

---

[5] ("And why should I have to obey it?"), he replied when they came to wave the public decree in his face before arresting him, "I don't even know what it means to be a foreigner. I'm a Gypsy from Granada and I'm very proud of it. I value it highly. This is my land; my parents were born here and so were my grandparents. If I travel repeatedly outside this city, it's just to go buy horses, but I always come back. I move around when I feel like it; nobody tells me either you go or you stay, because I'm a Gypsy and I'm from Granada.

y mis abuelos'" (38-39).[6] His insistence on his Christianity through his baptism and the payment of church tithes proves futile: the imperial difference is marked in his flesh.

Gerardo's mutilation by decree is also worthy of study because the graphic description and staging that Boullosa offers bring into stark relief the injustice of it, much in the same way that testimonial literature inspires indignation and judgment in the reader. As Gerardo's rejection of this othering is a decolonial response to an imperial imposition, Boullosa's narration of his torment is also a decolonial and epistemically disobedient act against the tendency to glorify the civilizing postures implicit in western Christianity's "reconquest" of the Iberian Peninsula. Indeed, the notion of the *Reconquista* has been questioned in recent decades as a misrepresentation of Spanish history (the implication being that Spain was always Christian before the Moors came and that it always should be Christian). Gerardo's mutilation also represents the Spanish empire's campaign to eradicate cultural differences by erasing any notion of the beauty and splendor of the Andalusian communities in the sixteenth century. The description of his handsomeness, he is given the epithet "el bello Gerardo (Gerardo, the handsome)," and the luxuriant descriptions of the exquisite taste, dress, and beauty of the Moriscas María befriends are juxtaposed with the dangers the Moriscas face, such as rape during the purge and slaughter in the depiction of the siege of Galera. The manifestations of beauty, as well as María's dancing, function as territorial representations; they denote a symbolic attachment and affiliation to the earth, to Andalucía.[7] They can appear as an inscription on the skin, henna, or tattooing, but can also be expressed through dress and dance. The opulence and sumptuousness of Farag's home and the Moriscas' clothing also contrast the harsh, austere ambiance of the convent in which María had previously taken refuge.

The build-up of Gerardo's and María's beauty makes his mutilation by royal decree all the more horrific. While this public mutilation may recall Michel Foucault's discussion of public torture in the Middle Ages as a representation of the physical presence of the king's authority in *Discipline and Punish*, we read it here in the broader terms of what Gilles Deleuze and Félix Guattari called imperial representation. The territorial signs, namely the dress and

---

[6] María the dancer's father did not shout, no complaint came out of his mouth, he swallowed his pain, knowing his daughter could be watching what was happening. And he kept insisting: "Don't call me Egyptian! I'm a Gypsy from Granada, I was born here, I'm Christian, my parents were the same, I was baptized at birth, I pay my tithes just as they did and just as my grandparents did.

[7] The terms "territorial representation" and "deterritorialized subjects" derive from Gilles Deleuze and Félix Guattari's *Anti-Oedipus*. See in particular pp. 184-217.

beauty associated with morisco and gypsy culture, are substituted with imposed abstractions, "egipcianos y calderas extranjeras (foreign Egyptian and coppersmith gypsies)," that erase the specificity and splendor of local difference. Thus, the deterritorialization occurs not simply in the physical expulsion and enslavement that Gerardo suffers, imperial difference is also marked in the flesh. In this deeper sense, Gerardo becomes a deterritorialized subject through this forced erasure, this effacing of his beauty and dignity; and yet he inwardly persists in his insistence on being a gypsy from Granada.

This is an imperial representation at its darkest, and Boullosa brings it fully to light to undermine any civilizing pretense of Spanish imperialism, of western civilization and modernity founded in slavery. This is also very stark in comparison with Cervantes's depiction of Ricote, Sancho Panza's morisco neighbor, who gives an apologetic justification for the expulsion. Burkhard Pohl describes the ambivalent and at times stereotyping of Muslims in Cervantes's *Exemplary Novels*, despite the positive image one can occasionally find (such as that of Ricote), whereas in *La otra mano* the tables are turned: when faced with secondary characters who exalt religion, triumphant Christianity in particular, María responds with skepticism and religious indifference (179-80). Indeed, María's religious ambivalence and use of disguises are reminiscent of Ricote's shallow convictions and his clandestine cover as a foreign pilgrim. Despite his own claim to be Christian, Gerardo is cut loose from the forms of representation that associate him with Granada, while in contrast, María, through dancing, but also with the sword inscribed with *aljamia* lettering and the apocryphal silver books, carries these symbolic items with her and is able to adapt her appearance to whatever social milieu she moves in. The contrast is significant because Gerardo, stripped of any exterior manifestation of his origin, maintains a visceral attachment to his identity as a Granadan gypsy, while María is more fluid in her identity and outward appearance. Moreover, his awareness of how he will be perceived by his daughter intensifies the pain of imperial and colonial differences, the experience of coloniality and exile. Later, toward the end of the second part when María is in Naples, Gerardo, having paid his own ransom, is free and sees María, but does not approach her. He has changed; he is no longer "el hermoso Gerardo" and feels shame at his mutilation and exile: "Gerardo se esconde atrás de un árbol cercano, imantado por la belleza y frescura de María. Debería presentarse y decir: 'Yo soy Gerardo, yo fui el duque del pequeño Egipto, yo soy el gitano de Granada, yo soy tu padre, hermosa María,' pero le parece fuera de toda posible consideración. La pura idea de hacerlo le repugna" (247).[8] The narrator negates the idea that this repugnance originates in his consciousness because his mind is twisted from his mutilation and years of suffering as a galley slave, and states that Gerardo "rechaza la idea con las vísceras (he rejects the idea with his gut)" (247). Mignolo also emphasizes that many non-western cultures' "way of knowing and sensing" centers in the heart and organs in contrast to the cerebral focus of western rationality. Although his will is largely broken, Gerardo still maintains a visceral conscience of his identity as a gypsy from Granada. This image of him spying on María is key because it happens when she, María *la bailaora* de Granada, begins to assimilate to an imperial sameness. She pines for Jerónimo de Áquilar and begins to falter in her mission to legitimize the Moors of Granada by traveling to Cyprus to bury the apocryphal book. She dreams of marriage with a Christian man of rank. By following Jerónimo, and changing her appearance, she is led to Lepanto where she uses the swordsman skills she learned from the Morisco Yusuf to kill dozens of Muslim Turks. After the battle, she feels ashamed for having killed so many Muslims.

Pohl accurately describes María in contrast to Cervantes's Preciosa-Constanza in a succinct manner: instead of a Christian damsel disguised as a gypsy, María is a woman in disguise who represents the very fluidity of identity: "el personaje de María y sus experiencias transculturales cuestionan las identidades prescritas que tanto importan en el discurso binario colonial (María's character and her cross-cultural experiences question the rigid identities imposed in colonial binary discourse)" (178). At the end of the novel, Boullosa introduces the burlesqued character Saavedra, Miguel de Cervantes, and has María charge him with telling her story, a supposed inspiration for *La gitanilla*. According to Pohl, the story she wants Cervantes to tell suppresses her adventure as a spy-sailor-soldier, limits her life story to Granada, and demonstrates the grim consequences of her exile and the racism she suffered: "si me desgitanizo es porque si mi padre hubiese sido idéntico a quien era pero no gitano, no lo habrían tomado preso los guardas, ni lo habrían desorejado, apaleado y atado a una cadena" (420). [9] Pohl rightly concludes that María chooses assimilation to the predominant culture in order to survive (178). When she recovers her desire to complete the mission to help save the Moriscos of Granada, she waivers as she fantasizes about the future: "Que, ya entregado

---

[8] Gerardo hides behind a nearby tree, drawn in by María 's beauty and youthfulness. He should introduce himself and say: "I am Gerardo, I was the Duke of Little Egypt, I am the Gypsy of Granada, I am your father, beautiful María," but it seems beyond any possible consideration to him. The very idea of doing so repulses him.

[9] If I cease to be a Gypsy, it will be because if my father had been the same person but not a Gypsy, the guards would never have imprisoned him, mutilated his ears, beaten him mercilessly, and shackled him in chains.

el libro, dónde se irá a vivir, que si una ciudad flamenca; . . . que si vivirá en su propio palacio, . . . fantaseándose, María juega a ser su propia hacedora. . . Grita en silencio; "¡Soy de Granada, soy María la bailaora!" (424).[10] In the moment she begins to truly imagine a future she designs, she is assassinated by Zaida who is unhinged with hatred for María's betrayal. While for María there is no going back to Granada, Gerardo never loses his desire to return to his daughter. The news of her death kills him. The narrator gives an alternative obituary that imagines what life would have been without his expulsion: "que nadie lo hubiera echado de Granada, . . . que no hubiera perdido a su mujer, fallecida de tristezas por las persecuciones de que eran objeto. Que su hija no hubiera corrido con la suerte de ser criada en un convento, ni cautiva en Argel, . . . ni mucho menos guerrera de Lepanto" (429).[11] This alternate history highlights what he has lost personally, but also his importance as a victim of dispossession and imperial expansion.

Decolonial Responses in *Texas: La Gran Ladronería en el Lejano Norte*

In *Texas*, Boullosa confronts the imperial expansion of the United States and settler capitalism in her depiction of the events around the Cortina revolt. The novel begins with a brief description of the history and geography of the Texas border, which is followed by a broad, almost mural-like depiction of the diverse communities in the area and their responses to the report of an event, a conflict between the white Sheriff of Bruneville and a legendary Mexican rancher. The first seventy pages of the "Primera parte (First part)" follow the spread of the rumor of this conflict, and the reiteration of the offensive phrase Sheriff Shears made at Nepomuceno's expense, spitting four words: "Ya cállate, grasiento pelado. Las dice en inglés, menos la última, *Shut up, greaser pelado* ("Shut up, you dirty greaser." He says the words in English, all but the last word, "Shut up, greaser pelado.")" (17).[12] The technique is reminiscent of Twain's satirical short story "The Man that Corrupted Hadleyburg" (1899). Like the "remark" in Twain's story, "la frase (the sentence)" is repeated, allowing Boullosa to exhibit the multiple perspectives and interests of the different members of the community in their responses to the insult. Many give varying opinions regarding the character of both men, though the narrator and the community

---

[10] With the book now turned in, where shall she live? Perhaps a Flemish city...or maybe she'll live in her own palace...as she daydreams about being the author of her own story... She screams voicelessly: "I am from Granada - I am María , the flamenco dancer."

[11] That no one would have expelled him from Granada, ...that he would not have lost his wife, who died of sadness due to the persecution they suffered. That his daughter would not have endured the fate of being raised in a convent, nor held captive in Algiers, ...and much less been a warrior in the Battle of Lepanto.

[12] Translations from *Texas the Great Thief* are taken from the English translation of this book by Samantha Schnee.

generally do not have high opinions of the Sheriff. The opinions and judgments of Nepomuceno oscillate between those, mainly Mexican Tejanos but also members of many groups, who know him as "don Nepomuceno," respecting him as a handsome and capable rancher, and those, mainly racist Anglo Texans, who view him as a bandit and thief, and stereotype him. The diversity of the community and the wide variety of opinions have a decisive leveling effect: the opinions of Mexicans, Mexican Tejanos, Jewish and German immigrants, black ex-slaves, and the different Indigenous groups in the area carry the same weight as the white characters. The plethora of different voices gives the narration a deep authority notwithstanding the clearly partisan tone of the narrator.

When Nepomuceno finally speaks as a character, it is in response to one of the accusations he hears from the Jewish immigrant, Glevack, that he is a horse thief. His response is a tirade that rejects the accusation, and in a combative tone fulfills a similar decolonial response to the self-appellations of Gerardo and María. He turns the accusation back on the Anglo settlers who stole Texas from Mexico, but more importantly from the local community of Mexicans:

> ¡Ladrón de caballos, yo! ¡Se atrevan a decirme *a mí*, Nepomuceno, que soy ladrón de ganado! ¡Cuántas cabezas no arrebataron *a mí* los recién venidos, los que se creen mucho porque hicieron la República Independiente de Texas! . . . luego los yankees que nos vinieron a pegar con eso de la anexión, convencidos de que aquí había negocio rápido – arrebatarnos tierras, ganado, minas–, por no hablar de que luego nos comerían del Río Nueces hasta el Río Bravo –¡nos birlaron el territorio! porque bien mirado, ¿cuál compra? ¿cuál guerra?, por más que le den a la hilacha fue hurto–. Yo soy el último de la lista a quien pueden ir a colgarle ese sambenito. (118)[13]

Nepomuceno positions himself as judge of the invaders, turning the accusation of theft onto the Anglo settlers while simultaneously articulating a collective "us" ("nos") rooted in a local sense of belonging. The decoloniality here is the non-acceptance of the incursion, and the affirmation of the knowledge of the land, promoting a use-based approach in harmony and reciprocity with nature,

---

[13] Me, a cattle thief! How dare they accuse me, Nepomuceno, of stealing livestock! How many heads have these newcomers stolen from me, folks who think they're important because they "created" the Independent Republic of Texas! . . . And after they annexed our land, the Yankees showed up, thinking there were easy picking here -stealing our land, our livestock, our mines -they took over everything from the Nueces River to the Rio Bravo! Because let's call a spade a spade: they didn't buy it, they didn't fight for it. When all is said and done it was a theft, pure and simple. And I'm the very last person who could be accused of such a thing.

that presents itself as an anterior and, therefore, a more legitimate order of things. He dismisses the new laws imposed by the Texans and the "Yankees," which are based on capitalist notions of property and accumulation:

> . . . mire: una cosa es levantar las piezas sueltas que se encuentra uno en la corrida, echar mano del ganado nanita, se da por hecho que es un recambio porque uno deja algunas propias rezagadas en el camino, no hay cómo no, es un cambalache natural. A fin de cuentas, el llano es quien alimenta a los animales, al llano pertenecen, y el que sea bueno con el lazo tiene el derecho de llevárselos, si sabe que contribuye a la siembra de cabezas. Ése era el orden, antes que llegaran éstos y pusieran sus leyes muy como les plazca. A la brava, pues. Yo vaya que he contribuido mucho a la siembra de nanita y pastos. ¿Y quieren plantarme *a mí* el conque de que soy *ladrón de ganado?* . . . ¡Ladrones ellos y los procuradores de sus injusticias! (119)[14]

This rationale and sentiment regarding the conflict around cattle-rustling are well known, and here Boullosa, through Nepomuceno, describes well the ethos of the vaqueros of the northern Mexican frontier. As Friederich Katz pointed out in his monumental *The Life & Times of Pancho Villa*, cattle-rustling in Chihuahua (and all along the northern border) was met with widespread social approval because "for nearly two centuries, the public lands of the state had been an open range, where wild cattle could be hunted and killed or appropriated by anyone willing to make the effort." He goes on to explain that Villa rebelled against the efforts of the hacendados of Chihuahua to appropriate both the open range and the cattle, a similar phenomenon to what happened north of the border a few decades earlier. For the Mexican ranchers of Chihuahua, "stealing cattle from these hacendados was thus viewed, not as a crime, but rather as the restoration of traditional rights" (70). The indignation in Nepomuceno's tirade expresses his condemnatory decoloniality and reflects the tone of the narrator and the author's decolonial response. Nonetheless, he is considered a bandit by the white Texans before the outbreak of violence resulting from the Sheriff's brutal attack on Lázaro. While Boullosa's depiction

---

[14] You see, it's one thing to hustle the animals that get separated from the herd, help the animals that wander off, they're obviously surplus, because you always leave stragglers behind, that's just the way it is, it's only natural. It's the plains that feed the animals and the animals belong to the plains, and if you're handy with a lasso then it's your right to take them and breed them because you know you're gonna leave some others behind. That's how things were before these gringos arrived and laid down their newfangled laws. They're animals. I've done a lot for the breeding of herds and sowing grass. And they try to accuse *me* of being a *cattle thief?* Me?! They're the thieves, every last one of them!

of Nepomuceno is largely partisan, she does create a great deal of ambiguity regarding his character through the rumors about him, and by no means is the depiction of the Mexican and Anglo conflict Manichean. As John Alba Cutler pointed out, *Texas* "recognizes that from the point of view of indigenous peoples, both Anglos and Mexicans are violent colonizers" (no page).

When Nepomuceno revolts, he forms a small band of rebels, thus organizing his own war machine that engages in cross-border skirmishes with the law enforcement of Bruneville. In the afterword entitled "Agradecimientos y homenajes (Acknowledgments & Homages)," Boullosa pays tribute to the historical Juan Nepomuceno Cortina as "el Robin Hood de la Frontera" (359), and the character certainly fits the criteria that Eric Hobsbawm coined for "social bandits" (21-27): in the novel he is regarded as a criminal by the state, but is considered by many local Mexicans and black people to be a hero, a "living legend" (61), a fighter for justice. Indeed, when Sheriff Shears publicly pistol whips the drunken old *vaquero*, Lázaro Rueda, and Nepomuceno step in to try to calm the situation, the conflict that arises is typical of the ballads and legends of bandits. Nepomuceno defends the humanity and dignity of the old vaquero, and the narration valorizes the character through Nepomuceno's memory of learning roping skills from him when a child. After Lázaro is lynched by vigilante rangers, and his body is burnt, the narrator reveals the value of the man in collective memory, and his dying thoughts, with clear intertextual notes of the *payador* in *Martín Fierro*:

> Mientras quemaban la persona del vaquero bonito, el noble, el que cantaba y hacía coplas y era grato y no tenía tierras ni intereses más allá de hacer pasar buen rato a la vacada y complacer al dueño –andar por la cuerda floja, pué–, éste pensaba:

> "¡Ay, Lázaro tú ya no revives! Ya nunca más voy a montar, ni a lazar un caballo o . . .ni cantaré, ni tocaré violín. . .Ya no soy lo que fui ni nada . . ." (341)[15]

For Shears, Lázaro is a worthless drunk, even more lacking in value for what he represents as a local *tejano:* an obstacle to the Anglo Texans who have penetrated the region to get rich quickly (and in this, the white characters are

---

[15] While they burn the body of this gentle, *noble vaquero* who sang and wrote songs and was easy-going and owned no land and had no interest other than caring for herds and pleasing his masters -he thinks: " Ay, Lázaro, you won't survive this! You'll never ride again, or . . . you won't sing, you won't play the violin . . . You're no longer what you used to be, you're nothing . . .

reminiscent of the schemers and swindlers of Twain's *The Gilded Age*). In Nepomuceno's decision to defend Lázaro against the sheriff, and in the narrative voice's report both of the "vaquero bonito" and his last thoughts, what comes into relief is the collective esteem for Lázaro's knowledge of the land and of culture ("el que cantaba y hacía coplas (*noble vaquero* who sang and wrote songs)," and early in the novel: "pa'l alcohol no es bueno, en cambio pa'l violin (Booze isn't good for him, the violin, on the other hand)," 59). For the anonymous, collective voice of the narrator, Lázaro is "noble": earlier he demonstrated his bravery in the face of the lynch mob by deciding to not resist in order to save innocent lives (336-37). The intertextual play with *Martín Fierro*, moreover, puts *Texas* in the larger context of displacement and dispossession in Latin America by associating the novel with the vanishing of the gauchos and the Conquista del Desierto in Argentina during the nineteenth century, which led to the extermination of the native Argentine tribes.

Conclusion

To close, I would like to comment on two examples of intertextuality between Boullosa's novels and works by Twain and Cervantes that demonstrate Boullosa's decolonial reading of their work. *Texas* refashions Twain's story "The Celebrated Jumping Frog of Calaveras County" by having Jim Smiley challenge one of the Texas Rangers, "Rangel Phil," to bet on whether his frog can jump higher than any other. When the ranger asks incredulously where he can get a frog, the fisherman Santiago offers to fetch a frog from the river. Ranger Phil is surprised by the offer and decides to follow Santiago to the riverbank and notices the tracks left by Nepomuceno's band's horses at the site where they had come ashore to attack Bruneville. He asks Santiago about the tracks and the fisherman reveals that he knew of their presence before the attack happened. The ranger then shoots Santiago in the head and has him hanged from an acacia tree in front of the Hotel La Grande. A group of vigilante gunslingers also shoot and hang the ferry pilot Arnaldo from the tree. Arnaldo is similar to Lázaro as a representative of the historical and collective memory of the region. By inserting Jim Smiley into the border conflict and making him the catalyst of a lynching, Boullosa infuses Twain's satirical story with the racial violence of the frontier. Boullosa's decolonial response to both Twain and Cervantes is to parody their work in a way that brings into stark relief the limits both authors faced regarding what they could write about the racial violence of their respective times.

Boullosa challenges us with her more violently realistic depictions of life and prejudice in Spain during Cervantes's time: Gerardo's brutal mutilation and the depiction of his suffering as a galley slave, and the recasting of Preciosa as a true gypsy who nonetheless becomes part morisca spy, part Christian sailor-soldier.

Her corpse, as Pohl points out as well, is defiled and raped, something that surpassed the discursive limits of Cervantes's works.

In "Cervantes contra Cervantes," Pohl carries out an excellent analysis of the intertextual references to Cervantes's work in *La otra mano*. He studies several of the "novelas intercaladas" from *Don Quixote* and the *Exemplary Novels: La gitanilla, Las dos doncellas, El amante liberal,* and *La ilustre fregona (The Little Gipsy Girl, The Two Damseis, The Generous Lover, and The Illustrious Scullery-Maid)* (177). Pohl left out one work that is, in my view, crucial: *El cerco de Numancia (The Siege of Numancia)*. *La otra mano* begins with a chapter titled "Menos-uno: Galera (Minus-one: Galera)" which tells the story of the siege and massacre of Galera, a morisco town that was assaulted by overwhelming Christian forces. Pohl rightly focuses on the more direct precursor: *To Amar depués de la Muerte (Love Beyond Death)* by Pedro Calderón de la Barca which recounts the suppression of the Morisco revolt and glorifies Juan de Austria, who is presented as murderous in *La otra mano*. In Boullosa's version, Zaida is the only survivor of the slaughter of the town's women warriors: "Cuando los cristianos entran a Galera, caminan sobre una alfombra de jóvenes mujeres muertas, sus ropas de seda y sus velos empapados en sangre (When the Christians enter Galera, they walk upon a tapestry of dead maids, their silk clothing and veils soaked in blood)" (26). As Pohl points out, the siege and occupation of Galera by Juan de Austria lead to the extermination of its people and he wages a deliberate policy of erasing any memory of the town (177): "que no quede piedra sobre piedra en este pueblo, . . .Que no quede memoria. Que de ahora en adelante se diga que Galera no existió, ni su mezquita, ni sus tres mil guerreras" (26).[16] The tone of Boullosa's "Galera" is more heroic and tragic than that of Calderón de la Barca's version, and thus more reminiscent of Cervantes's *Numancia*. Boullosa's graphic realism, and her poetic use of "alfombra de jóvenes mujeres muertas (a tapestry of death maids.)," also reflect the horrific spectacle of death in *Numancia*: "De mirar de sangre un rojo lago, y de ver mil cuerpos tendidos por las calles de Numancia (To look upon a red lake of blood, and to see a thousand bodies scattered through the streets of Numantia)" and later "¡Oh cuán triste y horrendo se me ofrece a la vista! ¡Oh caso extraño! Caliente sangre baña todo el suelo; cuerpos muertos ocupan plaza y calles (Oh how sad and horrid is the sight set before me! Oh strange spectacle! Warm blood soaks all the ground; dead bodies occupy the plaza and streets)" (Cervantes 174). The focus on Juan de Austria's suppression of memory in Boullosa's "Galera" is also comparable in the negative: Escipión is obsessed

---

[16] That no stone be left upon stone in this town, ...That no memory remain. That from now on it be said that Galera did not exist, neither its mosque, nor its three thousand female warriors.

with being remembered and becoming famous, but the suicide of the entire town robs him of his fame and ensures Numancia's.

Cervantes's play was immensely successful in dramatizing one of the foundational myths of the Spanish nation: an Iberian town, Numancia, represents the Spanish people resisting the incursion of the Roman Empire. The play was written just a few years after the siege of Galera and the battle of Lepanto, in the context of Spain's imperial consolidation and competition with the Ottoman Empire. What does Boullosa's "Galera" do in comparison? *La otra mano* inverts the roles: Spain becomes the oppressive empire. Cervantes, of course, was sympathetic to the Moriscos' plight, as is clear in the second book of *Don Quixote*, but it is difficult to imagine him writing something as tragic and brutally heroic as Boullosa's "Galera" about the Moriscos. In sum, the decoloniality of *La otra mano* and *Texas* resides in raising the silenced voices of marginalized peoples who resist colonization and empire, who resist the othering and dehumanization of racist exclusion and dispossession.

Works Cited

Boullosa, Carmen. *La otra mano de Lepanto.* Fondo de Cultura Económica, 2005.

Boullosa, Carmen. *Texas. La Gran Ladronería en el Lejano Norte.* Alfaguara, 2012.

Braidotti, R. *Sujetos nómades. Corporización y diferencia sexual en la teoría feminista contemporánea.* Paidós, 2000.

Cervantes Saavedra, Miguel de. *Obras completas.* Aguilar, 1960.

Cutler, John Alba. "The New Border." *College Literature*, vol. 44, no. 4, Fall 2017, pp. 498-504.

Deleuze, Gilles and Félix Guattari. *Anti-Oedipus: Capitalism and Schizophrenia.* Translated by Robert Hurley et al., U of Minnesota P, 1983.

Foucault, Michel. *Discipline and Punish: The Birth of the Prison.* Translated by Alan Sheridan. Pantheon, 1977.

Estrada, Oswaldo. "(Re)Constructions of Memory and Identity Formation in Carmen Boullosa's Postcolonial Writings." *South Atlantic Review*, vol. 74, no. 4, 2009, pp. 131-48.

Hobsbawm, Eric. *Bandits.* The New Press, 2000.

Katz, Friedrich. *The Life & Times of Pancho Villa.* Stanford UP, 1998.

Kroll, Juli A. "(Re)Opening the Veins of the Historiographic Visionary: Clothing, Mapping, and Tonguing Subjectivities in Carmen Boullosa's *Duerme.*" *Hispanófila*, no. 141, May 2004, pp. 105-27.

Menton, Seymour. *Latin America's New Historical Novel.* U of Texas P, 1993.

Mignolo, Walter. *The Darker Side of Western Modernity. Global Futures, Decolonial Options.* Duke UP, 2011.

Montes Garcés, Elizabeth. "El nomadismo y el disfraz en *La otra mano de Lepanto* de Carmen Boullosa." *Actas del XVI Congreso de la Asociación*

Internacional de Hispanistas, Vervuert 2007, no pag. http://aihparis2007
.univ-paris3.fr

Moraña, Mabel et al., editors. *Coloniality at Large: Latin America and the Postcolonial Debate.* Duke, 2008.

Pohl, Burkhard. "Cervantes contra Cervantes: relecturas conmemorativas." *El Siglo de Oro en la España contemporánea, edited* by Hanno Ehrlicher and Stefan Schreckenberg, Iberoamericana Vervuert, 2011, pp. 169-91.

Pratt, Mary Louise. "In the Neocolony: Destiny, Destination, and the Traffic in Meaning." *Coloniality at Large: Latin America and the Postcolonial Debate, edited* by Mabel Moraña et al., Duke, 2008, pp. 459-75.

Quijano, Aníbal. "Colonialidad y modernidad-racionalidad." *Los conquistados: 1492 y la población indígena de las Américas,* edited by Heraclio Bonilla, Tercer Mundo Editores, Facultad Latinoamericana de Ciencias Sociales, Sede Ecuador, and Libri Mundi, 1992, pp. 437-50.

Schnee, Samantha, translator. *Texas: The Great Theft.* By Carmen Boullosa, Deep Vellum Publishing, 2014.

Twain, Mark. *The Mysterious Stranger and other Stories.* Signet Classics, 2004.

Chapter 2

Boullosa, Driver's License, and the Energy Gratitude Test

Emily Hind

University of Florida

Abstract: The critique of fossil-fuel-reliant infrastructure that Carmen Boullosa launches in her work never actually changes the characters' petroprivileges. Key among Boullosa's tropes of conjured crisis, that is, of fantasy threat, is the frightful possibility of literature speaking for itself and discarding the privileged literate human. To illustrate this point, the article takes up seven of Boullosa's fiction works, along with the collection of personal essays *Cuando me volví mortal/ When I became mortal* (2010). Boullosa's narrative tends to channel attention not toward any particular source of energy, but toward an imagined threat to the supreme value of literature, which leads to a kind of intellectual paralysis, or an inability to refocus attention from what Joseph Masco calls "the crisis in crisis." The article proposes that one method for breaking with energopolitical complicity that fears losing petroprivilege is to rework the Christian legacy with renewed secular attentiveness. Rather than follow crisis discourse, from distraction to distraction, and from panic to panic, mindfulness might give priority to values like gratitude. Thus, in the model of the feminist Bechdel test, the chapter proposes a secular heuristic register for energy attitudes.

Keywords: *Antes, Llanto:novelas imposibles, La Milagrosa, Cielos de la Tierra, Treinta años, La novela perfecta,* and *El complot de los Románticos, Cuando me volví mortal,* oil, *energo-tude,* energopower, energopolitics, energopolitical, energency, gratitude, petroprivilege

***

Carmen Boullosa, born in 1954, began her writing career in the 1970s, a timeline that roughly coincides with the boom of the Mexican miracle (1954-

70) (Llerenas Morales).[1] Her early years as a writer also overlap with the discovery of the Cantarell oil deposit, exploited by Petróleos Mexicanos (Pemex). More specifically, in 1961 a fisherperson in Campeche named Rudesindo Cantarell noticed bubbles of crude oil rising from the seafloor; in 1968 he reported the phenomenon to a Pemex office; in 1971, Pemex sent two engineers to find the fisherperson and ask about the site (Pérez 34). By 1976, the Cantarell deposit had become the second most productive oil reserve in the world and was only poised to expand (43). Nearly forty years prior, with the nationalization of oil in 1938, Mexico's fossil fuel resources had already "helped propel major biopolitical investments" (Boyer 17). Even so, the formative decade for Boullosa marks a peak of energetic achievement, and though "a Mexican petrostate was by no means conjured from thin air in the 1970s," the decade saw the country make a transition "from a net importer to an exporter of oil" (72). The Mexican state-owned oil business, Pemex, used its deep pockets to fund, on average, some 40% of the Mexican public budget (Pérez 39). Unfortunately, with the crisis of the early 1980s Mexico suffered dearly under "sagging Pemex revenues, high unemployment, and 100 percent annual inflation for most of the decade" (Boyer 73). Might hegemonic oil have supported a kind of prestigious, "experimental" literature in Mexico?[2] What if Boullosa's experimentalist style that shrugs off genre rules understood as "commercial," pitches the special status of literature that could transcend "the market," not in a move of economic resistance, but in complicity with state energy management? The approach to this question is more important than the answer, given that we see through the filter of oil and thus may not be able to differentiate reliably between complicity and resistance with the state management of oil.

Even if I cannot escape the influence of reading under oil, in the present essay, I hope to address, at least in part, Ignacio Sánchez Prado's complaint that studies of Boullosa's oeuvre unduly stress notions of "womanhood" and center on one of three novels, *Antes /Before* (1989), *Llanto: novelas imposibles / Crying: Impossible Novels* (1992), and *Cielos de la Tierra / Heavens on Earth* (1997) (Sánchez Prado, 148). While, in fact, my study does examine those three texts, I also read two more novels, *Treinta años / Leaving Tabasco* (1999) and *El complot de los Románticos / The Romantics' Plot* (2009), along with the personal essays

---

[1] Germán Vergara notes that the boom decades through the 1970s always concealed a bust; "the state itself became the main capitalist and investor" which explains how "Mexico's GDP grew at one of the highest rates in the world" (185). By the 1950s, fossil fuels, especially oil, "set the country on a path to becoming a nation with seemingly intractable social, urban, and environmental problems" (219).

[2] I borrow the notion of the hegemony of oil from Szeman (280).

included in *Cuando me volví mortal / When I became mortal* (2010). I contemplate these fictions in terms of their assumptions that quite possibly support oil thinking. On that note, it seems important to recognize the early financial gifts that helped Boullosa gain fame as a worthy poet, that is, as a sponsored practitioner of a genre relatively distant from the bestseller list and discussions of fossil fuel dependence.

In 1977, her earliest lyrical period, Boullosa held a grant sponsored by Salvador Novo's short-lived philanthropy for young poets (CME Boullosa 53). Boullosa remains one of the few to have held this grant, because the notorious oil-related peso crisis of the early 1980s evaporated the funding—or so Boullosa told me in a personal conversation on November 22, 2016. Aside from Novo's vanished legacy, itself amassed in part through employment with the Mexico City-based federal government, in part from a co-owned advertising agency, and in part from theater-restaurant ownership, another source came to the rescue of Boullosa's early aspirations: boom-and-bust Mexican government backing, including the federal funding of "INBA/ Fonapas," which she held in 1979, and the year-long grant from the federally and philanthropically funded Centro Mexicano de Escritores (CME), which supported Boullosa from 1980 to 1981 (CME Boullosa 53). In 1983, Boullosa assumed co-ownership of the theater-bar El Hijo del Cuervo, located in the same Coyoacán neighborhood where Novo had established his theater ("Historia"). Writing of Novo and Boullosa in the same sentence might strike some readers as a lane-violation that confuses, respectively, a conservative and a leftist, but energetic thinking encourages a new alignment of orientations. A useful term for moving beyond notions of "right" and "left" under oil hegemony is Dominic Boyer's term *energopower.*

Energopower and the Colonial Complement to the Industrial Revolution

Coined in the model of Foucault's 1970s concept of *biopower,* the idea of *energopower* lends an important tool to address this oddly taken-for-granted subject, that is, "the contributions of fuel and electricity to the possibility of modern life and its ways of knowing and being" (Boyer 8).[3] Defining an overlapping governmentality of energopower from biopower inspires Cara Daggett's *The Birth of Energy,* in which she explains Boyer's reasoning for insisting on the first term as distinguishable from the second: "one cannot understand the biopolitical projects of Foucault's prisons, schools, and factories without attending to their dependence on industrial energy apparatuses to supply building materials, light, and heat" (124). Even as energy

---

[3] Boyer stresses the notion of "enablement" that underlies this notion of power (19).

management supports biopolitical aims, it establishes demands of its own, in Daggett's argument, by seeking "to put all the energy on Earth to work" (131). Troublingly, this governance mode also aims to "sacrifice any and all who are in the way of that vision" (112). Perhaps out of respect for the sacrifice that will be made of those rebels who would contest energopower, the fictional characters in Boullosa's novels neither review Mexican oil history in depth nor do they think deeply about their potential complicity with the ideology of energy and work ethic that Daggett traces.

Nevertheless, Boullosa's narrators evince an acute awareness of crisis and waste as moral problems, a thematic that links them to dominant energopolitics. The Mexican context pushes against Daggett's history as beginning in earnest in the 1840s with European WASPs, white Anglo-Saxon Protestants, and their influence over science and inventions. Mexico's energy history, of course, grows from deeper roots dismissed at our peril, as hinted at in Boullosa's fictions about social customs in New Spain. The horrific and less easily forgotten history of slavery and other relatively early oppressions signals patterns of governmentality available for repurposing in service of energy regulation during the industrial revolution and the rise of fossil-fuel dependence. Even as they reveal knowledge of New Spain, Boullosa's narrators deviate little from a script that rehearses moralistic anxiety over crisis and waste—a script familiar, for instance, from Daggett's definition of a set of energy assumptions created in the 1840s and upheld in the decades since: "Europeans had reached the top rung of the civilizational ladder by maximizing productive work and minimizing waste" (8).[4]

Certainly, in the Mexican context, the WASPy notion of the "work ethic" fits within an expansive notion of an allegedly non-wasteful "worth ethic," in which, following upon habits of Catholic, racist, and misogynist colonization, the twentieth-century oil economy retained control of workers through tactics such as unpredictable energy pricing and subjugation of individuals' status and safety to dominant energy interests. The value of "worth as work," abstractly, is risky for a narrator to dispute without jeopardizing the intellectual's status as a competent worker and thereby becoming "waste." Wary of this risk, perhaps, Boullosa's narrators tend to make compromises by way of erudition that wards

---

[4] Daggett traces the Christian moral framing of the "discovery" of energy and its units as we understand them now, such as the concept of energy transferable among various modes, e.g. calorie, joule, horsepower, and the like. This innovation can be attributed to "mostly northern British engineers and scientists" active at the apex of the Industrial Revolution, in the 1840s (3). According to Daggett, the WASP morality that guided these thinkers' view of energy spurred them to abhor waste and maximize efficient productivity, "a geo-theology that reverberates in energy politics today" (54).

off placement at the "bottom rung" of the "civilizational ladder," and by way of assuming ethics as "outsiders" meant to deny "top rung" ethical obliviousness—the latter understood as a quality of commercial or compliant literary narrators. Boullosa's narrators find a kind of conciliatory status for themselves by posturing as well-read unknowns, who can at once articulate anti-racist, anti-sexist, and anti-classist stances, informed by a rich historical understanding of Mexico's inglorious past, with a caveat: they decry this oppression *from* knowledgeable petroprivilege. I might call this fossil-fueled privilege *driver's license*.

Petroprivilege counts on secure oil access and reflects an elite's ability to view the world from a car without necessarily spending much time in one. Against the expansive freedoms of imagination under a *writer's license*, the narrower *driver's license* seems to limit the bounds of the imaginable in order to protect petroprivilege. A *driver's license* allows for a respectable narrative existence within an energetic system set up to assure the consumption of increasing amounts of nonrenewable energy, without any regard to human health. Management of high-burner energy under energopolitics imagines rising oil consumption as a goal in itself. The drivers licensed as intellectuals under this system, who would like to be seen as competent workers, only delicately question the priorities of energy management so as to avoid forfeiting driver's license privileges. One such privilege—posited as a kind of immunity—appears in an early lost story that Boullosa describes in the personal essay, "La hija del parque/ the daughter of the park." Among the lost juvenilia, Boullosa's autofictional narrator remembers having written about a well-dressed woman character who crosses the street, in defiance of the car that kills her: "La arrolla un coche. Queda muerta, pero sigue cruzando la calle, sigue su camino como si no hubiera pasado nada (A car strikes her. She is killed, yet perseveres crossing the street, continuing on her way as if nothing had occurred)" (*Cuando me volví mortal* 128). In the case of all Boullosa's narrators of interest here, the implicit claim to the transcendent value of their exceptional, even "outsider" suffering underpins the value of literature itself, as a defiance of the waste/work loop that drives energopolitical discrimination.

Driver's License in *Antes* or Juanita as "Asno/Donkey"

For a more developed case, I turn to the early novella *Antes*, winner of the Xavier Villaurrutia prize, which presents "Clavitos," an ex-voto-like drawing that the child protagonist, born in the same year as Boullosa, gives to her mother.[5]

---

[5] The folk genre of the ex-voto offers a format familiar to Mexican readers: "Most depict a miraculous cure through a portrayal of one or more persons praying for the sick individual who is usually prostrate in bed" (Castro-Sethness 21). That amateur genre was collected before Boullosa's time by such celebrities as Frida Kahlo.

"Clavitos" is executed in the naive mode of the ex-voto, through a supine, gender-neutral child, immobile, pierced by nails, who guards a resigned expression: "si no dejaba de sonreír, casi podría decirse que lo hacía. Ni una lágrima, ni una herida, ni una señal de dolor (If she didn't stop smiling, one could almost say she was doing it. Not a tear, not a wound, not a sign of pain)" (93). The mother character, named Esther, like Boullosa's own mother, pins "Clavitos" to her studio wall in an acknowledgment of the child's artistic capacity and, apparently, in approving agreement that the sketch wasn't meant for the Catholic school *serviam* assignment (*Antes* 93). Similar to experimental writing, "Clavitos" conveys an ambiguous message meant for a tenacious audience's interpretive labor. This unpragmatic art leaves the child protagonist to complete a second, obedient drawing for the official assignment that shows a figure washing dishes. The second drawing exemplifies the energopolitical hypocrisy, as identified in the narrator's bitter critique of her social class: "cuál serviam, cuál 'servir' si entre nosotros nos encargábamos de que el país entero nos sirviera (Which serviam? which to serve? When among us, we made sure the entire country served us)" (94). The demand to be served hides in the art that claims otherwise, and yet, even the artwork "Clavitos" is cleverly admirable for launching a critique that fails to bring down the system—like a Banksy shredding machine that fails to destroy the artwork halfway through.

To explore further the contents of "Clavitos," it is helpful to review the conclusion of the novella. After suffering through her mother's unexpected death, the narrator of *Antes* winds up the story by claiming that she herself died, while still a minor, which coaxes a kind of impossible plot, much like the inscrutability of the figure sketched in "Clavitos." Thus, upon a second reading, the drawing seems less rebellious and more like foreshadowing. Why isn't the "Clavitos" drawing more successful in staging a rebellion that would extract the child protagonist from the gothic world of invisible threat—of nameless energy—that seems to endanger her classmates, her mother, and herself at every turn? Perhaps because that unnamable energy menace has to win the conflict with the protagonist for the book to "work."

Certainly, the conclusion and the narrator's claim to have died seems to trigger the trap of collusion: in *Antes*, Boullosa's narrator can both "do nothing" and be seen to tinker with a "rebellious" or experimental and prestigious story, which saves her from falling out with the energopolitical values that privilege high burners' ambivalent relationship with work. As befits a narrator whose claim to heightened sensibilities pleases Boullosa's governmentally supported writing peers who control the Xavier Villaurrutia award, the child protagonist's rebellious intent in the drawing of "Clavitos," can be summarized as safely levying an ineffectual critique of the energy regime.[6] By claiming to have died, the narrator of *Antes* manages to strike a delicate balance between abject unproductivity in death, and normative productivity in life. She retains her capacity to narrate as if she were not dead, which only *seems* to manage a kind of privileged exception from the work regime. In completing the project, it seems that the author Boullosa (like the artist Bansky) still collects a check.

Racist discrimination inherent in this system is of great importance, and the child protagonist in *Antes* echoes this racist energopolitical rhetoric. As Daggett's *The Birth of Energy* points out, the pressure to work has been called into service to control minority populations, including people of color, by decrying these groups as inept, inefficient, or otherwise unsuitable workers, labeled derogatorily as *waste*: "Waste is generated at the intersection of race, gender, class, virtue, pollution, and ecological violence" (8-9). The discrimination in *Antes* predetermines a rejection of the minor character Juanita, albeit for the same reasons that turn out to be positive when related to the child protagonist. In other words, Juanita will never draw "Clavitos," because even if she did, it would *only* be an ex-voto.

"Clavitos" enjoys a privileged *birth within energopower*, to play with Daggett's title, because it emerges framed in petroprivilege, already created in the painter's studio, and already assessed by a generous audience. By contrast, the barely mentioned character Juanita is perceived as failing to adapt to the household, and the narrator's family returns her to a program of technical education in Michoacán, funded by the Opus Dei (*Antes* 84, 87). Before that ignominious exit, the narrator labels Juanita "un asno/a donkey," and scoffs at the memory of Juanita operating an appliance for fun: "era aficionada a la licuadora, a la que prendía para jugar, vacía, bien acomodada, puesta la tapa de hule sobre el vaso, y le jalaba hacia arriba la palanca de controles para oírla 'cantar,' según me dijo la misma Juanita" (84).[7] The narrator can levy a rejection of the young assistant without much explanation and dismiss the playful young woman with such vehemence because she assumes readers' prior sympathy to the direction of the complaints.

Indeed, perhaps nothing defines high-burner status in Mexico like complaining about the help; as Salvador Novo himself would write in a newspaper column published on March 22, 1958: "Hace mucho tiempo que nadie tiene completa la planta de sus criados. Si no le falta el jardinero, se le va

---

[6] Other critics propose alternative interpretations. Melgar Pernías, for example, argues that "Clavitos" reflects both the daughter protagonist and the soon-to-be-deceased mother.

[7] She was a fan of the blender, which she would turn on to play, empty, well arranged, with the rubber lid placed on the jar, and she would pull the control lever upwards to hear it 'sing,' as Juanita herself told me.

el chofer, o el mozo recibe un telegrama que lo conmina a irse a su tierra, o la cocinera deja el trabajo, o la recamarera desapareció con los relojes" (Novo 267).[8] The more diplomatic Boullosa would never write such a haughty paragraph, and yet she can channel the tone. The narrator in the novella *Antes* delivers the snobby treatment of Juana in the tradition of the unempathetic assessment of service workers performed by Novo's privileged narrative voice in the newspaper.

Intriguingly, in *Antes* Boullosa's narrator speculates spitefully about what Juanita will do once returns to Michoacán: "seguramente que tomará más cursos que le enseñarán a no hacer nada, a despreciar todo cuanto era su mundo con mayor perfección (surely, she would take more courses that would teach her to do nothing, to disdain everything that was her world with greater perfection)" (87). Daggett would likely explain the technical school as an instrument of colonization; an example of "the parody of education set up by white imperialists, who set about converting students into docile, low-paid wage laborers" (161). While Boullosa's narrator also views education as a parody, she describes her own experience as similar, though with different ends: "Distraída aprendía. ¿Aprendía qué? ¡Quién sabe! No me acuerdo de una sola palabra. No sé ni qué temas. Estaba absolutamente fuera de mí (Distracted, she was learning. Learning what? Who knows! I don't remember a single word. I don't even know what topics. I was absolutely beside myself)" (*Antes* 31). The narrator never suggests herself to be "un asno," of course, but someone whose worthy mind is distracted by the meaningful torment of a haunting energy. The trick of energopolitical governmentality is revealed in its discrepancy: while the narrator disparages Juanita for her implied ignorance and laziness, the narrator herself represents similar habits coached during her childhood—but with a different slant: now these same qualities hint at the child protagonist's artistic sensitivities.

In astonishing contradiction with the critique of Juanita's education, the narrator of *Antes* never bothers to apply *to herself* the condescending statements she makes about Juanita's nonsensical training in "doing nothing" and her alleged contempt towards "her world." The reader is left to wonder to what extent this world is "hers" and requires a possessive pronoun to demarcate Juanita's world from that of the narrator. This conundrum is particularly tricky given the narrator's claim to idle dead person status that

---

[8] It's been a long time since anyone has a complete staff. If it's not the gardener missing, the driver leaves, or the servant receives a telegram compelling them to return to their homeland, or the cook quits, or the chambermaid vanishes with the watches.

alienates her, in turn, from the world, if not from "her" world. In sum, the empty blender concert is a "waste" when Juanita plays it, and yet the narrator derived from the child protagonist's experience values the latter's starring games with art that merit space on the studio wall. The narrator assigns merit to "Clavitos," as a piece with the serious interpretation granted the life and death stakes endured by this child (but not Juanita) who suffers at the mercy of transcendent energy forces.

Of course, Boullosa's narrator faces discriminatory challenges herself. The intersectional nature of heteropatriarchal oppression means that the narrator rightly extends at least some sympathy to the girl protagonist's battles. Privileged women in the time of the protagonist's childhood were not necessarily applauded for being seen as laborers. As Daggett writes, inspired by Anne McClintock's *Imperial Leather*, the Victorian-rooted censure of illegitimate idleness was counterbalanced by an idealization of leisure; the latter was imposed in a contradictory performance of whiteness and womanliness and requires a pattern of illusion and concealment that conditions the problems of the Anthropocene (158).[9] Again, it bears cautioning that the application of Daggett's work to Boullosa's writing comes with an additional heaping dose of Catholic and colonial tradition: the most consistent prejudice that guides the Mexican etiquette might simply be that of rabid classism. Thus, in the context of *Antes*, the position of the feminine "white" ideal in the schematic cuts both ways, as Esther's decision to be a painter and a mother challenges the ideal of "unemployed" household dedication, while elegantly sidestepping the debates on other prejudices about office work.

The move *toward* innovative and admirable art by way of labor concealed in the home, as in the model of *Antes*, touches on the zone of energopolitically compliant behavior that unites more secular views on "productivity" with the historically religious roots of detecting "inefficiencies" and eliminating "waste from one's schedule" (Gregg 56). These games of revealing and concealing human labor compare to similar attitudes toward oil. Just like the expectation that "decent" white women in Mexican culture, over the period lasting from colonization until near the end of the twentieth century, oil is not to be seen working. That is, according to Daggett, aside from coercing feinted leisure and exposing idle "waste," energopolitics collude with the program of concealing "those threatening economies and ecologies, just as subterranean oil pipelines, refineries sited in poor, industrial zones, and opaque gas pumps help to

---

[9] Daggett summarizes McClintock's work with the contradictory type of productivity demanded of Victorian women who were at once held to a standard of productivity and required not to be seen managing it: "The goal was to discredit the importance of women's labor, which was ironically increased to meet the demands for cleanliness" (158).

conceal our sensory awareness of the ubiquity of oil" (158). In *Antes*, when Boullosa's narrator excessively polices the unfit worker Juanita, always within a context of liberal sympathies for the oppressed, she also covers over some of the labor of oil and the concealment of where the "waste" winds up: not so much in wealthy neighborhoods and cities, as in dumping grounds perceived to be more rural or lower-status because they burn resources less conspicuously, like the agricultural state of Michoacán, to where Juanita is returned. The ex-voto of *Antes* gives only equivocal resistance to *serviam*, but clearly avoids any real threat to the surrounding fossil-fuel-reliant infrastructure.

Treinta años or How Delmira Judges Dulce and Deforestation from Europe

The novel *Treinta años* returns to this tactic. Dulce, employed in Delmira's family since age seven, receives something other than a scornful description on page 224 of a 259-page novel, when narrator Delmira assesses the household helper more empathetically:

> Me avergoncé frente a Dulce, de mí misma y del papel que me tocaba representar. Las dos hacíamos una persona completa, las dos éramos fragmentadas mitades [:] ella tenía de su lado la complicidad y el calor de la abuela que la obligaba a una esclavitud. Yo tenía una habitación para mí misma. (*Treinta años* 224)[10]

Dulce's lack of meaningful mobility suggests that if Dulce and Delmira form one person, then for Delmira to arrive at a kind of social justice enlightenment after the protest march, Dulce must remain at home where she can be seen again upon Delmira's return. Importantly, Delmira's reassessment of Dulce occurs after a street demonstration, a distinctly pedestrian event. A march in the street literally places all protestors on more equal footing and sets up Delmira upon her return to take the measure of her privilege by *seeing* Dulce, rather than passing over her with the usual gaze through a windshield. That is, in the context of driver's license, Delmira doesn't just have "a room for herself." Like Virginia Woolf, she has secure access to fossil-fueled vehicles. In Delmira's case, before riding a plane into exile, she rode regularly in the priest's Jeep with her mother. Riding in the Jeep provides occasion for a half-hearted critique, by way of the role the vehicle plays in making possible the priest's consensual sexual relationship with Delmira's mother. The priest's hypocritical exercise of

---

[10] I was embarrassed in front of Dulce, of myself and of the role I had to play. The two of us made up one complete person, we were both fragmented halves[:] she had on her side the complicity and warmth of the grandmother who imposed slavery upon her. I had a room to myself.

driver's license never finds its comeuppance. It almost goes without saying that Indigenous people, portrayed as such, do not ride in the Jeep.

Delmira never contemplates these petrosegregations in so many words. Instead, she indulges in a critique of Dulce, now familiar from *Antes*. If Juanita's mistake is to entertain her fascination with the blender, Dulce's error is to feed herself baked goods, thus gaining a lower-classed physique as, "un ser Redondo (a round being)" in the style of "las gordas del mercado (the fat ladies from the market)" (*Treinta años* 121). This physical change ages Delmira: "A los diecisiete tenía el aspecto de una señora (at seventeen she had the appearance of a mature woman)" (121). Of course, a viewpoint less enthralled by the notions of energopolitical efficiency might not view Juanita's and Dulce's indulgences as blunders, but as strengths. What would happen if Delmira of *Treinta años* decided to imitate Dulce and stay in Tabasco and eat baked goods? What would happen if the narrator of *Antes* were to mimic Juanita and listen to the blender "sing"? Possibly, the result would shift ideas about worthy art.

Possession of a driver's license allows for any critique launched by Delmira to undermine itself through discrimination supported by the topic of waste, which comes to haunt the environmental concerns stated within *Treinta años*. In that sense, it is important to stress that the very notion of the "environment" finds traction among the concerns of oil companies in the 1970s, as worries about a finite amount of oil came to the forefront (Mitchell 189). Thus, like knowledge of the economy (what Mitchell calls "petro-knowledge"), knowledge of the environment legible to the compatible form of knowing, also probably depends on "abundant and low-cost energy supplies" (139). In acquiescence to the "environment" as a compensation for the "economy" which could prevent "environmentalism" from developing beyond energopolitical notions of waste and work, Boullosa's novels display a kind of moralistic and academic environmentalism, narrated briefly, pedagogically, and at a relative emotional remove. The novels therefore seem unlikely to threaten the established energetic order.

Treinta años never burdens any individual character with ecological blame, and instead Delmira's rather numb lament for the destruction of the forests of Tabasco underway in the 1960s and 1970s delivers a relatively abstract lamentation for the ruined jungle habitat: "Entre el petróleo, la explotación de los bosques tropicales y el ganado, han barrido con ella [la selva] (Between oil, the exploitation of tropical forests, and cattle, they have swept it [the jungle] away)" (250). Without mentioning any steps needed to remedy the problem, Delmira's distanced perspective simply offers complacent speculation on the presumed destructive effects of oil and cattle: "no sé cómo será el cielo donde la tierra ha borrado la selva, supliéndola por potreros o pozos (I don't know what the sky is like where the land has erased the jungle, replacing it with pastures or wells)" (257). Delmira may not know what the sky looks like under this context of destruction because she consumes others' data, available thanks to cheap, abundant, and often nonrenewable energy supplies. If legible, printable knowledge of the environment functions on the same level as knowledge of the economy, then access to it, as well as the skills to decipher and circulate it, practically require petroprivilege. Delmira's environmental knowledge is already conditioned by oil, in other words. Thanks to her privileged spot on the consumption ladder, Delmira finds sophisticated phrasing to hide her failure to renounce petroprivilege. Her suffering as an exiled "outsider" thus conveniently facilitates a kind of complicity. As with *Antes*, in *Treinta años* Boullosa's plot hints that the literary wielding of a driver's license is done best by those who deny a comfortable relationship with it.

Moctezuma of *Llanto: Novelas imposibles* and Dante of *El complot de los Románticos*: Classic Juanitas?

The driver's license wielded by worthy narrators in Boullosa's experimental, genre-bending, thickly ambiguous style carves out privilege that cannot be fully enjoyed, perhaps because the latter enjoyment might flirt with "commercial" qualities, or a lack of artistically ambitious worth ethic. To explore the point another way, I note that in *Treinta años* Delmira's assessment of environmental damage seems to spring from crisis talk. As Joseph Masco complains, no programmatic efforts result from the current state discourse that doubles down on "repeated failure as well as totalizing external danger without generating the need for structural change"—what can be called *analysis paralysis* (240). The utility of crisis themes in maintaining the status quo leads me to Masco's important question: "if we were to remove crisis talk from our public speech today, what would remain?" (237). Literary critics can reappropriate Masco's query by replacing "public speech" with "prestigious literature." What would remain if in admired fiction the notion of crisis were removed? Perhaps below the crisis there lies an even more obvious remainder of collusion.

The possibility of "another way" is sometimes shut down even in Boullosa's fantastical reach to historical characters who wield a pre-petro, pre-windshield gaze. The fifteenth-century Aztec emperor Moctezuma of *Llanto: Novelas imposibles*, and the late-thirteenth and early- fourteenth-century poet Dante of *El complot de los Románticos*, end up nearly as mute as Juanita in *Antes* and Dulce in *Treinta años*. In *Llanto: Novelas imposibles* Moctezuma reacts with amazement and terror to car culture (55, 56). His surprise seems misguided rather than contestatory. Moctezuma's estrangement from petroculture leaves one of the contemporary women narrators repeating "coche, coche (car, car)" to herself in imitation of the emperor, but without developing the possible idea

(120).[11] For the narrator, the joylessness of car culture matches her inexpressiveness regarding its purpose. The refusal to make car culture into a transferable lesson with a meaning almost seems to lead to a more superficial level of analysis than the starting point of Moctezuma's shock would indicate, like an Escher stairway that seems to lead into a profound critique of energopower, but by a trick of perspective winds up at the level plane it began on. This trick avoids the active solutions, such as renouncing petroprivilege.

Petro-infrastructure as an unexaminable given reappears in *El complot de los Románticos*, when Dante reacts with similar astonishment to cars, but across many more pages, as if Boullosa's narrator's second pass at the pre-petro anachronism were to stretch horizontally in reaction to implausible depth.[12] One of Dante's encounters with cars has the poet watch the Britney Spears video, "Stronger." Dante sees the cars in the video, shouts about "chairs," and launches a string of questions (89). The contemporary narrator, the president— since 2002—of the dead writers' club called El Parnaso (25), answers simply, "Es un coche, Dante, (it is a car, Dante,)" and from there the explanation only grows more tautological: cars require a highway and driving cars at night requires headlights, and so on (89). Finally, the narrator responds to Dante's query about the video, "¿Qué está diciendo? (what is it saying?)" with the resigned, "Diciendo, nada; significando, nada tampoco (saying, nothing; meaning, nothing either)" (90). All attempts at an explanation lead Dante to more questions—seemingly all the wrong ones.

Cielos de la Tierra and the Algorithmic Return of Petroprivilege

Perhaps Dante, like Moctezuma of *Llanto* and like Juanita of *Antes*, is supposed to play the role of "ass" in a state of unlicensed ignorance as compared to the narrator. As in *Antes*, in *Llanto* and *El complot de los Románticos* review of the significance of a car doesn't go anywhere because it becomes an exercise in writing for itself. In the latter two fantasy anachronism novels, these educated, laborious descriptions of historical shock at self-explanatory car culture ensure that the contemporary narrators will not renounce their privileges, which they require in order to dismiss this shock. Their retention of privilege hints that it cannot be conferred upon others and at the same time cannot be responsibly admitted as pleasurable.

---

[11] Ferrero Cándenas gives a detailed review of Moctezuma's function for Boullosa through the framework of surrealism (110-115, for example).

[12] For a review of the novel as a parody of Dante's work and for reference to the initial US-Mexico border crossing accomplished on giant rats, see Mohssine (247).

Perhaps the most paralyzed of all these narrators is Estela Díaz from *Cielos de la Tierra*. Estela's privileged viewpoint remains defensive of petrosegregration and has her omit the mode of transportation she uses to arrive at her preferred (non-)work spot, El Colegio de México, an institution anchored in a largely car-dependent zone of Mexico City. The unreferenced car that the reader suspects may deliver Estela during her sabbatical in the late 1990s to the library lurks in insinuation as a privilege that cannot be acknowledged because a driver's license is most expertly wielded when taken for granted. The unhappy Estela uses her sabbatical to insist she is not working—at least not pragmatically—because she translates for herself a manuscript by a sixteenth-century disabled Indigenous man, named Hernando, from Latin to Spanish. She views her labor as resistance to what I have been calling energopolitics: her translation should be "*inútil*, como un juego (*useless*, like a game)" (65, italics in original). But is this translation *really* a resistance to the worth ethic? Estela thus defends the academic project as determined leisure but the critique from *Imperial Leather* might overturn this negation, or at least incite the reader to wonder if Estela conceals her labor for reasons that in the end are not all that resistant to hegemonic energy management. The related fact that Estela narrates from a white perspective is clear from her autobiographical notes on her family's hypocritically unrecognized racism (43). In recompense for this legacy of colonialism, Estela takes an interest in Hernando's view: a safely pre-petro one. In the same way that Moctezuma and Dante provide little to no insight into energopolitics in their respective novels, in *Cielos de la Tierra*, Hernando holds no authority over a (car) culture he never saw.

The fact that Estela narrates from contrasting petroprivilege is clear: for example, she rode in a vehicle as a child when her family traveled in a Jeep that got stuck in mud during a missionary visit to a rural area (54). These details overlap with information that Boullosa's autofictional narrator will later share in the personal essay "Mis cadáveres," first published in *Debate Feminista* in 2003, and later reproduced in *Cuando me volví mortal*. In the original version of "Mis cadáveres," Boullosa recalls experiences with her family's missionary activities over the course of a year in Huejutla, Hidalgo; the family piled into a Jeep and brought the Christian message to primarily Otomí-speaking audiences by way of a record player, projector, battery, screen, and film strips that showed the lives of the saints (34). In the context of energopolitics, it is important to note that the missionaries used religious pedagogy as a cover for perhaps the real lesson: placing the unconverted into the energetic grid by instructing them to want to consume electricity and fossil fuels.

Estela never mentions that the missionaries gave the Indigenous people a battery or a Jeep. It seems that the conversion idea regarding fuel consumption centers at least initially on implanting desire, not satisfying it. The notion of an energy story that practically tells itself, using impersonal modes to complete its ends, leads to unsettling doubt regarding the true identity of the "child martyr," when in *Cielos de la Tierra* Estela projects *Mambo, el niño mártir (Mambo, the child martyr)*: "y yo giraba una perilla que hacía correr la tira de celuloide, cambiando de una proyección a la siguiente, tan fácil como darle cuerda al reloj (and I turned a knob that made the celluloid strip run, changing from one projection to the next, as easy as winding a clock)" (*Cielos de la Tierra* 53). What damage happens to children's mental health when they serve (perhaps simplistically, perhaps obscuring the labor) the ends of petroprivilege? In the case of Estela's conversion audience, do the Indigenous viewers learn to perceive themselves compliantly as an energopolitical "waste," for their apparent lack of consumption of fossil fuels and batteries? Estela shows her disagreement with the decision through such acidic phrasing as the commentary on petrochemical delousing without consent: "sin preguntarles su opinión, los rapábamos y les aplicábamos con una bomba manual flit mata piojos, un D.D.T., seguramente dañino en todos sentidos para la salud, pero que acababa de una vez por todas con cualquier piojo vivo o en estado latente" (55).[13] For all her disapproval of this fossil fuel-consuming Christian project, Estela never suggests that illiterate people are a solution to the woes, an omission that ultimately leaves intact the insinuation of them as nearer the category of "waste" than the narrator. Higher levels of consumption come to define an energopolitically complicit sort of worth ethic.

The most tangible result of all the historical genocide and environmental destruction narrated in *Cielos de la Tierra* is a proselytizing mission regarding the gospel of "high" literature. A third narrator, the posthuman Lear, narrates from the postapocalyptic Age of Air (17) and delivers a metafictional product called *Cielos de la Tierra*, which consists of her own writing, plus Estela's narrative and the latter's translation of Hernando's text. The productiveness of Lear's final solution, that of the novel *Cielos de la Tierra*, hardly reassures the reader that somehow literature has solved the waste/work conundrum. Indeed, by her own description, Lear insists on virtuous occupation and spends her centuries rescuing books and manuscripts from the ruins of Earth, after humans are extinguished by a nuclear disaster-like calamity. Lear excels at crisis talk and fears what she views as another apocalypse: she becomes the lone hold-out to her lobotomized companions' new society; the others destroy their language capabilities—and, in another sign of decline—begin to eat meat.

---

[13] Without asking their opinion, we shaved their heads and applied a DDT lice killer to them with a hand pump sprayer - surely harmful to health in every way, but which finally eradicated any living louse or nit.

By contrast, Lear retains language and insists on the exceptionality of books: "Porque los libros vencen la Muerte (Because books conquer death)" (21).

For Lear, the written page transcends the material, that is, those objects likely to become waste, unlike all the other detritus left from human occupation of planet Earth. Therein, this post-petro gaze fails to differ from Boullosa's other narrators' worshipful appreciation of literature—always operant within the bounds of a driver's license. Lear's canon embraces male writers of the fossil-fuel age, with brief admiration paid to Octavio Paz (24) and lengthy citations of Álvaro Mutis (25, 27, 28-29) and Federico Gamboa (29-30). Estela perhaps helps to coach this view; she discusses the novels *Pedro Páramo* and *Cien años de soledad/ One Hundred Years of Solitude* as significant books (199). In a way, Lear's duplicate prejudice, shared with other narrators from Boullosa's oeuvre, anticipates the biases built into algorithms that know only the historical injustice baked into the discriminatory logic of the archive: the petro-knowledge that ends up coded as "impersonal," taken-for-granted patterns (McKittrick 104, 117, 121). Like an algorithm, Lear never appreciably separates herself from the usual prejudices of the energopolitical design and thus confers a depressing immobility regarding her assumptions, with such implications that the elimination of cars would fail to eliminate the driver's license.

Of all Boullosa's novels, *Cielos de la Tierra* suggests most clearly that if readers were to examine literature as a fossil-fueled force compliant with analysis paralysis, then Lear's version of high literature might lose its special status as supposedly transcendent. That is to say, of all Boullosa's fiction, *Cielos de la Tierra* implies most strongly that if crisis talk were removed from the text, what would remain is compatibility with unsustainable oil economies. This collaboration explains why Lear, like Estela before her, cannot win, even in her own narrative. The always ineffective resistance that Boullosa's thoughtful and poetically talented narrators offer to energopolitics never overthrows it. They likely do not dare such a rebellion in part because they benefit from arguing literature as a special endeavor, cognizant of and yet transcendent of crisis. The governmentality that Boullosa's narrators promote, which even in Lear's posthuman Age of Air runs on petroknowledge and considers problems through the circumscribed driver's license, leads me to wonder if the first step toward breaking complicity with energopolitics is an attitude shift. For example, might one problem be a lack of gratitude that favors the crisis discourse and thus distracts from programmatic action?

The *Energo-tude* Test: Trying Gratitude for a Change

Possibly, criticism, as a genre that does not view itself as transcendent, holds part of the answer. Criticism, like the piece I have written here, rather than fiction narrated from a driver's license, might help us break with the narrowness and alienation coached by the windshield perspective. Criticism might reach beyond the "crisis of crisis" that circles around the same fears rather than acting to curtail them. The lack of plotting in criticism might also help to answer Jennifer Wenzel's query regarding the need to frame the predicament of the Anthropocene through something other than rule-bound literary terms, such as the genre term *tragedy*, along with the plot points of *crisis* and *catastrophe* (15). Criticism might devise alternative heuristics, such as an energy attitude registry—call it an "*energo-tude* test." In the model of the feminist Bechdel test, an energy heuristic test would ask about energy attitudes. Though a more subjective enterprise than the Bechdel question of whether two women characters speak to one another about something other than a man, an energy gratitude test might reject the usual taking-for-granted of energy sources and the self-congratulatory habits of privileged narrators who implicitly or explicitly label some characters and endeavors as "waste" and others as transcendent wielders of energetic license. The tool would aid us in discovering which stances are especially prevalent among prize-winning Mexican texts, also known as oil-subsidized literature. The test might even help us to think about what attitudes we *should* be subsidizing with oil. Deciding what responsible oil knowledge *should* be seen to work on seems an excellent question. Oil knowledge already discusses the topic of environmental crisis, so far to little avail if the goal is to avoid sweeping changes in the planetary climate and loss of biodiversity. What else should/can petro-knowledge be made to do?

Perhaps the benefit of such a highly subjective *energo-tude* exam would be the discussion, rather than any one judge's rating. In *Antes*, the narrator suggests that Juanita might fail such a test because she exemplifies obliviousness toward waste: Juanita is unto herself an *energency* of wasted electricity and effort. Nonetheless, a reader unsympathetic to the classist system of energopolitical Mexico might rescore Juanita, rating her highly for joy over the grid, a low-burner celebration of the possibilities of mindful presence. Juanita might not evince a crisis unto herself, but an appreciative *energo-tude*, aware of and even grateful for energy from the grid, however precarious she might find it. Juanita's main problem might be the narrator's assumption of a closed energy system that reflects the laws of thermodynamics as articulated in scientific theory and that may serve as classist justification for restricting upward mobility in Mexico (for the point regarding the assumed closed system, see Daggett 48).[14]

---

[14] Daggett, citing Bruce Clarke, questions the literary implications of this second law as perhaps cultural and not necessarily scientific in its "inevitable and tragic" frame (Daggett 75).

The proposed solution in criticism through an energo-tude test leads me to the beginning of the present article, with the history of the Cantarell discovery. Is another key to breaking complicity with energopolitics the insistence that energy ties explicitly into criticism? What have we been missing by helping to conceal oil? What happens if I decide not to conclude this article with mentions of the decline in production in the first decade of the twenty-first century from Cantarell, that spectacular "heritage of apocalypse" (Breglia 259)? What happens if I fail to mention that in early 2022, President Andrés Manuel López Obrador announced the purchase of the ownership that Shell held in the Deer Park refinery in Houston, Texas, making Mexico the sole owner of the facility (Domínguez)? Maybe the first step in finding "another way," is to be mindful of *the way*. I don't know what would have happened if I hadn't given those last two petro-data points. It's the way I'll end it: without crisis talk about another way from within something I helped to control from the beginning. *The way* is how we critics decide to do it.

So, what's your energo-tude?

Works Cited

Boullosa, Carmen. *Antes.* 1989. Suma de letras, 2001.

—. *Cielos de la Tierra.* Alfaguara, 1997.

—. *El complot de los Románticos.* Siruela, 2009.

—. *Cuando me volví mortal.* Cal y Arena, 2010.

—. *Llanto: Novelas imposibles.* Era, 1992.

—. *La Milagrosa.* Era, 1993.

—. "Mis cadáveres." *Debate Feminista*, vol. 28, pp. 23-50., JSTOR, 2003, https://www.jstor.org/stable/42624768.

—. *La novela perfecta.* Alfaguara, 2006.

—. *Treinta años.* Alfaguara, 1999.

Boyer, Dominic. *Energopolitics: Wind and Power in the Anthropocene.* Duke UP, 2019.

Breglia, Lisa. *Living with the Oil: Promises, Peaks, and Declines on Mexico's Gulf Coast.* U of Texas P, 2013.

Castro-Sethness, María A. "Frida Kahlo's Spiritual World: The Influence of Mexican Retablo and Ex-voto Paintings on Her Art." *Woman's Art Journal*, vol. 25, no. 2, 2004-2005, pp. 21-25. JSTOR, www.jstor.org/stable/3566513.

CME Boullosa, Carmen. Archive Centro Mexicano de Escritores. Box 6, File 30. Fondo Reservado of the Biblioteca Nacional de México, UNAM, Mexico City.

Daggett, Cara New. *The Birth of Energy: Fossil Fuels, Thermodynamics, and the Politics of Work.* Duke UP, 2019.

Domínguez, Pedro. "AMLO agradece a Shell tras compra de refinería Deer Park en EU; 'nunca se agandallaron.'" *Milenio.* 21 Jan. 2022, https://www.milenio.co m/politica/deer-park-amlo-agradece-shell-y-eu-compra-refineria. Accessed 3 Feb. 2022.

Ferrero Cándenas, Inés. "Carmen Boullosa's *Llanto: novelas imposibles*: Narrating history and herstory." *Journal of Iberian and Latin American Studies*, vol. 14, no. 2-3, 2008, pp. 109-121. Taylor and Francis Online, DOI: 10.1080/14701840802543936.

Gregg, Melissa. *Counterproductive: Time Management in the Knowledge Economy*. Duke UP, 2018.

"Historia." *El Hijo del Cuervo*, www.elhijodelcuervo.com.mx/acerca-de/. Accessed 25 December 2020.

Llerenas Morales, Vidal. "El desarrollo estabilizador." *El Economista*, 5 April 2018, www.eleconomista.com.mx/opinion/El-desarrollo-estabilizador-2018 0405-0138.html.

Masco, Joseph. "The Crisis in Crisis." *Infrastructure, Environment, and Life in the Anthropocene*, edited by Kregg Hetherington. Duke UP, 2019, pp. 236-260. De Gruyter, DOI: 10.1515/9781478002567-012.

McKittrick, Katherine. *Dear Science and Other Stories*. Duke UP, 2021.

Melgar Pernías, Yolanda. "Madres e hijas en los 'Bildungsromane' femeninos de Carmen Boullosa: *Mejor desaparece, Antes y Treinta años*." *Iberoamericana*, vol. 10, no. 40, 2010, pp. 27-45. JSTOR, www.jstor.org/stable /41677232.

Mitchell, Timothy. *Carbon Democracy: Political Power in the Age of Oil*. Verso, 2011.

Mohssine, Assia. "'Ratalgando' con Los 'clásicos.' Parodia y juego literario en *El complot de los Románticos* de Carmen Boullosa." *Pensar en activo: Carmen Boullosa, entre memoria e imaginación*, coordinated by Assia Mohssine. UANL, 2019, pp. 243-257.

Novo, Salvador. *La vida en México en el periodo presidencial de Adolfo Ruiz Cortines*. Memorias mexicanas, vol. 3, 1994. Conaculta, 1997.

Pérez, Ana Lilia. *Pemex rip: Vida y asesinato de la principal empresa mexicana*. Grijalbo, 2017.

Vergara, Germán. *Fueling Mexico: Energy and Environment, 1850-1950*. Cambridge UP, 2021.

Sánchez Prado, Ignacio. *Strategic Occidentalism: On Mexican Fiction, the Neoliberal Book Market, and the Question of World Literature*. Northwestern UP, 2018.Szeman, Imre. "Conjectures on World Energy Literature: Or, What is Petroculture?" *Journal of Postcolonial Writing*, vol. 53, no. 3, 2017, pp. 277-288. Taylor and Francis Online, DOI: 10.1080/17449855.2017.1337672.

Chapter 3

The Decolonial Option in Carmen Boullosa's *Llanto. Novelas imposibles*[1]

Assia Mohssine

Université Clermont Auvergne

Abstract: In her work *Llanto: Novelas imposibles/Crying: Impossible Novels* (1992), Carmen Boullosa undertakes an exercise of the decolonial option to rethink the figure of the Aztec emperor Moctezuma II, based on the epistemic proposal of Walter Mignolo who argues that the decolonial alternative can only be affirmed in diversity, as critical border thinking (Capitalism 2004). Indeed, the novel privileges local histories in the geopolitics of historical knowledge and incidentally imposes the decolonization of the Indian imagination by inserting, from the outside, its word, even if it is imaginatively recreated. In other words, Boullosa uses the figure of Moctezuma which the colonial discourse has tried to make negative, to make room for a relegated and subaltern knowledge, and to open a gap in the epistemic hegemony of modernity.

Keywords: decolonial option, decoloniality, Walter Mignolo, Carmen Boullosa, colonial, Moctezuma, gender

***

Argentinian semiologist, Walter Mignolo, identifies the field of epistemic disobedience, upon which his work is based, and simultaneously analyzes the rhetoric of modernity, the logic of coloniality, and the grammar of decoloniality:

> La diferencia epistémica apunta hacia otra dirección: al pensamiento a partir de los saberes relegados y subalternizados no ya como una búsqueda de lo auténtico y de lo antitético, sino como una manera de pensar críticamente la modernidad desde la diferencia colonial. Esto es,

---

[1] The original text "La opción descolonial en *Llanto. Novelas imposibles* de Carmen Boullosa" was published in *Cuadernos Americanos* 166, México, 2018/4, 133-153. Traducción del francés por Hernán G. H. Taboada. Traducción del español por Nicolás Kulisheck-López, revisado por Assia Mohssine.

desde una epistemología fronteriza que, desde la subalternidad epistémica, reorganiza la hegemonía epistémica de la modernidad. Esta epistemología fronteriza puede pensarse como descolonización, o si se quiere, como desconstrucción desde la diferencia colonial (234).[2]

Based upon the epistemological posture towards decoloniality, we too propose a reading of *Llanto. Novelas imposibles* (1994) as a decolonial exercise conceived from two perspectives: First, it gives privilege to the local stories and the geopolitics of historical knowledge and, in passing, imposes the second perspective, which is to decolonize the imaginary of the Indians, as we insert their words *a posteriori* - even though they may be fabricated. To this end, we will expose the lines of coloniality to great lengths, branching from Mignolo's contributions, who postulates that "the progress of modernity moves parallel to the violence of coloniality" (234) and, consequently, the decolonial alternative may only affirm in diversity, and in a vision defined as a critical conception of "the border." In other words, a place of enunciation must be established that displaces the epistemology regarding "detachment," viewed as unlearning, liberation, emancipation, and decoloniality.

The Colonial Horizon of Modernity According to Mignolo

Born under the aegis of the research group Modernity/Coloniality, the decolonial posture of Latin America promoted by Mignolo, among others, is defined as a critical perspective that reconfigures the narrative regarding modernity, stemming from the notion of "coloniality."[3] Mignolo's statement

---

[2] All Spanish quotations translated into English by María del Mar López Cabrales. The epistemic difference points in another direction: toward thinking based on relegated and subalternized knowledges, no longer as a search for the authentic and the antithetical, but rather as a way of critically thinking about modernity from the vantage point of colonial difference. That is, from a border epistemology that, from a position of epistemic subalternity, reorganizes the epistemic hegemony of modernity. This border epistemology can be thought of as decolonization, or if one prefers, as deconstruction from the perspective of colonial difference.

[3] "Del grupo Modernidad/Colonialidad forman parte el filósofo argentino Enrique Dussel, el sociólogo peruano Aníbal Quijano, el sociólogo venezolano Edgardo Lander, los semiólogos argentinos Walter Mignolo y Zulma Palermo, el filósofo colombiano Santiago Castro-Gómez, el antropólogo colombiano Arturo Escobar, el filósofo puertorriqueño Nelson Maldonado Torres, el sociólogo puertorriqueño Ramón Grosfoguel [y] también la teórica de la cultura norteamericana Catherine Walsh" (The Argentine philosopher Enrique Dussel, Peruvian sociologist Aníbal Quijano, Venezuelan sociologist Edgardo Lander, Argentine semioticians Walter Mignolo and Zulma Palermo, Colombian philosopher Santiago Castro-Gómez, Colombian anthropologist Arturo Escobar, Puerto Rican philosopher Nelson Maldonado Torres, Puerto Rican sociologist Ramón

becomes one of the most influential, as it leans on transdisciplinary concepts, such as coloniality of power, transmodernity, and the notion of the border (introduced respectively by Peruvian sociologist, Aníbal Quijano, the Argentinian philosopher, Dussel, and the Chicana intellectual, Gloria Anzaldúa), it presents issues of coloniality of knowledge, and of being, as an extension of the epistemic colonial difference.[4]

In *La idea de América Latina: la herida colonial y la opción de-colonial* (2007), which carries into and is developed in *Desobediencia epistémica* (2010), Mignolo calls attention to the need to consider coloniality as an intrinsic corollary to modernity and the discovery of the Americas as the founding element of that global project, which Mignolo redefines in terms of a "modern/colonial world," marked by violence that is as much epistemic as it is material. With this aim, coloniality is, most of all, a tool of analysis that makes it possible to reveal the logic that drives coloniality and which remains hidden below a rhetoric of rendition, progress, modernization, and the common good, all native languages to those who have served colonialism and imperialism, in turn.[5] Considering Quijano's work regarding the four fields of human experience in which colonial logic operates (economic, politic, social, and epistemic),[6] Mignolo pays particular attention to the conceptual square which

---

Grosfoguel, and also the American cultural theorist Catherine Walsh, are part of the Modernity/Coloniality group), Claude Bourguignon- Rougier, Philippe Colin y Ramón Grosfoguel, dirs., Penser l'envers obscur de la modernité, Pulim, 2014, p. 13.

[4] "Para Dussel, la transmodernidad no sólo es la caracterización histórica que incluye lo que se entendió hasta ahora como modernidad localizada geohistóricamente en Europa, a la que se atribuyó como un bien de pertenencia, sino también las modernidades periféricas o subalternas que quedaron ocultas en la construcción eurocéntrica de la modernidad. Es decir quedaron ocultas junto con la diferencia colonial" (For Dussel, transmodernity encompasses not only what has hitherto been understood as modernity - geohistorically situated in Europe, and claimed by Europe as its own - but also the peripheral or subaltern modernities that were obscured by the Eurocentric conceptualization of modernity. That is, these other modernities were rendered invisible, as was colonial difference), Walter D. Mignolo, "Capitalismo y geopolítica del conocimiento" [n. 1], p. 229.

[5] Transmodernity "consiste en develar la lógica encubierta que impone el control, la dominación y la explotación, una lógica oculta tras el discurso de la salvación, el progreso, la modernización y el bien común" (consists in unveiling the concealed logic that imposes control, domination, and exploitation, a logic hidden behind the discourse of salvation, progress, modernization and the common good), Walter D. Mignolo, *La idea de América Latina: la herida colonial y la opción decolonial*, Barcelona, Leidsa, 2007, p.32; del mismo autor, *Desobediencia epistémica: retórica de la modernidad, lógica de la colonialidad y gramática de la descolonialidad*, Buenos Aires, Ediciones del Signo, 2010.

[6] Quijano describes them: "(1) economic: appropriation of land, abuse of workers, and control of finances; (2) political: control over authority; (3) social: control of gender and

denies "epistemic colonial difference" in order to show the ways in which the hegemonic discourse locked the inhabitants of colonized territories in categories and taxonomies that are diminishing and racist, and which treat their knowledge, their history, and their humanity with contempt. A similar approximation makes it possible to say that the permanence of coloniality beyond colonization can only be understood as a system of domination that, through the difference, exerts its control over knowledge and subjectivity. Mignolo invites us to extend the coloniality of power to knowledge and being, "with the end of unveiling the processes of subjectivation which colonization has ingrained in its colonized subjects" (Bermudez 25).

Lo que caracteriza a los indios (y también a los negros, los criollos, los indios de India desde la llegada de los británicos, los africanos del norte del continente etc.) es que su interpretación subjetiva se construye, como la de los pueblos colonizados en general, sobre la herida colonial. Por el contrario, la interpretación subjetiva europea se apoya en el liderazgo imperial y no en la herida colonial (Mignolo 140).[7]

Taking advantage of the Latin American experience of coloniality and theories of Mexican philosopher, Edmundo O'Gorman, Mignolo demonstrates that the construction of a common Euroamerican knowledge crystallizes around the *discovery* while, in the light of that fact, the American perspective is described as an invention. Beyond its antinomy, the ways of naming it allow for reference to differing postures and perspectives regarding the same event, behind which two representations of the world and two opposite paradigms are profiled: the first is close to Eurocentric discourse that, beyond what is geographical, Quijano defines in epistemic and historical terms as the control lever of subjectivity and knowledge, where, at its core, the pathologization and *inferiorization* of what is the Other, form part of the constitutive process of modernity.[8] This is not the case with the second point of view, which is really

---

sexuality, and (4) epistemic and subjective/personal: control of knowledge and subjectivity," Migonolo, *La idea de América Latina* [n. 5], p. 36.

[7] What characterizes indigenous peoples (as well as blacks, creoles, Indians under British rule, North Africans, etc.) is that their subjective self-interpretation, like that of colonized peoples broadly, is constructed upon the bedrock of their colonial wound. The European subjective self-interpretation, conversely, rests its assumptions on the foundations of imperial dominance rather than any colonial wounding.

[8] "Quijano defined Eurocentrism not in geographical terms, but in epistemic and historical terms: control of knowledge and subjectivity. That is, coloniality of knowledge and being. He characterized decolonial thinking as a 'detachment' from Eurocentrism as

just a critical perspective regarding coloniality, thrown around by all who have been beaten by epistemic silence, for those who understand the term *discovery* as an obstacle because of the designation of a place as having no history, being outside of history itself. O'Gorman theory of the invention of America represents one of the fundamental bases of decolonial thought, as it marks a historical inflection point and, in agreement with Mignolo, aspires to demonstrate that:

> para los pueblos indígenas, la invasión de América es un desastre, una violencia que reorganiza su vida y su tejido social; para los europeos [es] el cumplimiento de su destino histórico que abre una brecha entre la historia de Europa y sus colonias, las que siempre estarán más atrás pues siguen una historia que no es la suya (*La idea de América Latina* 259).[9]

Within coloniality, there is a violence of epistemic and ontological order. This last point presents the occasion to interrogate the coloniality of knowledge, and what Mignolo considers the hidden side and most somber counterpart to modernity. Situating himself in the same plane, Frantz Fanon sees in coloniality a way of transfiguring and annihilating the history of others:

> Quizás no ha sido suficientemente demostrado que el colonialismo no se conforma con imponer su ley al presente y al futuro del país dominado. El colonialismo no se satisface con encerrar al pueblo en sus redes, de vaciar el cerebro del colonizado de toda forma y todo contenido. Por una suerte de perversión de la lógica, se orienta hacia el pasado del pueblo oprimido, lo distorsiona, lo desfigura, lo aniquila (201).[10]

As Mignolo underlines in a very logical manner, the historiographical discourse is racist and patriarchal, as it naturalizes the colonial difference in the way it

---

a sphere of knowledge from which it is possible to control the economy, authority, gender and sexuality and, ultimately, subjectivity." (Mignolo, *La idea* 257).

[9] For indigenous peoples, the invasion of the Americas was a catastrophe, a violence that radically disrupted their lives and social fabric. For Europeans, it represented the actualization of their purported historic destiny - widening a gap between Europe's history and that of its colonies, which would forever trail behind, compelled to follow a history not of their own making.

[10] Perhaps it has not been adequately shown that colonialism does not merely content itself with imposing its law upon the dominated country's present and future. Colonialism is not satisfied by simply ensnaring the people in its web, emptying the colonized mind of all forms and content. Through some perverse bend of logic, colonialism sets its sights on the oppressed people's past, distorting, disfiguring, and annihilating it.

alternates this epistemic silence and attempts the essentialization of the natives; in passing, it also sustains categories that aspire to trace a divisive line between the invisible, idealized native, and the reified native. From this point, the promotion of a different vision, one open to diversity, would have to pass by a reference to the trauma of history and participate in the grammar of the decoloniality proposed by the Argentinian semiologist.

The decolonial Option in *Llanto: Novelas imposibles*

To reflect on the possibilities of resistance offered by literature, in the face of the rhetoric of coloniality of knowledge, imposes the determination of the supposed antecessors and especially takes into account the critical gesture that causes literature to become a place of epistemic disobedience. While servicing itself of the anachronic representation of Aztec emperor Moctezuma II, which magnifies meaning in the narration, the historic metafiction *Llanto: Novelas imposibles* specifically insists on liberating this ambiguous character (at times victim, at times responsible for the disaster that was the Spanish Conquista) from the historic and epistemic ballast fomented by the rhetoric of modernity. As a historiographical counterpoint, generally confused and contradictory, there is a need to situate Carmen Boullosa's interest in reconfiguring Moctezuma – a historical and marginalized character – from the perspective of gender and the urban, quotidian frame of reference.

Centered in the memory of the colonized subject, *Llanto* endeavors an effort to dismantle colonial logic that presides over the hegemonic tale. From the beginning, the reader confirms that the dismantling the author attempts to realize does not consist of a sterile critique that shows the shortcomings of historiographical, colonial rhetoric; on the contrary, it orients and pushes with effort the word "Other" from the side of relegated and subalternate knowledge. Preceding from an appropriation of narrative strategies of historical metafiction from the twentieth century, the perspective of Boullosa announces an interpretative turn that, as said by Menton, reclaims history, stripping away its guise of state sanction in order to place it under the light of unrelenting criticism and restorative interpretation (42).[11] As it favors the superposition of

---

[11] Six traits of the new historical novel are highlighted: "The subordination of historical content, the distortion of history through omissions, anachronisms, and exaggerations, the fictionalization of historical figures compared to fictional ones, metafiction, intertextuality, the inclusion of multiple voices, parody and carnivalization" (Menton, 42-44). Fernando Ainsa mentions the questioning of historiographic discourse, the dialogue with the past abolishing epic distance, the degradation of the myths that constitute nationality, the freedom to document or invent the historicity of fictional discourse, the superimposition of temporalities, the narrative polyphony that dilutes a single version of events, the variety of expressive modalities and languages, and pastiche" Nueva novela 9-18). For more information, see Ainsa, "La reescritura de la historia en la nueva narrativa latinoamericana," *Cuadernos Americanos*, núm. 28 (julio-agosto de 1991), pp. 13-31; and

space and time, voice and knowledge, past and present, what is hegemonic, what is subaltern, what is historical, what is poetic, the fictional text is positioned at a border between what pretends to question the lineage of occidental thought and its paradigms of singular knowledge. The affirmation of a thought "from the colonial subalternity" (Mignolo, "Géopolitique" 181) therefore constitutes the fundament of a borderline epistemology engaged with the decolonization of thought and being.

Published in 1992, the context of the "celebrations of the Quincentennial since the discovery of the Americas," *Llanto. Novelas imposibles* confirms the will of its author to reinterpret the history of Mexico, using the chronicles of the time of the *Conquista/Conquest* (Madrid 138-146). Thanks to anachronisms, the plot takes a temporal jump and an ellipsis spanning five centuries of colonial wounds to place the death of the tlatoani Aztec, Moctezuma, occurring in 1520, at the heart of its historical debate. Far from being a stumbling block, those narrative resources subject the story to a new circulation of sense:

> por heterotemporalidad leemos el rechazo de la visión historicista eurocéntrica, la puesta en cuestión de las tesis esencialistas, evolucionistas y teleológicas que han participado, durante toda la época moderna, en la cristalización de las nociones binarias y dicotómicas como la de civilización/barbarie, colonizador/colonizado modernidad/ tradición, primitivo/ civilizado (Lani and Neiva 13).[12]

Running countercurrent to the grandiloquent rhetoric of celebration, the novel sides directly with the chronicles of conquest like *Historia general de las cosas de Nueva España/ General History of the Things of New Spain* (1540-1585) by Bernardino de Sahagún or *Cantares tristes de la Conquista/Cantares Mexicanos: Songs of the Aztecs*, among others. In this intertextual dialogue, of special interest is book 12, "Del llanto que hizo Motecuzoma y todos los mexicanos desque supieron que los españoles eran tan esforzados/ Of the weeping that Motecuzoma and all the Mexicans did when they found out that the Spanish were so mighty/valiant" where the Spanish chronicler established: "Todos lloraban y se angustiaban, y andaban tristes y cabizbaxos, [...] las madres llorando, tomaban en brazos a sus hijos, y trayéndoles la mano sobre la cabeza, decían ¡Oh, hijo mío! ¡En mal tiempo has nacido!? Everyone wept and felt anguish, and they walked sad and downcast, [...] mothers crying, taking their children in their

---

María Cristina Pons, *Memorias del olvido: Del Paso, García Márquez, Saer y la novela histórica de fines del siglo XX*, Siglo XXI, 1996.

[12] By heterotemporality we understand the rejection of Eurocentric historicist vision, the questioning of essentialist, evolutionist and teleological theses that have contributed, throughout the modern age, to the crystallization of binary and dichotomous notions such as civilization/barbarism, colonizer/colonized, modernity/tradition, primitive/civilized.

arms, and placing their hands over their heads, said, "Oh, my son! You were born in such an unfortunate time!" (Sahagun 40).[13]

This song of mourning, supported by the subtitle *Novelas imposibles*, immediately establishes the lineaments of a story and a speech that cannot be reconstructed. It is also the song that characterizes the narrator when she must abandon, dead in her soul and beyond her control, the presentation of the encounter between the two worlds: indigenous and Western. The tale of the encounter (or rather non-encounter) between two worlds (new and old, occidental and native, colonial knowledge and other knowledge) becomes historically impossible, refractory to any attempt of reconstruction, a zone situated in the thresholds of thought, negated by modern history. For the narrator, to perceive the emancipatory potential of subaltern knowledge and the inability to vocalize it is an overwhelming defeat.

> Empiezo a llorar.//No sé de qué lloro. Todo fue mentira. Pero no puedo desprenderme de la imagen del hombre recostado cerca de mí, en el pasto del parque, vestido como un Tlatoani antes de la caída de la Gran Tenochtitlan, y sin dejar de llorar pienso en la novela que yo hubiera querido escribir sobre este encuentro, la novela que las musas me decidieron imposible (Boullosa, *Llanto* 120).[14]

Llanto is disconcerting to readers, as much through its dispersed, fragmented structure, as it does through the plurality of its narrative voices; there are no less than ten narrators, not always identified, with the exception of three women: Laura, Margarita, and Luisa, and Moctezuma himself, to which is added the voice of Wind.

> Tenemos diecinueve capítulos sin título, a excepción del primero ("La aparición"), que están entrecortados por una segunda estructuración en nueve fragmentos de la novela imposible que se intercalan en cualquier

---

[13] Carmen Boullosa seems to corroborate that the chronicles are the anchorage of her novel: "De Moctezuma II he devorado toda la información que llegó a mí. Me he leído a los cronistas, a López Austin, a Todorov, a todo lo que he encontrado, todo, todo, todo, todo/ I have devoured all the information that has come to me about Moctezuma II. I have read the chroniclers, López Austin, Todorov, everything I have found, everything, everything, everything" (Pfeiffer 40).

[14] I begin to cry. // I don't know why I'm crying. Everything was a lie. But I can't get rid of the image of the man lying near me in the park grass, dressed like a Tlatoani before the fall of Great Tenochtitlan, and without stopping crying I think about the novel I would have wanted to write about this encounter, the novel that the muses deemed impossible for me.

momento de la historia y además de esta doble organización del texto, algunas páginas no llevan número de capítulo ni número de fragmento sino un título ("otra voz," "aquella voz," "addenda"). Últimas curiosidades, el capítulo 18 falta, mientras que después del capítulo 17 se encuentra una página que lleva el título de "último capítulo," bajo el cual viene inmediatamente "octavo fragmento," ¡que no es por lo tanto el último! Los narradores dicen haber sentido molestia en comenzar y terminar esta novela imposible y esta "sobrefragmentación" es consecuencia en primer lugar del gran número de narradores (una decena, masculinos y femeninos), de los cuales la mayoría no están identificados a excepción de tres mujeres y de Moctezuma (Palaisi 159).[15]

The universe as presented is similar, in this case, to a body without backbone, a narrative chaos where anachronism and contemporaneity are coded spectacularly with minor modality and canonical tale, quotidian and colonial rhetoric. By way of polyphony and the narrative fragmentation designed to relativize and distort historical knowledge, the author succeeds in freezing the supremacy of hegemonic discourse in the image of a perspectivism that enables partial interpretations and subjectivizes historical truth.

The effects of that distortion in history can be found, according to Ainsa, in a truth that is pluralized and in a hybridization that denies the possibility of a clear generic affiliation. One of these techniques, that participates in the crumbling of any historic retelling, relates to the use of anachronisms that start as gross errors of historical marking. Eventually, they become true aesthetic strategies of an ideological nature that ceaselessly interrogate the politics regarding the representation of Amerindians in historiography and literary tradition. In contrast to modern colonial epistemology, the novel takes a decolonial stance, reconfiguring Moctezuma on the basis of what he might have been his word and vision, in the light of his humanity, fears, and doubts. And it is this reversal that seems innovative to us.

---

[15] We have nineteen untitled chapters, except for the first one ("The Apparition"), which are interspersed with a second structuring of nine fragments of the impossible novel that are inserted at any point in the story. In addition to this double organization of the text, some pages do not have a chapter or fragment number but rather a title ("another voice," "that voice," "addendum"). As a final curiosity, Chapter 18 is missing, while after Chapter 17 there is a page titled "last chapter," under which immediately follows "eighth fragment," which is therefore not the last! The narrators claim to have felt discomfort in beginning and ending this impossible novel, and this "over-fragmentation" is primarily a consequence of the large number of narrators (about ten, male and female), most of whom are not identified except for three women and Moctezuma.

A brutal cut in time and space marks the opening in medias res of the narrative. "La aparición/The apparition" announces the return of Xocoyotzin Moctezuma II, by decision of the Aztec gods, on August 13th, 1989 in Parque Hundido of Mexico City, "nueve veces cincuenta y dos años (nine times fifty two years)" after the fall of Tenochtitlan to establish the truth about his death and expose a memory of the past:

> Moctezuma pensó "mis macehuales no tienen por qué pensar que yo fui un cobarde o un traidor, voy a regresar para decirles que no morí como se dice, que si leen con detenimiento las fuentes se verá que fui asesinado por los conquistadores." Esto pensó, pero cuando se vio en el parque tirado con una cruda tremenda olvidó por completo que lo había pensado (Boullosa, "La destrucción" 218).[16]

In the first chapter, it is possible to notice the power of poetic writing that has a tendency to be over-precise and to de-chronologize the exposition of the facts. In this mode, readers see themselves immediately transported to a preterit temporality, projected over a utopian horizon. At its center, we find the antique, and majestic Tenochtitlan. We will have to wait until the second chapter to clarify the reasons and circumstances of that brutal rebirth that the guardians of the park provoked:

> Se enojaron los dioses cuando los guardianes del parque echaron el veneno que tapara los túneles del hormiguero. Se enojaron los dioses pero no tenían cómo externarse, atrapados en una tierra que los desconocía, encerrados en un tiempo que no los recordaba, hundidos entre restos de tiempo que no había tenido nunca noticias de ellos, casi inexistentes, porque su realidad sólo era conocida por ellos y por el gran Moctezuma (Boullosa, *Llanto* 35).[17]

---

[16] Moctezuma thought, "My macehuales (commoners) don't have to think that I was a coward or a traitor; I will return to tell them that I did not die as it is said, that if they read the sources carefully, they will see that I was murdered by the conquerors." This is what he thought, but when he found himself lying in the park with a tremendous hangover, he completely forgot that he had thought this.

[17] The gods became angry when the park guardians poured poison to seal the tunnels of the anthill. The gods were angry, but they had no way to express it, trapped in a land that did not recognize them, enclosed in a time that did not remember them, submerged among remnants of a time that had never heard of them, almost non-existent because their reality was only known to them and the great Moctezuma.

The wrath of the gods is superimposed by the presence of Moctezuma, who has come to disseminate the truth about his death from a space-time unknown to all, and to remedy the misinterpretations and omissions that have fed colonial/modern and subaltern historiographical discourse. His reincarnation ensues after the return of his favorite sacrificed ones, brought in with the goal of accompanying him in his voyage to the kingdom of Mictlantecuhtli, the place of the dead. Next to those women, reduced to fine dust and tears of defeat, Moctezuma closes his eyes, alien to the beauty of the garden where he finds himself, letting run the grateful memories of his times in the ceremonious Tenochtitlan, where he has royal etiquette, and was "Lord over all Lords and the greatest of all:" "En el estero rodeado de manglares, atenazado de manglares, sobre el agua del río las balsas contienen flotando al cortejo. Los músicos irrumpen al silencio. Con enormes abanicos de plumas remueven el aire alrededor de Su Persona alejando a los insectos" (Boullosa, *Llanto* 15).[18] The image of the great Moctezuma, accompanied by the court of his favorites, proudly strutting over the waters of lake Texcoco, acts as a visual counterpoint to his vile assassination at the hands of the Spaniards.

> Recuerda lo hermoso que lo percibió [al lago] a la distancia y se acrecienta el desagrado. El hombre verdura cocida, el hombre puerco de monte, saca una daga de sus ropajes y lo toma por el cuello; no puede verlo, sólo siente su brazo bajo la barbilla y la daga empujando las carnes bajo su ombligo, en la espalda, entre sus nalgas (Boullosa, *Llanto* 21).[19]

In this oniric-ritual hetero-temporality, where incantation tackled the prosaic everyday life of the park, the anachronistic Moctezuma, resurrected on the very site of his cremation, adorned with his royal attributes and speaking rudimentary Spanish, meets the bewildered gaze of three slightly tipsy women, who decide to take him to the home of one of them. At once diegetic relays, postmodern declensions of the favorites with whom Moctezuma liked to surround himself, and avatars of the Llorona, the 3 nurturing and protective women operate here processes of symbolization: they are those who name, those who transmit and tirelessly repeat history in this vast struggle against oblivion. This is undoubtedly a significant gendered perspective that makes

---

[18] In the estuary surrounded by mangroves, ensnared by mangroves, the rafts containing the entourage float on the river water. The musicians disrupt the silence. With enormous feather fans, they stir the air around His Person, keeping the insects at bay.

[19] He recalls how beautiful he perceived the lake from a distance, and his displeasure intensifies. The man, the cooked vegetable man, the wild boar man, draws a dagger from his garments and grabs him by the neck; he cannot see him, only feels his arm under his chin and the dagger pushing into the flesh below his navel, in his back, between his buttocks.

Laura, Luisa, and Margarita the guardians of historical memory, which they try to perpetuate as a space of resilience.

The man once considered a demigod, reigning at the head of one of Mesoamerica's most powerful empires, appears in the novel endowed with human characteristics: the horizontality of the body stretched over the grass of a garden clearly opposes the hieratic majesty of a tlatoani:

> Así se formó, otra vez, sin madre, el cuerpo a que aquello todo se había visto en otros tiempos adherido, el que no había alcanzado a ver caer lo que hacía nueve veces cincuenta y dos años él había dejado desplomándose, y así fue como llegó, el 13 de agosto de 1989, acostado sobre el húmedo pasto, durmiendo, soñando, envuelto en trece mantas bordadas y descansando el peso sobre las plumas de águila y la piel de jaguar que un día recubrieron su asiento, aún creyéndose colibrí aleteando en el azul que antes rodeaba los bosques hasta imbricarse en las minucias de las ramas. Así fue como apareció (Boullosa, *Llanto* 11-12).[20]

To establish his identity, the Aztec emperor agrees to the removal of his royal garments for submission to the scrutiny of archeologists and ethnologists. Stripped of his hieratic iconography, Moctezuma turns into a form of humanity whose contours we are allowed to see not from the deforming prism of historiography -colonial or nativist- but through the quotidian and carnal relationship he has with Laura, one of his protectors. This specular image of Cortes and Malintzin seems to rearticulate what it means to be Mexican around the binding that brings together all the present people and their past. In the novel, Moctezuma is much more than the body adorned by attributes of power, he is a spectral figure, a living dead who can contemplate "its death" and its "resurrection," his body and his "shadow" and as he contemplates his present, he can internalize his past.

The phantasmal Moctezuma, who originally thought he was in Seville, is invited by his protectors to wander the streets of Mexico City, "nine times fifty and two days" after the fall of his empire. The laugh as a "syncope of himself and of what makes sense" (Droit), the laugh as the only response to Margarita when she shows him the statue of Cuauhtémoc, elevates the level of

---

[20] Thus was formed, once again, motherless, the body to which all that had once been attached, that had not lived to see the fall of what he had left collapsing nine times fifty-two times years ago, and so was how he arrived, on August 13, 1989, lying on the damp grass, sleeping, dreaming, wrapped in thirteen embroidered blankets and resting his weight on the eagle feathers and jaguar skin that had once covered his seat, still believing himself a hummingbird fluttering in the blue that once surrounded the forests until blending into the details of the branches. That was how he appeared.

incomprehension regarding the accumulation of images and antinomic testimonies: what sense would there be in the placement face to face of victors, and those defeated, Aztec heroes, and Spanish conquistadors, effigies of a remote past, and illustrious characters of the Reform, and of modern Mexico?

> Me di cuenta que él veía todas nuestras estatuas iguales, la inmensa que reproduce a Cuauhtémoc con un raro penacho vertical y una lanza a punto de escapársele de las manos, y las pequeñas estatuas que bordean el Paseo de la Reforma, vestidas con casacas y pantalones entallados, usando lentes y barbas de candado, algunas con libros en las manos y las manos atrás de la espalda [...] Más le impresionaba lo demás [...] la disposición de la calle, los otros autos, el camellón al centro [...] como si él, suponiendo que fuera el Tlatoani salido de otros siglos, fuera todavía quien gobernara el imperio, la región donde estaban los cimientos del cielo (Boullosa, *Llanto* 57).[21]

Moctezuma enters the contemporary world of Mexico under the banner of modernity, and this discordance prevents him from recognizing himself in his descendants and in the values of the new nation reformulated, in his opinion, in the categories of the conquistador and in a disembodied language... So far from the glorious Tenochtitlan, foreignness is the aura of this city, which tells of the violence of a devastating modernity whose paradigmatic choices turn their backs on the past. The narration, in conflict with a present worker by heterotemporality, structures itself into an initiatory voyage with the purpose of building bridges between the past and present, and above all else, of questioning the place of indigenous memory in Mexican identity, individually, and as a collective. Focused from the angle of modernity, Mexico City resists all tentative assimilation to the old Tenochtitlan. There is no remembrance of the Mexica Empire, the glamour of its palaces, its temples, not even its gods, it all seems to have vanished. In the face of such a predicament, Moctezuma invokes, in a gesture of desperation, his own memories and the testimony of Ortequilla, the Spanish pageboy placed at his service: "¿Dónde estamos? ¿Qué ciudad?... ¿De dónde he de venir? Soy el Tlatoani, mis palacios están en

---

[21] I realized he saw all our statues alike, the immense one reproducing Cuauhtémoc with a strange vertical headdress and a spear about to escape his hands, and the small statues lining Paseo de la Reforma, dressed in frock coats and tailored pants, wearing glasses and handlebar mustaches, some with books in their hands and hands behind their backs [...] What impressed him more was everything else [...] the layout of the street, the other cars, the median strip in the center [...] as if he, assuming he was the Tlatoani emerged from other centuries, was still the one ruling the empire, the region where the foundations of the sky were laid.

Tenochtitlan/Where are we? What city?... Where am I to come from? I am the Tlatoani, my palaces are in Tenochtitlan" (Boullosa, *Llanto* 62), he cries.

Quickly sweeping aside this painful present, the narrative proposes, from the outset of this visual exploration, to summon the ancient capital of the Aztec empire, Tenochtitlan, a specular counterpart and reassuring flux that allows this resurrected body to still be the Tlatoani of other centuries:

> Laura le contestó entonces, tomándolo de la mano: "Está usted en Tenoch-titlan, pero mucho tiempo después," y como él pareció no escucharla, ella repitió "Estamos en Tenochtitlan, en otros tiempos, en otra era, en otros años" y él le preguntó quién es ahora el Tlatoani, quién gobierna, y si no es mexica de qué ciudad es el que nos gobierna y si acaso era Carlos el de Cortés (Boullosa, *Llanto* 62).[22]

The novel invites readers to an authentic change in perspective: The *Discovery* is described from the point of view and the counternarrative of the native who explores this *New World of modernity*, made indecipherable to him despite the vertiginous efforts of Laura to make it legible:

> Laura le volvía a decir que por el teléfono podían hablar a cualquier parte del mundo con quien él quisiera y cuando dijo mundo abrió un libro hermoso que tiene Laura de mapas y empezó a enseñarle a Moctezuma los mapas, y le enseñó uno que había sido hecho a imaginación tratando de copiar lo que sería el que Cortés mandó a Carlos V, otro que mostraba la extensión del imperio mexica en el reinado de Moctezuma Xocoyótzin, le mostró Europa, Asia, África, un mapamundi y luego un plano de las estrellas y él escuchaba con una cara extraordinaria como si ahora él fuera el que descubriera el mundo. Nueve veces cincuenta y dos después de la caída de Tenochtitlan, presenciábamos, sí, un verdadero Descubrimiento (Boullosa, *Llanto* 87).[23]

---

[22] Laura then replied, taking him by the hand, "You are in Tenochtitlan, but much later in time," and as he seemed not to hear her, she repeated, "We are in Tenochtitlan, in other times, in another era, in different years," and he asked her who the Tlatoani is now, who governs, and if he's not Mexica, from which city the current ruler is, and whether it was Carlos from Cortés.

[23] Laura kept telling him that through the telephone, they could speak to anyone in the world he wished. When she mentioned the world, she opened a beautiful book of maps that Laura had and began to show Moctezuma the maps. She showed him one that had been created using imagination, attempting to replicate what Cortés sent to Charles V,

Thanks to the reference to the Aztec calendar, and in particular to the 52-year solar cycle, the text claims heterotemporality to be useful in order to reread Mexico in the twentieth century, subdued to prove its modernity, and drowned in treason and violence, as testified by this acerbic diatribe:

> Sí que el siglo veinte se parece a la época de la conquista. Nos enfrentamos a nuestro propio dominio: no entendemos con qué nos estamos dominando. El triunfo de la tecnología, los alcances de la tecnología, el modo de vivir de la modernidad arrasan al hombre de ayer, nos arrasan a nosotros. Con dificultad nos hacemos a la idea de que lo que el hombre ni se atrevió a soñar es ahora cierto. Los inventos, los dominios sobre la materia van más allá de lo inimaginable. También las armas y la violencia. También la crueldad, también los regímenes que nos avergüenzan de ser humanos. No hemos crecido: nos hemos hinchado. Tal vez, si aceptáramos nuestra situación de conquistados por nosotros mismos, nuestra situación de ser, como fue Moctezuma, personajes en la frontera, seres situados entre dos territorios, expulsados tal vez de ambos por nuestra incertidumbre, tal vez si lo viéramos... (Boullosa, *Llanto* 98).[24]

The impossible word

Despite all, Moctezuma continues to be an inapprehensible object and both the colonial and native versions are contaminated. The Aztec emperor, and especially the facts regarding his death, contribute to an ambiguous space, fragmented, always brought into question due to the silence that surrounds it, characteristics that cause it to become an epistemological issue:

---

another depicting the extent of the Mexica empire during the reign of Moctezuma Xocoyótzin. She showed him Europe, Asia, Africa, a world map, and then chart of the stars. He listened with an extraordinary expression, as if now he were the one discovering the world. Nine times fifty-two years after the fall of Tenochtitlan, we were witnessing, indeed, a true Discovery.

[24] Indeed, the twentieth century resembles the time of the conquest. We face our own domination: we do not comprehend with what we are dominating ourselves. The triumph of technology, the reaches of technology, the modern way of life overwhelm yesterday's man, they overwhelm us. With difficulty, we come to terms with the idea that what man did not dare to dream of is now real. Inventions, dominion over matter go beyond the unimaginable. So do weapons and violence. So does cruelty, and so do regimes that shame us for being human. We have not grown; we have swollen. Perhaps, if we accepted our situation as conquered by ourselves, our situation of being, as Moctezuma was, characters on the border, beings situated between two territories, perhaps expelled from both due to our uncertainty, perhaps if we saw it that way...

Este tema es uno de los más espinosos de la conquista, ya que existen dos versiones opuestas: por un lado, aquellas que sostienen que Moctezuma murió a causa de la pedrada que el pueblo le asestó: dentro de este grupo está la versión de Cortés, la de Gómara, quien afirma que la piedra no iba dirigida a Moctezuma sino a los españoles, pero los aztecas no alcanzaron a reconocer el rostro del emperador ya que lo tapaba un escudo; Cervantes de Salazar y Bernal, por su parte, sostienen que la piedra desde el principio iba dirigida a él pero la muerte se debió al estado de aflicción del propio Moctezuma; por otra parte, la versión de las fuentes indígenas, como la de los Códices Ramírez, interpreta que Moctezuma fue asesinado por los soldados españoles por mandato de Cortés, mediante una puñalada en la parte baja de su cuerpo para que cuando lo sacaran ante su pueblo éste no se percatara de la herida. Es la versión que apoyan Las Casas, Durán y Acosta, entre otros y la que plantea Boullosa a lo largo de la novela como alternativa a la que tradicionalmente la historia de los conquistadores ha proclamado (Madrid 141).[25]

Faced with such a concert of historiography, Boullosa tries to establish a direct dialogue with the principal hypotexts of the Conquista, whole sections of which are summoned, in particular those that are based on founding texts such as *Historia verdadera de México* (1648) by Antonio de Solís, *Nueva España* (1568) by conquistador Bernal Díaz del Castillo, *Cartas de relación* (1519-1526) by Hernan Cortés, *Historia de la conquista de México* (1684) by Antonio de Solís, *Historia general de las cosas de Nueva España* by Bernardino de Sahagún, *Codice Aubin* (1576), *Codize Ramirez* (1587); chronicles that are referenced, in part, by recent works such as *La conquista de America: la cuestión del otro* (1982) by Tzvetan Todorov. The author even dares to grant a fictional status to certain Mexican informants (such as Eduardo Matos Moctezuma,

---

[25] This topic is one of the thorniest of the conquest, since there are two opposing versions: on the one hand, those who argue that Moctezuma died as a result of the stone-throwing that the people inflicted on him. Within this group is Cortés's version, as well as Gómara's, who claims that the stone was not aimed at Moctezuma but at the Spaniards, but the Aztecs failed to recognize the emperor's face as it was covered by a shield. Cervantes de Salazar and Bernal, for their part, argue that the stone was initially directed at him, but Moctezuma's death was due to his own distress. On the other hand, the version of indigenous sources, such as the Ramírez Codices, interprets that Moctezuma was murdered by Spanish soldiers on Cortés's orders, by stabbing him in the lower part of his body so that when he was presented before his people, they wouldn't notice the wound. This is the version supported by Las Casas, Durán, and Acosta, among others, and the one that Boullosa proposes throughout the novel as an alternative to what the conquerors' history has traditionally proclaimed.

anthropologist and archeologist, and historian Alfredo Lopez Austin). Despite this, far from being about a simple hypertextual relation that would inscribe the text (letter, chronicle, codex) as forms of citation or loan, the effects of the transposition impose upon this goal the creative stakes of the anachronism, dedicated to "dialectize" the image of Moctezuma and, more broadly, the colonial history from which it is necessary to separate ourselves as shown by this example of Moctezuma's death, taken from Hernán Cortés' second letter:

> Y el dicho Muctuzuma, que todavía estaba preso,//y un hijo suyo, con otros muchos//señores que al principio se habían tomado,//dijo que le sacasen a las azoteas de la fortaleza//y que él hablaría a los capitanes de aquella// gente y les haría que cesase la guerra. E yo lo//hice sacar, y en llegando a un petril que salía//fuera de la fortaleza, queriendo hablar a la//gente que por allí combatía, le dieron una//pedrada los suyos en la cabeza, tan grande,// que de ahí a tres días murió; e yo lo fice saber//así muerto a dos indios de los que estaban//presos, e a cuestas lo llevaron a la gente, y no sé//lo que dél hicieron, salvo que no por eso//cesó la guerra, y muy más recio y muy cruda//de cada día (Boullosa, *Llanto* 83).[26]

The fragment Hernan Cortes wrote -here transcribed literary- is just one example of the historical tension that pits the version told by the victors against that told by the defeated. It should be noted that Boullosa analyzes the death of the Aztec tlatoani, in this key of ambiguity, without agreeing on either side. Thus, by suggesting that the stone thrown by one of his subjects caused Moctezuma's death, Cortes' version conflicts with the facts presented by Sahagun's native informants in the *Codice Florentino*,[27] as well as with the

---

[26] And the aforementioned Moctezuma, who was still imprisoned,//and one of his sons, along with many other//lords who had initially been taken,//said to be taken to the rooftops of the fortress,//and that he would speak to the captains of that//people and make them cease the war. And I//had him taken out, and upon reaching a parapet that extended//outside of the fortress, wanting to address the//people who were fighting there, his own people threw//such a large stone at his head, that within//three days he died; and I had it made known//to two Indians among those who were//imprisoned, and they carried him on their backs to the people, and I don't know//what they did with him, except that the war did not//cease because of it, but it grew much fiercer and bloodier//every day. See Hernán Cortés, *Cartas de relación* (272) for the original text by Cortés.

[27] One of the aforementioned informants acknowledges both perspectives: "Dicen [los españoles] que uno de ellos [sus vasallos] le tiró una pedrada de lo cual murió, aunque dicen sus vasallos que los mismos españoles lo mataron, y por las partes bajas le metieron una espada/They [the Spaniards] say that one of them [Moctezuma's vassals] threw a stone

allegations of other conquistadors such as Diaz del Castillo[28] and the Dominican missionary Diego Duran.[29] To escape the dilemma, between an intrinsically ambiguous history, embodied by short-sighted and biased visions, and the historical impossibility of filling in the silences, Boullosa makes the choice of orienting the narrative towards the rehabilitation of indigenous voices, in order to delve deeper into their thoughts and the way they experienced the violence of the Conquista.

What interest could have been awoken in them by the encounter with those foreign men with strange manners? What would happen if that memory had not been lost and overthrown forever? The answer to those questions would imply, without doubt, the development of another version of history, and forces us to affect the rescue and preservation of subaltern knowledge to transcend the colonial wound and build a Mexican identity that is balanced, in consonance with the local legacies.

Making little of the scattered and controversial versions of Moctezuma's death, Boullosa chooses to offer the Indian Moctezuma a narrative identity through which he can deliver his own vision of history. In other words, to decolonize history, Boullosa suggests a new locus of enunciation, rooted in local history and colonial wounds. Thus, within the Eurocentric monologism, the Aztec emperor's voice triggers the interpretive act that casts doubt on the

---

at him, from which he died, although his vassals say that the Spaniards themselves killed him, and they thrust a sword into his lower parts" (Alva Ixtlilxóchitl, 828).

[28] "Le dieron tres pedradas, una en la cabeza, otra en el brazo y otra en la pierna; y puesto que le rogaban se curase y caminase y le decían sobre buenas palabras, no quiso, antes cuando no nos catamos vinieron a decir que era muerto/They threw three stones at him, one at his head, another at his arm, and another at his leg; and even though they begged him to tend to himself and walk and spoke kind words to him, he refused. Instead, when we least expected, they came to tell us that he was dead," (Díaz del Castillo, 391).

[29] "Diego Durán desmiente que la pedrada fuera la causa de la muerte de Moctezuma pues a raíz de la llamada "noche triste," los mexicanos "hallaron muerto [a Moctezuma], con una cadena a los pies y con cinco puñaladas en el pecho, y junto a él, a muchos principales y señores [...] todos muertos a puñaladas [...] Lo cual, si esta historia no me lo dijera, ni viera la pintura que lo certificara, me hiciera dificultoso de creer, pero como estoy obligado a poner lo que los autores por quien me rijo en esta historia me dicen y escriben y pintan, pongo lo que se halla escrito y pintado/Diego Durán denies that the stone blow was the cause of Moctezuma's death, as following the so-called "night of sorrow," the Mexicans "found [Moctezuma] dead, with chains around his feet and with five stabs in his chest, and next to him, many nobles and lords [...] all dead with stab wounds [...] If this history did not tell me, nor if I had seen the painting that certifies it, it would be difficult for me to believe. Still, as I am obligated to report what the authors whose accounts guide me in this history tell me, and write, and depict, I present what is written and painted," (qtd in Baudot and Todorov, 423).

information about his death, by pointing to the perfidious action of his assassins, who did not hesitate to present him dead on the roof of Axayacatl's palace, so that he could harangue his people and ask them to lay down their weapons, while it was all a masquerade and deception:

> Cuando sacaron el cadáver para engañarlos con que iban a oír la voz de su emperador, olvidaron poner la música que antecede su aparición, los tambores, la invocación, porque aunque fuera su prójimo en cuanto al ser de hombre, en cuanto al oficio era como un dios. Todo era falso, y el cuerpo que alguien detenía para que no cayera (pues sí era un muerto) se repetía a sí mismo las palabras que le habían sido dichas el día de su coronación [...] Pero dejó el orden de sus recuerdos cuando sintió sobre su carne muerta, en la frente, una Piedra lanzada desde allá abajo y se dijo: "No es para mí, es para Hernando Cortés, porque quién no se dará cuenta que me han matado, pero me ha atinado a mí, en la frente" (Boullosa, *Llanto* 32).[30]

With this corollary, the truth about the assassination of Moctezuma, while in question and in denial, remains unresolved. The aforementioned Eduardo Matos Moctezuma summarizes here the dilemma:

> Dos versiones conocemos del fatal acontecimiento: por un lado, la de cronistas españoles como Hernán Cortés y Bernal Díaz del Castillo, quienes achacan la muerte de Moctezuma a los indígenas, y por el otro, la de cronistas de estirpe indígena como Fernando Alvarado Tezozómoc y Francisco de San Antón Chimalpahin, que, por el contrario, dicen que fue muerto por los españoles (88-89).[31]

---

[30] When they brought out the corpse to deceive the people into thinking they would hear the voice of their emperor, they forgot to play the music that precedes his appearances - the drums, the invocations - for though he was their fellow man, in his role he was like a god. Everything was an illusion, and the body that someone held back from falling (for he was indeed dead) repeated to himself the words spoken on the day of his coronation [...] But his train of thought was interrupted when he felt a stone thrown from below strike its lifeless flesh, on the forehead, and he said to himself, "This is not meant for me, but for Hernando Cortés, for who will not realize they have killed me, yet it is I who has been struck, on the forehead.

[31] Two versions of the fateful event are known: on one hand, there is that of the Spanish chroniclers such as Hernán Cortés and Bernal Díaz del Castillo, who attribute Moctezuma's death to the indigenous people. On the other hand, there is the version of the indigenous chroniclers such as Fernando Alvarado Tezozómoc and Francisco de San Antón Chimalpahin who, on the contrary, state that he was killed by the Spaniards.

The same confusion presented in this fact (about the death of the Aztec emperor) is reproduced, in a much more vertiginous manner, in the story of his burial, oscillating between two historiographical postures. For some, Moctezuma had a solemn funeral, while for others, Moctezuma was abandoned by all and his funeral was more pitiful, without the honors he deserved for his rank as tlatoani. The truth is that it is impossible to describe Moctezuma's funeral, as Patrick Lesbre recalls, the information generally appears fragmented, confused, and even contradictory. To begin with, the narration claims not to attribute credit to the burning of Moctezuma, since it suggests that it was carried out in accordance with the Aztec ritual, that is, after placing the jade stone in his mouth, symbolizing power and regeneration.[32] But very quickly, Laura, who understands neither its meaning nor its function, except that it is a dangerous object that can suffocate Moctezuma, decides to take it away from him, thus sealing the desecration of the Tlatoani.

> Todo en él era extraño […] Me miró con los párpados entreabiertos mientras yo, sin ningún recato, como una niña, miraba qué era lo que no le dejaba cerrar la boca: sostenía entre las dos mandíbulas una redonda piedra pulida, un enorme jade verde y en los dientes pequeñas piedrecillas empotradas […] Sentí preocupación, ansiedad, de que esa piedra lo fuera a ahogar, y se la saqué de la boca, usando los dedos como pinzas (Boullosa, *Llanto* 49).[33]

Without the chalchihuitl, a symbol of power and immortality, Moctezuma definitively loses his regenerative powers: from there he is dissolved into cosmic dust and becomes forever elusive, dragging Laura with him in a final orgasm. Returned to the dust of time, the spectral figure who calls himself Moctezuma, Motecuhzoma, Motecuzomatzin, Motecuzohma, Motecuhzoma

---

[32] Patrick Lesbre in "L'impossible description? Les funérailles de Moctezuma" notes how "in the Florentine Codex, the indigenous informants of Friar Bernardino de Sahagún provide additional details about Moctezuma's funerals, although with considerable historiographical distortions made in retrospect, more than fifty-five years after the events transpired. Moctezuma had become, in the indigenous consciousness, the one responsible for the disaster of the conquest. Indigenous painters deliberately contrast the lamentable funeral of Moctezuma (fol. 447v°; lib. xii, fol. 40v°), depicted as abandoned by all, with the magnificent funeral of the Lord of Tlatelolco, who perished around the same time (just before the Noche Triste) (fol. 448v°; lib. xii, fol. 41r°)."

[33] Everything about him was strange […] He looked at me with half-closed eyelids as I, without any shame, like a child, examined what was preventing him from closing his mouth: he held between his jaws a round polished stone, an enormous green jade, and in his teeth, small embedded stones […] I felt concern and anxiety that this stone might choke him, so I removed it from his mouth using my fingers like tweezers.

Xocoyotzin, the ninth Aztec Tlatoani, Tlacatecuhtli, The Emperor M.X., Moctezuma II, reduced to dust, mixes and blends into the identity of each Mexican driven by the need to give meaning to their present. In reality, a collective memory cannot exist without individual memory; there is no present without critical readings of the past, and there is definitely no sense of identity without reference to one's origin. Ainsa clarifies, "inscribed into this perspective is the idea that all narrative discourse is, above all else, a recreation created with the attempt of preserving memory" (Aínsa "Guardianes"). From this angle, Moctezuma has no individual memory; Boullosa's novel is her attempt to find one, particularly in communion with his peers, in a universalist and symbolic scope: "El no es un indio, un mexica, no tiene raza ni patria. Él es un hombre que mira el fin del Hombre/ He is not an Indian, a Mexica; he has no race or homeland. He is a man who sees the end of humankind." (*Llanto 39*). The disappearance of Moctezuma and Laura, at the end of the novel, suggests a possible union in their differences:

> entre un muerto y una viva, un indio y una blanca, un rey y una súbdita, un espectro y un cuerpo, volviéndose ambos un solo polvo de muerte y para la muerte. Espectro Moctezuma y cuerpo escritora, fantasmas que transitan para asegurarse que alguna vez irrumpirán, pasarán de éste al otro lado y viceversa, absolutamente extraños, absolutamente cómplices, absolutamente imposibles (s./p.).[34]

The open and deconstructive will of the narration serves as a testimony of an attempt to make intelligible the confused memory of those colonized, buried, transfigured, and to simultaneously liquidate hegemonic discourse and the native sources, by proposing a third voice, a road traced by the word of the Native American Moctezuma. In this way dealing with the silences of history, opening a discourse in the exterior of what is the colonial retelling, self-inscribed as a necessary demand to comprehend the colonial wound referred to by Mignolo, and to break this sense of "epistemic indifference." In other words, to the epistemic privilege of modernity which "generates and maintains coloniality," Boullosa opposes the "epistemic rights" of indigenous peoples as a decolonial option, centered on the other face of history. Certainly, the voice

---

[34] Between a dead man and a living woman, an Indian and a white, a king and a subject, a specter and a body, both becoming a single dust of death and for death. Specter Moctezuma and writer's body, ghosts who pass by to ensure that at some point they will erupt, cross over from this side to the other and vice versa, absolutely strangers, absolutely complicit, utterly impossible.

of the native does not represent the voice of all natives; however, it offers a valid alternative, necessary to complete and counteract the colonial, native projects.

This innovation in narrativity is significant, although it derives, above all else, from the utopian-poetic word, it continues to be inscribed in the wake of border thinking, detached from colonial, hegemonic knowledge, constructed from the "epistemic exteriority," as put by Mignolo. But in this specific case, Boullosa argues that the biography of Moctezuma is impossible to create as there is no historical knowledge without memory.

> Es una necedad estúpida querer escribir una novela de Moctezuma II. Sabios quienes al contar nuestra historia olvidan disertar acerca de las razones de su raro comportamiento, como los que lo adjudican a que en la llegada de los españoles él vio el retorno de Quetzalcóatl y lleno de culpa y temor dejó que tomaran lo que les pertenecía y de inmediato pasan a disertar durante cientos de cuartillas acerca de lo que representó para Occidente el encuentro con este mundo (*Llanto* 75).[35]

Moctezuma's confession is therefore only understandable within the framework of his own geopolitics of knowledge and from collective memory. That world and that memory, marked by epistemic violence and the colonial wound, have disappeared forever. Thus, anyone who attempts to rewrite Moctezuma's history is condemned to a shortsighted perspective, "visto antes de ver, para que cuando el otro se le aproxime [...] vea en él la cara que él sabe que le será vista, que el otro quiere que le sea vista/Seen before seeing, so that when the other approaches, [...] he sees in him the face that he knows will be seen, the face that the other wants to be seen" (Boullosa, *Llanto* 91). With lucidity, Boullosa faces this myopia transformed into impossibility: "No hay novela en el Mexica/ There is no novel in the Mexica" (112), and concludes that only the metaphor can provide the ability to appropriate native knowledge, as Palaisi points out: "The poetic word is therefore, curiously enough, the creative word (meaning of Aristotelian *poiesis*), that which constructs History: the ashes of Moctezuma, these dust carried by the wind, symbolize the word of Moctezuma" (162). To reach the truth about Moctezuma there must be a detachment from history towards fiction, and from fiction towards poetry.

---

[35] It is foolish nonsense to want to write a novel about Moctezuma II. Wise are those who, when recounting our history, neglect to elaborate on the reasons for his odd behavior - those who ascribe it to him seeing the return of Quetzalcóatl in the arriving Spaniards. Filled with guilt and trepidation, he let them seize what was theirs. Immediately, they expound for hundreds of pages on what the encounter with this world represented for the West.

> Sin embargo, no escapa a mi entendimiento de escritor el que esta novela sea imposible. La confesión de Motecuhzoma el joven tiene que ser hecha en el marco de su cultura para ser comprensible. Empresa inútil: Tenochtitlan ha muerto y su memoria es confusa (Boullosa, *Llanto* 39).[36]

In the novel, this utopian idea is taken up through the voice of the wind which scatters, here and there, the ashes of Moctezuma, exasperated in the face of distracted writers, and their inability to understand the emancipatory perspective that a more dispersed memory allows. Today more than ever, it is the wind, subversive, and playful, which blows to awaken the conscience of Mexicans, guilty of indifference towards the past, or making this woman – totally foreign– believe that she is about to bite into a sugar cookie, when in reality, the sugar in her mouth is only the sacred dust of Moctezuma.

> El vientecillo siguió adelante. Aventó de nuevo otro puño a los pies de un atolondrado escritor, enviándolo en un chorro de viento tirado a morir, y ésta fue la constancia que dejó [...] Pero un viento así, mudo y no anónimo, un viento que casi no camina y avanza, un viento así no pertenece a un país o a una patria...Aquí y allá sin disolverse, va dejando la forma de un pasado que nadie quiere ver, que no detesta ni ama ni al cual se arrima, un pasado que no es nada porque no tiene memoria, porque empequeñece (Boullosa, *Llanto* 60, 65-66).[37]

Any narrative project would be doomed to failure if it were expected to recreate an indigenous memory. For this reason, the writing moves away from certainties and advocates that poetry is the only medium capable of extracting indigenous peoples from epistemic violence. Certainly, poetry does not tell stories, as Henry Meschonnic asserts in *États de la poétique*, but it remains nonetheless true that the poet is the one through whom salvation comes.

---

[36] However, as a writer, I understand that this novel is impossible. Motecuhzoma the Younger's confession needs to be framed within his culture to be comprehensible. A fruitless pursuit: Tenochtitlan has perished, and its memory grows hazy.

[37] The gentle breeze moved onwards. It flung another fistful at the feet of a bewildered writer, sending him adrift in a gust of wind, left to perish. Such was the record it left behind [...] But a wind like this—noiseless and not anonymous, a breeze scarcely inching ahead—belongs to no country or homeland... Loitering without fading, now here, then there, it outlines remnants of a bygone era that no one wishes to regard; a past vilified by none, loved by none, drawn near to by none. A past rendered null for having no remembrance, for it withers away.

Works Cited

Aínsa, Fernando. "Nueva novela histórica y relativización del saber historiográfico," *Casa de las Américas*, vol. 1, No 202, 1996, pp. 9-18.

—. "Los guardianes de la memoria: novelar contra el olvido," *Amerika. Mémoires, Identités, Territoires*,141 No. 3, 2010 , http://journals.openedition.org/amerika/1442&gt. Accessed 19 Nov. 2018.

—. "La reescritura de la historia en la nueva narrativa latinoamericana," *Cuadernos Americanos*, núm. 28,1991, pp. 13-31.

Baudot, Georges y Todorov, Tzvetan eds. *Historia de las Indias de Nueva España e islas de la tierra firme: relatos aztecas de la conquista.* Grijalbo, 1990.

Bermúdez, Juan Pablo. "Qui est Walter Mignolo?," *Critique Sociale et Pensée Juridique*, No. 2, 2014.

Bernardino de Sahagún (Fray). *Historia general de las cosas de Nueva España.* Vol. 2 Alianza, 1988.

Boullosa, Carmen. *Llanto. Novelas imposibles*, Era, 1992.

—, "La destrucción en la escritura," *Inti. Revista de Literatura Hispánica*, vol. 1, No 42, 1995.

Bourguignon- Rougier, Claude, Colin, Philippe y Grosfoguel, Ramón dirs. *Penser l'envers obscur de la modernité.* Pulim, 2014.

Cortés, Hernán. *Cartas de relación.* Castalia, 1993.

Díaz del Castillo, Bernal. *Historia verdadera de la conquista de la Nueva España.* Porrúa, 1960.

Droit, Roger-Pol. "Les sens du rire et de l'humour de Roger Sibony," *Le Monde* (París), section "Le Monde des livres," 18 March 2010, https://www.lemonde.fr/livres/article/2010/03/18/les-sens-du-rire-et-de-l-humour-de-daniel-sibony_1320811_3260. Accessed 10 Nov. 2018.

Fanon, Frantz. *Les damnés de la terre* (1961). La Découverte/Syros, 2002.

Jerez Garcés, Gabriela. "Llanto de Carmen Boullosa: notas a una novela imposible," www2.udec.cl/postliteratura/docs/artilinea/Llanto.pdf&gt, Accessed 10 May 2016.

Lani, Soraya y Neiva, Saulo coords. *Temporalités amériendiennes. Représentations de l´Autre et racahat du passé*, Clermont-Ferrand, PUBP, 2021.

León-Portilla, Miguel. *Visión de los vencidos: relaciones indígenas de la conquista.* UNAM, 1959.

—. *Los antiguos mexicanos a través de sus crónicas y cantares.* FCE, 1961.

Lesbre, Patrick. "L'impossible description? Les funérailles de Moctezuma," *e-Spania* (clea), No. 17, February, 2014, http://dx.doi.org/10.4000/e-spania. 23246 &gt. Accessed 12 Feb. 2016.

Madrid Moctezuma, Paola. "Las narraciones históricas de Carmen Boullosa: el retorno de Moctezuma, un sueño virreinal y la utopía de futuro," *América sin nombre. Recuperaciones del mundo precolombino y colonial en el siglo XX hispanoamericano*, No 5-6, 2004, pp. 138-146.

Matos Moctezuma, Eduardo. "¿Quién mató a Moctezuma II, los mexicas o los españoles?," *Arqueología Mexicana*, vol. XXI, No 123, 2013, pp. 88-89.

Menton, Seymour. *La nueva novela histórica de la América Latina, 1979-1992.* FCE, 1993.

Meschonnic, Henri. *Les états de la poétique.* Puf, 1985.

Mignolo, Walter. "Capitalismo y geopolítica del conocimiento," *Modernidades coloniales: otros pasados, historias presentes* edited by Saurabh Dube, Ishita Banerjee-Dube. El Colegio de México-Centro de Estudios de Asia y África, 2004.

—. *La idea de América Latina: la herida colonial y la opción decolonial.* Leidsa, 2007.

—. *Desobediencia epistémica: retórica de la modernidad, lógica de la colonialidad y gramática de la descolonialidad.* Ediciones del Signo, 2010.

—. "La idea de América Latina (la derecha, la izquierda y la opción decolonial)," *Crítica y Emancipación,* año 1, No 2, 2009, pp. 251-276.

—. "Gépolitique de la sensibilité et du savoir. (Dé)colonialité, pensée frontalière et désobéissance épistémologique," translated to English by Vanessa Lee, revised by Seloua Luste Boulbina, *Mouvements. Des idées et des luttes,* No. 73 (2013/1), pp. 181-190 https://www.cairn.info/revue-mouvements-2013-1-page-181.htm&gt. Accessed 17 Nov. 2018.

Mohssine, Assia. "L´option décoloniale dans *Llanto. Romans impossibles* de Carmen Boullosa," en *Temporalités amériendiennes. Représentations de l´Autre et rachat du passé,* Saulo Neiva y Soraya Lani Silva dirs., Clermont-Ferrand, PUBP, coll. Littératures, 2021, pp. 157-179.

— (coord.). *Pensar en activo, Carmen Boullosa entre memoria e imaginación.* Editorial Universidad Autónoma de Nuevo León (UANL), 2019.

O'Gorman, Edmundo. *La invención de América* (1958). FCE, 1995.

Palaisi, Marie-Agnès, "Fonction de l'hypertexte dans la rénovation du genre romanesque. Une application: 'Llanto' de Carmen Boullosa," in Milagros Ezquerro y Julien Roger, comp., *Le texte et ses liens/El texto y sus vínculos: cultures et littératures hispano-américaines,* Indigo et Côté femmes éditions, 2006, pp. 157-166.

Pfeiffer, Erna. *Entrevistas: diez escritoras mexicanas desde bastidores.* Vervuert, 1992.

Pons, María Cristina. *Memorias del olvido: Del Paso, García Márquez, Saer y la novela histórica de fines del siglo XX.* Siglo XXI, 1996.

Chapter 4
Symbolic Violence: Virgins, Witches and Cooks in Carmen Boullosa's Dramaturgy

Ericka H. Parra Téllez
Valdosta State University

Abstract: This essay discusses how desire for material goods and sexual desire is performed in the binary witch-virgin representations. Carmen Boullosa's characters problematize their material and sexual desires within their traditional women's roles; the witches create a man from the traditional role of cooking, while virgins denounce representations of women in media and advertising. According to Parra Téllez, Carmen Boullosa applies experimental theater techniques to illustrate the connections among media, fantasy, legends, and myths while she recreates stories in which the narrative techniques: parody, irony, the juxtaposition of times, and fragmented structure voice women's concerns in different plays. The plural voices of the witch, virgin, and cook seek to recount their stories or their desires with postmodern aesthetics. The performance and reading of her works would allow viewers and listeners to rethink ways of ending unseen violence toward women by discussing and inquiring critically about women's roles today.

Keywords: Symbolic violence, dramaturgy, postmodern, *Teatro Herético*, motherhood, Mexico

***

This essay examines how the dramaturgy of Carmen Boullosa (1954) scrutinizes different forms of desire that dealt with characters who represented stereotypical roles given to women such as the virgin, cook, or witch who seek equality. Yet, the performance of sexual and materialistic desires symbolized an unseen imposition of social norms that became actions of symbolic violence towards women. Among literature, the study on desire dates to the psychoanalyst Sigmund Freud (1932) who argued how women felt "castrated," and the resolution allowed them "feeling desire for the father/penis/baby" (McEnery-West 358). Whereas Freud's study focused on the symbolic meaning of the Oedipus stage and examined the connection with the male power, the term desire could be narrowed to passionate sexual desire, motivation, pleasure, or reward. On one hand, the feminist psychoanalyst Julia Kristeva (1981) argued for the specificity of women and suggested a rethinking of gender power relations from a standpoint of gender difference. In this regard, Third Wave Feminists in the nineties discussed "women's agency" and the creation of new spaces to discuss sexuality, culture, and politics of desire (McEnery-West 362; Ferreira-Pinto). On the other hand, one area that has been developed in recent gender studies discussions is symbolic violence.

Symbolic violence is generally an unperceived form of violence. It is a type of nonphysical violence to maintain social hierarchy and manifest an imposition of social norms across different social domains. According to the French sociologist Pierre Bourdieu (1930-2002), it is an unconscious reinforcement of social norms through language, self-representation, bodily care, and adornment (Grenfell 180; Burawoy). Although Carmen Boullosa's work did not apply directly both terms, desire, and symbolic violence, she addressed how both forms manifested themselves in cultural expressions.

This essay addresses desire and symbolic violence performances. The first section began with Boullosa's trajectory on experimental theater which exemplified various types of desire represented in her work. Then, the second section examined cultural expressions of symbolic violence, the virgin, witch, and cook.

Carmen Boullosa's Experimental Theater

Experimental theater was a scenario for women's narratives to voice women's desire for equality and the creation of new social spaces. In the seventies, experimental theater impacted the Mexican authors as a result of the 1968 student demonstration, known as the Tlatelolco Massacre (2 October). The context of sociopolitical events and women's rights upsurges denoted a rupture in the traditional Mexican theater. The political activism precipitated the entrance of women and other marginalized groups into a reconfigured public space. Within this context, Carmen Boullosa joined the "Martín Pescador" Workshop directed by Juan Pascoe and conformed by Roberto Bolaños with writers like José Luis Rivas, Francisco Segovia, and Verónica Volkow, among others. In fact, most of her work has been translated into English, Chinese, Dutch, French, German, Italian, Portuguese, and Russian. The Mexican writer has received national and international literary prizes and awards for her theater adaptations, acting skills, and production.

Carmen Boullosa's contemporary authors Alicia García Bergua (1954), Jesusa Rodríguez (1955), and Antonio Serrano (1955) promoted Mexican theater with innovative postmodern aesthetics that voiced women's social problems. The questions of power relationships and fragmented narratives echoed feminism through its mid-twentieth-century manifestations in Latin America and became "instrumental in motivating more women to write theater" (Larson and Vargas xi). Thus, Boullosa, in a similar way to other dramatists (such as the Mexican, Pilar Campesino; the Argentinean, Griselda Gambaro; and the Brazilian, Consuelo Castro), was influenced by social movements and committed to self-reflection about modern societal experiences. "Motherhood, communication, personal and social relationships" were performed in Campesino's plays (Larson and Vargas xv). In Mexico, the editor José Ramón Enríquez compiled theater pieces in the anthology *Teatro para la escena/ Theater for Settings* (1996) to outline contributions of works that were the result of the civil rights events.

Carmen Boullosa also directed her plays, group stages, and cabaret shows at the bar-theater, "El Cuervo." In 1983, the plays *Cook Men* and *XE-Bululú* reached "250 representations" (Alarcón 2). The Theatrical Unions honored *Los totoles* directed by Alejandro Aura. In the nineties, *Roja doméstica/Domestic Red* (1996) played in the Museum Rufino Tamayo Forum. The plays in the *Teatro herético/ Heretic Theater* (1987) collection were also staged at the bar-theater. Altogether, her plays represented Mexican theater in Germany and the United States, among other international festivals.

Boullosa's postmodern dramas crossed the boundaries of literary genres. Poetry and short stories became drama stage adaptations. As an example, the drama *Vacío/Emptiness* (1979) originated as a stage adaptation of the poem "Tres mujeres" ("Three Women") by the American poet Sylvia Plath (1932-1963). She wrote the script *Vacío* in collaboration with Julio Castillo and the group members of "Sombras Blancas:" Jesusa Rodríguez, Isabel Benet, Paloma Woolrich, and Francis Laboriel. The play ran in Mexico, and at the Theater Festival in Cologne, Germany, representing Mexico (Enríquez 329). According to Alessandra Luiselli, the poem involving three voices examined the topics of giving birth, abortion, and adoption. In other words, "Boullosa reconfigured the three women as the internal voices of a motherhood assumed with deep anguish" (my trans.; 57-66). Boullosa's theater described fragmented stories to highlight different motherhood identities.

In contrast, the play *13 señoritas, homenaje a Frida Kahlo/Thirteen Young Women* (1983) explored a soliloquy that unfolded multiple images, interested in different women's portrayers. The soliloquy lasted forty-five-minutes in which the actress and dramatist Jesusa Rodríguez performed as Frida Kahlo. Jesusa Rodríguez embodied different viewpoints inspired by thirteen paintings. The scenario "portrayed Kahlo's surrealist paintings" and "lacked unity" (Rabell 4). According to Boullosa, as a teenager, she often saw Frida Kahlo. Thus, for Boullosa, this play honored Frida Kahlo before the artist became "an international icon" (Hind 57). The purpose of this experimental approach was to show a dramatic monologue and fragmented narratives: Boullosa described different women's stories.

The pattern of voicing women's acts of political violence also remained on stage as cabaret. Boullosa and Rodríguez directed the political drama *El tour de corazón/The Heart Tour* (1989). The cabaret piece lasted months on stage, making the audience laugh and have fun. The main character could resemble any Mexican president. One of them, Carlos Salinas de Gortari who launched the country "into the global market through neoliberal economic policy has affected most acutely (and negatively) the middle and lower economic classes" (Constantino 58). As stated by Boullosa, "the meaning changed" based on different political governments as leadership shifted in the political government (my trans.; Hind 60).

The playwrights were included in textbooks and became a pedagogical tool of experimental theater used to question women's roles in relationships. For instance, *El muerto vivo: obra de teatro en cuatro cuadros/ The Death Alive: A Play in Four Piece* (1988). The play had four scenes and the conflict focused on the lack of communication in personal relationships such as extramarital relationships. With humor and irony, the conversation between a dead husband, his wife, and his lover became soliloquies. By itself, death seemed an extension of life whereas a dead body criticized those who were alive. The pedagogical selection facilitated reading aloud and performing as a learning experience.

In sum, the idea of experimental approaches engaged with multiple possibilities of constructed identities that aimed to open avenues by the desire of voicing self-representations and active representation in social issues.

Cultural Expressions of Symbolic Violence: Cooks, Virgins, and Witches

Boullosa expressed in several interviews that she advocated for the voices and images of different women whose stories included diversity in modern society. Thus, her plays opened spaces for those cooks, virgins, and witches found in fairytales, legends, and fantastic stories; and allowed them to perform those stories of different social backgrounds, including those in which they played roles behind the scenes.

In the art of cooking, the kitchen set up a space to reflect on how women talked back and told another version of their stories. The kitchen became a space where women exchanged conversations and philosophical ideas. For example, since the XVII century, Sor Juana Inés de la Cruz in *Respuesta a Sor Filotea de la Cruz/ Answer to Sor Filotea* (1691) said, "But, lady, as women, what wisdom may be ours if not the philosophies of the kitchen?" (54). In reconstructing other women's social places, the symbolic action of cooking opened spaces for oral expression and creation. But how did the spaces open to women symbolize a trap?

a) A Talkative Cook: *My Version of Events*

First, in the drama, *My Version of Events/ My Version of Events* (1987), such a "version" did not find a public space. The cook, who performed as a secondary character, found herself displaced, and trapped in a tower where she remained uncommunicated. The discussion on gender in reference to fairy tales and social issues showed female characters unable to communicate with each other. In this paradox, the main character Margarita, kept asking the talkative cook where she found herself. Whereas the story's fantastic plot resembled a dream in which the author or cartoonist drew and erased the characters, the background framed a place of mystery and danger from which the cook, a talkative woman, also vanished.

In the prologue to the play, Bruce Swansey proposed multiple readings. One of them recalled *Rapunzel,* the German fairy tale by the Brothers Grimm published in 1812. She lived locked up in a tower with neither stairs nor a door, but only one window. The second way to read the play focuses on the confusing, repetitive, and meaningless nature of the language used. Lastly, drawings framed spaces surrounding the protagonists that later were erased (Boullosa, *My Version* 10). The plot outlined the nonexistence of freedom while the setting encompassed a room deprived of windows, even though the blinds simulated their existence. The illusion of staying in a closed place conspired and contradicted the experience of each character. The scenario embodied a tower without stairs.

The story had multiple characters that developed throughout the drama. For example, the men who interrogated Margarita created the illusion that they were many men. To distinguish each other, they took names after their blue, brown, and gray suits. Other characters included a woman who performed multiple roles such as a saleswoman, hungry cook, hairdresser, and caretaker: all of the characters suspected each other. The drama's narrator represented a Mexican intellectual from the eighties who had ideological conflicts. Thus, the unfolded image of the actors ensembled many stories of people who were trapped in their dreams. In the ensemble acting the cook also disappeared without evidence; although she seemed unsteady, she served Margarita.

Then, a new character unfolds. It is the saleswoman. She advised Margarita to forget the cook, and without adding anything, she told her to get used to only dream:

VENDEDORA. (*Entrando*) Así es siempre, con los dibujos. Al contacto de cualquier mirada. Llamas que parecen ni quemar. A eso estamos ya acostumbrados. A lo que todavía no nos acostumbramos es a ver la misma manifestación en seres humanos. ¿Te acuerdas de la mujer gorda que venía a vestirte?

MARGARITA. ¡Cómo no me voy a acordar! (97)

VENDEDORA. Pues vete olvidando de ella. Le pasó lo mismo, quien sabe por qué, dice el del traje café que se le quedó viendo y ante su mirada ¡zas! Nada. Ni humito (riéndose). ¡Esa gordita no era gran cosa! Yo también soñé que me pintaba el pintor.

MARGARITA. ¿Y no pudo hacer nada por ella?

VENDEDORA. ¿Por quién? ¿Por la gordita? Aquí nadie puede hacer nada por nadie. No nos queda más que soñar y soñamos poco porque todos acostumbramos a interrumpir nuestros sueños.... (98)[1]

In other words, the saleswoman's message was to forget because it was just a dream. Women's conversation about the cook focused on the prohibition of helping each other and insisting that it was a dream. However, the secret dialogue between the cook and Margarita did not exist. Thus, the desire to subvert silence and challenge hegemonic power might just be a vision. The enclosed space without stairs symbolically obliterated those women who expressed their ideas. In the end, Margarita opened the door; she also vanished. At the same time, the author repeated the other way around the phrase: I can't, "Odeuponoy, odeuponoy" ("T'nac I, t'nac I"; my trans.; 103). Then, he also disappeared. The plot related to the allusion of a tower, as the place in which

---

[1] SALESWOMAN. (*Entering*) That is the way it always is, with the drawings. At the contact of any gaze, flames. Flames that do not seem to burn. We are already used to that. What we still do not get used to is seeing the same manifestation in human beings. Do you remember the heavy woman who used to come to dress you?
MARGARITA. How can I not remember!
SALESWOMAN. Forget about her. The same thing happened to her, who knows why, says the brown suit that stared at her before her gaze, bang! Nothing. Not even hazy (*laughing*). The heavy woman was not a big deal! I also dreamed that the painter was painting me.
MARGARITA. And, couldn't you do anything for her?
SALESWOMAN. For whom? For the heavy girl? No one can do anything for anyone here. We have nothing left but to dream, and we dream a little because we all are used to interrupt our dreams...(my trans.)

women's dreams vanished, was a technique to break through the narrative of unpowered women.

Carmen Boullosa addressed in an interview with Emily Hind that the playwright of *My Version of Events* did not stage. However, the irony and parody were different from the other plays: Humor resulted in harsh and irritating situations because of the "political Mexican context" where not only women but all citizens could not speak out (Hind 55-56). In particular, the plot denounced how governments did not hear people voicing disappeared students and women's violence. The title itself conveyed that "one's version of events" resulted in invalid proof to decry corruption. Thus, the Mexican writer intended to make the audience laugh spontaneously. Boullosa answered "Incluso ante el dolor, la risa aparece como una salida mágica/ Even in the face of pain, laughter appears as a magical way out" (my trans.; 55). Nevertheless, the drama led to gaining awareness of confined spaces where symbolic violence seemed to transform into a mental matter for those talkative women. In sum, women's voices in different settings were suppressed.

b) The Antagonistic Cook: *Los totoles*

Second, in the drama *Los totoles / The Turkey* (1985), Carmen Boullosa adapted a traditional Nahuatl fable to point out that if the cook dared to speak became a cultural decorative artifact. For instance, the function of the cook was to reclaim her space in the kitchen. In this drama, Sebastiana's control over the food set boundaries for workers who went to work in the kingdom of King Totol. Boullosa adapted *Los totoles* story from the Nahuatl short story *Los totoles* by Armando E. Martínez. In oral tradition, the story told how the character of Pascuala transformed into a mermaid. Nowadays, the mermaid with a guitar has become a cultural artifact made of wood for tourists, another way to silence women.

The drama's adaptation represented an empowered cook who rejected the action of cooking for workers. Yet, Boullosa's adaptation anticipated themes such as migration, and women's empowerment was represented by the cook. In the social structure, the characters were ants, a donkey, a coyote, and a stork, while the *totoles*, the Nahuatl word for turkeys, represented King Totol Santiago. But the conflict between Chunel and the cook Sebastiana Pascuala had to do with her resistance to cook.

She wanted Chunel and other indigenous to abandon the kingdom of King Totol Santiago. Consequently, the malevolent cook set obstacles and manipulated the King, and so Chunel gave up on impossible tasks such as separating the corn from wheat, training maroon horses, or having a child in one night. In response to these difficulties, the humanized animals helped Chunel achieve those tasks. Julio Ortega discussed that in *Los totoles* the story of facts transformed the fable and became the story itself wherein the fantasy-reality frames everybody as helping each other (my trans.; 145).

In Boullosa's *Los totoles* version, one cook's quality resembled her as a mediator between the workers and King Totol. She impeded Tunel from talking directly with King Totol. In this regard, she said,

> SEBASTIANA. "Espéreme aquí (*cierra la puerta, camina hacia la habitación principal del castillo del rey.*) Oiga, Totol Santiago, ahí afuera hay un hombre que dice que quiere trabajo"(18).[2]

Sebastiana left Tunel waiting and closed the door before him. In closing the door, she built a frontier that prevented laborers from meeting directly with the King. This way, she manifested her power as the liaison between the people and the patriarchal power.

She had controversial opinions about the workers, particularly if the situation related to her eagerness to free herself from serving others. She justified her action and remarked, "Then they do not even work well and eat a lot" (my trans;19). She also restricted access to the kitchen: it became her space in which she gained power by controlling the food for workers.

The cook's constant resistance to serving the workers may also represent a subversive action towards women's traditional roles. However, in the end, King Totol achieved justice for workers by transforming the cook into an art craft. She became a quiet enchanted mermaid with a guitar. Indeed, she continued as an eternal cultural artifact standing for what could happen to talkative women who resisted cooking and serving. The fable's morality reconfigured society's responses to those women who dared to cross the patriarchal power borders.

c) *Mary, Why Don't You?* (Impossible Dialogue in One Act)

In other cultural traditional settings the stereotype of the "virgin" is represented. In *Mary, Why Don't You?* (1987) the main theme echoed the last conversation between Mary and Joseph as a form to exemplify women's agency. The set reproduced the times of the catholic origin of the family; Mary and Joseph symbolized the traditional family. Therefore, the deconstruction of the patriarchal model could create awareness of how these culture manifestations express symbolic violence. According to Marta Cabrera, a Colombian cultural studies critic, the forms of symbolic and cultural violence existed since the Middle Ages and have continued through to today's context of economic

---

[2] SEBASTIANA. Wait for me here (closes the door, walks toward the main room of the King's castle.) Listen, Totol Santiago, outside there is a man who wants a job (my trans.).

globalization (344). Carmen Boullosa went back to the story of Mary to portray the virgin image as an active inquiring woman. The deconstruction of the patriarchal model could create awareness of how these cultural manifestations express symbolic violence.

In *Mary, Why Don't You?* Boullosa attempted, for her audience, to find evidence of the last conversation between Mary and Joseph by recording their voices. This element of experimental theater consisted of rethinking how Mary, according to the Catholic tradition, configured the image of a virtuous woman. In the play, Mary's character knew her destiny as the Holy Mother. Therefore, the performance of the last conversation between Mary and Joseph expressed her curiosity regarding her sexual desires.

The play had Act One and time stamps to indicate subtitles. At the beginning of Act One, the narrator introduces an "Important Note" as a preface, explaining how he secretly received the anonymous transcription from the voice recording of Mary and Joseph's last conversation. The omniscient narrator confessed that he hid tapes at the foot of Joseph and Mary's bed.

In searching for evidence from the "last conversation," the readers learned about Mary's struggles on her mission as a mother. Thus, the recording corroborated how by using anthropological instruments readers could find Mary voicing her version and desires. At the opening of each scene, the titles were numbers displayed as clips from a recorded tape featuring time stamps. These inconsistencies carried the idea of veracity. Later, the narrator exposed that the message was cut, and incomplete, stating that these time markings could also represent the length of the tape or other measurements. The application of this fragmented technique told a story with questionable results since the truth was altered and edited out.

According to the tapes as evidence, the couple encounter before Jesus's birth and Mary's ascension to Heaven. In the last conversation, they were listening to the Radio announcing women's latest fashion while Mary asked Joseph about sexual desire. The story in this drama featured the motif of two lovers talking about their desires. Interrupting that mindset, the poetic voice of the radio personified economic globalization. The radio commercials blended into the scene, advertising fashion and clothes as material desires. García Canclini in *La globalización imaginada* (1999) also argued that economic globalization appropriated media and culture to incorporate hegemonic models. Thus, in *Mary, Why Don't You?*, the motif of radio commercials configured the idea of women's beauty standards and the push of women to resemble society's ideal woman in order to please men.

To illustrate, Mary argued that diet entailed unnecessary tributes to beauty because of how colors and style shaped women's bodies, including "a veil in a softer shade covering the neck, and bare to the waist" (Boullosa, *Mary* 198). Joseph complained about the commercials and asked her to change the station since he preferred to listen to the news. At that moment, Mary interrupted him, allowing herself to listen to the radio because she recognized the woman talking about hairdos. In the meantime, Mary and Joseph's voice-recorded last conversation had radio commercials playing as background noise. In other words, the message was unclear.

Women's fashion reinforced the image of desirable women, while Mary posed the idea of gender power over women starting with everyday scenes to express fascination for the latest style. In particular, Mary told Joseph a story about a wife who dressed in a "low cut in front and her back covered" (198).

> MARY: Do you know what they told me? A husband would always force his wife to wear dresses cut very low in the back, and when he invited people to the house, after dinner he gave her a signal and she got up from the table and returned with the dress on the backward: the low cut in the front and her back covered ... (198)

Then, she vocalized, "This fashion is going to look terrific on her" (198). In particular, she voiced how fashion symbolically shaped a desirable image of a wife/woman through the way she looks according to the model proposed by radio announcements.

On the other hand, Mary inquiring her role as a chosen mother and her sexual desire. Mary kept asking questions to avoid being close to him since the religious principle prohibited women's sexual experiences before motherhood. According to Michela di Giorgio, the virtuous feminine model discussed moral principles inspired by Marianistic devotion (231). In addition to fashion shaping beauty, an example that voiced women's sexual desire repressed was included in a letter. It contained another clue in which Mary and Joseph talked about desire.

They found a note that posed the problem of how women's attitudes towards good manners were mistaken as submissive actions while the author moved to talk about sexual desire. The letter below introduced the topic of conversation to which Joseph pointed out, "Listen to this, it's hilarious." Next, he read it aloud to Mary:

> *I can tell you that the better we get along in our daily life, and the more time we spend together, the worse we understand one another in bed. The more I respect her as a person, the less I desire her as a woman. Is what is happening to me **is** normal? Is there some way to fight against this?* (Boullosa 199; italics in original)

The discussion on desire transcended the couple's conversation about fashion. Indeed, the above intertext led to Mary's inquiring about how a man and woman's sexual relationship happened. Joseph unreciprocated with her concerns, and instead said she would not understand. He silenced her questions on desire.

Culture also shaped women's silent desires by justifying that "she would not understand." When Joseph talked to Mary, he called her "little girl," each time she asked for a "night of desire" (203). In a way, his response denoted her curiosity as an irrational query. Even so, they would not experience passion, and she would be kept wondering how sexual desire would feel. Joseph idealized Mary by expressing his love, then he repeated, "You are my little girl, my little sister" (203). In this regard, Cabrera examined that one could find cultural violence "in the hegemonic practices of everyday life, is key, in the opinion of feminist and subalternist critique, in articulating relations of domination and subordination" (344). According to "Catholic culture, women lacked an adult body" (Boullosa, *Interview* 56). The *Marianism* myth prevented women's participation in economics, jobs, and sexuality. In the play, Joseph treated Mary as a child. To mirror the past with the present, the Marxist feminist Lillian Robinson also discussed that "women's traditional roles have also shaped an established patriarchal aesthetic" (Robinson 33). Boullosa's scenario placed the conversation between traditional icons out of time, to add a humorous tone, entertain the audience, and reflect on women's stereotypes and how women have found ways to voice their desires and passions.

Overall, whether the last conversation between Mary and Joseph happened or not required more evidence. Mary's doubts remained unanswered in Boullosa's drama because the tape ran over. Since then, the collected evidence failed to uncover the truth. In this case, the way to deconstruct chastity's patriarchal discourse opened a space to rethink Mary's questions on social manners, fashion, and women's desires. In general, the Virgin Mary's image culturally constructed acceptable relations between wives and husbands. However, the drama *Mary, Why Don't You?* promoted awareness and opened forums to discuss and extract new meanings from the image of the holy mother as a symbolic and cultural gender construction. With this experimental approach, the author posed a dilemma that could be self-reflected and challenged ideas of devotion to rethink *Marianismo* influences that suppressed women's desires and passions.

d) *Aura and the Eleven Thousand Virgins*

Beauty consumerism and sexual desire are manifested around cultural representations in very subtle ways that convey symbolic violence toward women's desires. An example of denouncing symbolic violence to silent women's desires has also ensued in *Aura y las once mil vírgenes/Aura and the Eleven Thousand Virgins* (1986). The drama portrayed the experience of the symbolic and multifaceted character named Eleven Thousand Virgins. One actress performed it to trigger Aura's creativity and inspiration for television-commercial acting. The Postmodern paradigm of art intersects mass media and advertising to configure a "hyper-representation" of the Mexican culture landscape altered by foreign consumer products, using "the mass media to perpetuate a myth of national unity and democratic reform" (Constantino 55-58). Thus, the ensemble of the virgin represented women's multiple constructed identities to voice different perspectives and explore how women's desires became acts of symbolic violence in the media.

The two acts of this drama outlined the acquisition of material goods and allowed the audiences and readers to discuss how commercialism increased the proliferation of erotic portrayals of women. In the first act, the conflict focused on Aura having writer's block. He worked at his friend Juan Ramon's Advertising Agency as director. However, Aura felt unhappy and frustrated because he wanted to become a famous actor. El Único, the antagonist character, performed as the omnipresence of patriarchal power. This parody focused on a hierarchical structure that invested "all power and wisdom in one *masculine* figure" similar to "Mexico's political, social, religious and economic institutions" (Constantino 61). Indeed, El Único's role entailed manipulating Aura's inspiration and desires. Therefore, Aura's desire as a television star would be granted if he deflowered the Eleven Thousand Virgins' multifaceted character. The reading of the virgin image represented the imaginary of eleven thousand virgins who symbolized women's disappearance. One version of the legend told that Saint Ursula and the eleven thousand virgins joined Ursula's pilgrimage to Rome from Cologne, Germany. On the journey, all of them were killed. However, another Christian version stated that only eleven women made the pilgrimage to symbolize missing women. Therefore, the disappearance of the virgins symbolizes the suppression of women who voice their concerns and organize pilgrimages.

The drama also portrayed innumerable actions against women's real desires and passions. For example, the motif questioned whether Aura harassed and abused two thousand virgins just to become a famous actor. The plot focuses on the transformation of virgins into women and the increased desire to obtain material goods for beauty. At the same time, Aura gained inspiration to design creative advertisements such as shampoo, creams, and beauty magazines for women. Beauty images portrayed the new women as beings without free will to think. In sum, the virgins' motif criticized the consumerism of material things in exchange for their virginity, but still, the media represented the polyphony image as irrational beings.

In the second act, Aura refrained from continuing with Unique's plan. Unique, the antagonist character, threatened Aura, using the same recording technique used in *Mary, Why Don't You?* Again, the evidence pointing towards the intellectual as the perpetrator of the crimes waned. The voice message from Unique emphasized, "Sabrás lo que es tener toda mi fuerza en tu contra, mis ejércitos, mis … (Entra interferencia en la cinta y no se oye más)" 'You will know what it is to have all my power against you, my armies… (An interference breaks the tape, and it is no longer heard)'; (my trans.; Boullosa, *Aura* 36). Hence it appears that the proof against the patriarchal voice Unique died out, signifying the death of the patriarchal voice.

Right after, the police became involved in the crime of missing the two thousand virgins that Aura deflowered and those "whose bodies were still missing" (36). In this frame, the television news denounced the problem of missing women due to violence. However, Aura escaped the police and hid in a Mennonite Church. In other words, the man who deflowered the symbolic Eleven Thousand Virgins found refuge in a church, the institution where the myth of the virtuous women began. In the discussion on cultural violence, Galnung argued that social structures were exploited and discriminated against when using symbolic mechanisms such as "language and art" (qtd. in Cabrera 344). Indeed, the drama related the image of the female in television commercials as a social and national commodity, where women's desires for beauty are interconnected with consumerism in such a way that "selling" the idea of beauty caused violence in the action of deflowering the Eleven Thousand Virgins multi-faced character, to continue as dependent or "subservient" of male desire (Ferreira-Pinto 8).

The juxtaposition of the Eleven Thousand Virgins' parody intersected television commercials with gender in economic globalization. Characters resembling virgins prompted the audience's self-reflection on the virgin myth as a continuous model in the present time. Thus, the image of a virgin was reconfigured as a woman who subverted everyday roles in media and performances in society to provoke awareness of symbolic forms of violence. Overall, the juxtaposition of corruption and media reached a broader audience searching for evidence of missing women due to violent social acts in contemporary Mexican society (Constantino 56).

e) Witches or Creators of Man in *Cocinar hombres/Cook Men*)?

The last example was to illustrate the action of cooking a man to challenge the patriarchal power of creation. Thus, a witch challenged the desire of women for the creation of man. In *Cook Men* (1984), the structure's drama had an introduction, a dream, and two Acts. The story recounted how two teens could not remember how they became 23-year-old women at an initiation ceremony.

However, these two new women, Wine and Ufe, realized they could fly and lure men. With the new power, both imagined how to create the ideal man.

In the Introduction, the author underlined that the witches were different from the traditional model of French witches or *lamias* (Boullosa, *Cocinar* 46). In fact, Lamia was a "grief-crazed woman...Her own children were killed by Hera, who was jealous of Zeus's love for her; thereafter Lamia, out of envy for happy mothers, stole and killed the children of others" (qtd. in Wehling 52-53). However, the play questions the creation of gender roles designed by patriarchy. In the Dream chapter, the characters Ufe and Wine appeared on stage, having a conversation after they were taken away. Ufe recalled herself driving her mother's car and living in her mother's body. In the first Act, they talked about the events of the night before. In the second Act, both characters talked about cooking a man. The unexpected changes to their bodies happened at an initiation ceremony, where they became witches. Wine and Ufe remembered how they were violently caught and taken to the ceremony and forced to drink. The following day, they were floating except when they were wearing shoes. Their bodies also changed; the nails grew longer, and the head seemed heavy. Their bodies began to metamorphose (52). Wine confirmed what Ufe started remembering, and she told Ufe her version of the fantastic experience, using the personal "I" she joyfully expressed:

> WINE. Antes de que cruzara la noche montada en un pez, antes de que viajara como en agua, antes de que sintiera el frío de la luna brillando en las escamas de ese pez inmenso, antes de que oyera todo tan lejano mientras él me llevaba rápidamente, jugando, saltando, zigzagueando, rodeada de esa risa inexplicable, sintiendo en los hombros y en los pechos la cabellera larguísima que ahora no tengo pero que anoche, tibia, tupida, me cubría para acariciarme …. (52).[3]

The above fantastic scene detailed how Wine expressed how she felt towards her body's transformation. Although Wine argued on the importance of desire, Wine geared "to feel less" breaking through the stereotype that women were more emotional.

---

[3] WINE. Before I crossed the night riding a fish, before I traveled as in water, before I felt the cold of the moon shining on the scales of that immense fish, before I heard everything so far away as he carried me quickly, playing, jumping, zigzagging, surrounded by inexplicable laugher, feeling on my shoulders and breasts the very long hair that I do not have now but that last night, warm, thick, covered me to caress me...(my trans.).

Ufe refused to accept her body's transformation while Wine talked about desire as a territory that she did not lose. Wine told Ufe,

> WINE. De eso que ocurre sin que lo podamos compartir con nadie, de eso que sólo se platica uno a sí mismo y a solas y que a veces no podemos ni platicarnos a nosotros mismos porque no encontramos las palabras para hacerlo, ese territorio inmenso donde siempre estamos solos (56).[4]

In the example above, Wine argued that the body became women's territoriality where they expressed desire. In this regard, Ufe contradicted her by saying that the body or territoriality "hinges on social roles." Then, she noted, "we have a body tied to our gender roles" (66). By this, she referred to motherhood as a means of uniting man and woman. Ufe revisited the theme of desire from another perspective after recalling how witches cooked the other girls; then, she proposed "cooking a man" to do wherever she asked him to do (68). But also, Ufe desired a man to whom to love and who loved her, a man who felt passion and motherly love towards her, meaning to have unconditional love. The action of "cooking men, rather than cooking *for* men" took on "an anti-patriarchal stance suggesting nothing less than a revolution" (Wehling 52). In Act two, they created a man before they vanished. Ufe described her ideal man:

> UFE. Que sólo me quiera a mí y que yo lo adore; que no haya para mí nada más que él. Y lo quiero cálido y expresivo…y más que nada quiero amarlo. Que apenas lo vea sienta que lo adoro, que inexplicablemente no puedo vivir sin él. Que sea él mi lazo con el mundo, que sea mi padre, mi hermano, mi madre, y que yo lo sea para él. Eso quiero. (79).[5]

Although Ufe focused on ideal love, cooking a man transformed her into the protagonist of her dream. The symbolic way to gain power is through her discursive recipe inserted in the traditional binary model of a sensitive woman redesigning a sensitive man. Her description also echoed Joseph's fraternal

---

[4] WINE. Of what happens without us being able to share it with anyone, what one only talks about to oneself and alone and that sometimes we cannot even talk to ourselves because we cannot find the words to do so, that immense territory where we are always alone (my trans).

[5] UFE. May he only love me and that I adore him; may he be nothing for me but him. And, I want him warm and expressive… and more than anything, I want to love him. That as soon as I see him, he feels I adore him, that inexplicably I cannot live without him. May he be my link with the world, may he be my father, my mother, and may I be more for him. That is what I want. (my trans.).

discourse in the drama *Mary, Why Don't You?* After everything, the stage and the dramatic time departed radically from conventional dramatic forms. The end was not a synthesis of the old and the new. Ufe decided to join Wine in her departure from her patriarchal Mexican roots, entering a new system beginning with "appropriating language, signifying and narrative practices" (Wehling 55). The witches flying to a world beyond patriarchy incarnated "women's desire, women's sexuality" and the vindication of a type of woman that tradition has deemed evil or a witch (Flores 63). In sum, the teenagers' transgression to women and then to witches opened a possibility of resigning stereotypes and designing a subject with whom the relationship remained equal.

Conclusion

The term desire, rooted in the search for power, motivation, pleasure, or agency to open new spaces, enables us to uncover unseen elements of symbolic violence that prevent women to perform as agents in different social spaces. Even more, desire has been silenced by men against women and sometimes has been misinformed to confuse women's suppression of their feelings and wishes. Therefore, the experimental approach engaged ideas of challenging what could have happened if there were evidence of those role models imposed by patriarchal cultures, such as Mary and Joseph's last conversation. Or, by deconstructing the images of virgins and witches that conformed to the binary of good and bad women. Or, by transforming the role of the cook to voice her desire not cooking or creating a man.

Indeed, women's social constructions as virgins, witches, or cooks represent subtle forms of symbolic violence since society continues accepting those culturally imposing roles. The social dramas above represented a parodical fantasy created to produce the illusion of reality transgressing spaces and roles of power. As a consequence of that irreverence, one cook vanished and the second became a cultural artifact; one virgin continued her role as a mother but asked about sexual desire; and the teen witches wished to create a man to promote awareness of gender equity in which everyone was involved, everyone.

Overall, Carmen Boullosa's theater represented how culture had delved into traditional gender roles, using language to configure women's representations. Performances mirrored symbolic and cultural elements of violence across historical times to bring media to evidence symbolic elements such as calling Mary "little girl" or "my little sister." For instance, the settings of fashion or cleaning products assessed the validity of virgins' irony and witches' performances by allowing readers to critique what Aura or the cartoonist considered insignificant actions, such as women's intellect or the fact they inquire critically about traditional roles.

In summation, Carmen Boullosa's theater plays a crucial role in deconstructing the binary virgin-witch to include the cook, and to re-signify the creation of men. The connections among media, fantasy, legends, and myths recreated stories in which the narrative techniques: of parody, irony, the juxtaposition of times, polyphonic voices, and fragmented structure were techniques of the experimental theater. Language also intersects reality and fantastic events. Therefore, the ensemble acting and reading aloud mirrored symbolic and cultural forms of violence. The hope is that each woman within the stereotyped roles assigned by men could perform their own change and breakthrough attitudes that allowed unequal viewpoints towards women's material and sexual desires.

Works Cited

Alarcón, Justo S. "Biografía. Carmen Boullosa." *Revista Literaria Katharsis*, no. 7, 2008, pp. 1-9. revistaliterariakatharsis.org/Carmen_Biografia.pdf.

Boullosa, Carmen. *Aura y las once mil vírgenes* (comedia). *Teatro herético*. Universidad Autónoma de Puebla, 1987, pp. 9-41.

—. *Cocinar hombres: obra de teatro íntimo*, *Teatro herético*. Universidad Autónoma de Puebla, 1987, pp. 43-82.

—. *El muerto vivo: obra de teatro en cuatro cuadros*. *Voces de Hispanoamérica. Antología Literaria*, edited by Raquel Chang-Rodríguez and Malva E. Filer, 2015, pp. 613-627.

—. *Los Totoles*, Editorial Alfaguara, 2000.

—. *Mi versión de los hechos*, Arte y Cultura ediciones, 1987.

—. *Mary, Why Don't You? (Impossible Dialogue in One Act)*. *Contemporary Mexican Women Writers: Five Voices*. Translated by Gabriella de Beer, U of Texas P, 1996, pp. 196-208.

—. *Propusieron a María (Diálogo imposible en un acto)*. *Teatro herético*. Universidad Autónoma de Puebla, 1987, pp. 83-101.

—. *Vacío. Teatro para la escena*. Edited by José Ramón Enríquez, Ediciones El Milagro, 1996, pp. 327-363.

Burawoy, Michael. *Symbolic Violence: Conversations with Bourdieu*. Duke University Press, 2019, https://doi.org/10.1515/9781478007173.

Cabrera, Marta. "Violencia." *Dictionary of Latin American*, edited by Robert Mckee Irwin and Mónica Szmurk, U of Florida, pp. 342-347.

Constantino, Roselyn. "Postmodernism and Feminism in Mexican Theater: *Aura y las once mil vírgenes* by Carmen Boullosa. *Latin American Theater Review*, vol. 28, no. 2, 1995, pp. 55-72. *EBSCOhost*.

Cruz, sor Juana de la. *Respuesta a sor Filotea de la Cruz*. Fontamara, 1998.

Enríquez, José Ramón, editor. "Textos nacidos en el escenario." *Teatro para la escena*. Ediciones El Milagro, 1996, pp. 9-12.

Ferreira-Pinto, Cristina. *Gender, Discourse, and Desire in Twentieth-Century Brazilian Women's Literature*. Purdue U P, 2004. *JSTOR*, https://doi.org/10.2307/j.ctt6wq4tx.

Flores, Yolanda. *The Drama of Gender: Feminist Theater by Women of the Americas*. Peter Lang, 2000.

García Canclini, Néstor. *La globalización imaginada*, Paidós, 1999.

Giorgio, Michela de. "El modelo católico." *Historia de las Mujeres. El siglo XIX.* Edited by George Duby and Michelle Perrot, Taurusminor, 1993, pp. 206-258.

Grenfell, Michael, editor. *Pierre Bourdieu: Key Concepts*. Routledge, 2014.

Hind, Emily and Carmen Boullosa. "Carmen Boullosa." *Hispanoamérica*, vol. 30, *no.* 90, 2001, pp. 49-60. www.jastor.org/stable/20540327.

Larson Catherine and Margarita Vargas, editors. *Latin American Women Dramatists: Theater, Texts, and Theories*. Indiana U P, 1998.

Luiselli, Alessandra. "*Vacío* de Carmen Boullosa y Sylvia Plath: Performatividad, textualidad y adaptación." *Latin American Theatre Review (Project Muse)*, vol. 48, no. 2, Nov. 2015, pp. 55-70.

Ortega, Julio. "Fabulaciones de Carmen Boullosa." *Celehis: Revista del Centro de Letras Hispanoamericanas*, vol. 2, no. 2, 1992, pp. 145-157.

Rabell, Malkah, "Se alza el telón. *Trece señoritas*, ¡viva la audacia!" *El Día,* 27 Jul 1983, p. 24, criticateatral2021.org/transcripciones/2507_830727.php.

Robinson, Lillian S. "Canon Fathers and Myth Universe." *Left Politics and the Literary Profession*. Edited by Lennard J. Davis and M. Bella Mirabella, Columbia U P, 1990, pp. 147-161.

Wehling, Susan. "Cocinar hombres. Radical Feminist Discourse." *Gestos: teoría y práctica del teatro hispánico*. Vol. 8, no. 16, Nov., 1993, pp. 51-62.

Chapter 5

Las Paredes Hablan a Crossroad between Time and Memory

María R. Matz

University Massachusetts, Lowell

Abstract: In a loop of three centuries (1810, 1910, and 2010), Boullosa narrates the History of Mexico while presenting an impossible love-story between the two main characters. In a non-chronological narration located in the neighborhood of San Ángel in Mexico City and inspired by Elena Garro's novel *The Memories of the Future*, history, passion, hate, corruption, and the repetition of past errors are what keeps memories alive. Using the History of Mexico as a fictional element in the novel *Las paredes hablan*, its narrator is a house, *Casa Espíritu*, whose voice is located in a perpetual present, offering the reader an account of how Mexico became an independent country. Matz's essay illustrates how memory is a puzzle in three dimensions and *Casa Espíritu* becomes, through its memories, a metaphor for modern Mexico.

Keywords: Mexican bicentenary, *Las Paredes hablan*, memory, history, art, official history, Casa Espíritu, Mexico

***

Critics have defined Carmen Boullosa's writing as multilayered and complex, occupying the margins between discourse, the body, and subjectivity. Her works resist reductionist readings, with plots and characters that shift, and transform based on historical and cultural contexts. According to Julio Ortega, Boullosa's narrative zigzags among styles, as each beginning emerges from its own creative nothingness, separate from any tradition. Rather than building on preexisting texts and ideas, Boullosa starts anew each time with an intransigent inventiveness. Every work is a fresh challenge, in her works, she transcends genre constraints and traditional narrative forms through constant reinvention at the levels of style, structure, and subject matter. Critics emphasize this refusal to be pinned down as a defining feature of Boullosa's body of work, which occupies an ever-transforming space between the written word, human experience, and systems of meaning (Ortega, 10). Furthermore, as she states in several interviews: "Writing a novel is a bestial effort. You face your own demons. The effort is not just intellectual or emotional but physical: I finish my novels with a destroyed neck" (Flores).[1]

Casa Espíritu and Mexico

As a reflection of the Mexican bicentenary, in *Las paredes hablan* (*The Walls Speak*, 2010), Boullosa, once again, focuses on the history of Mexico and the micro-stories of everyday life. In this novel, her use of historiographic metafiction has enabled her "to create upon a historical basis, to surpass historiography with her imagination, to continue a history's intertextual discourse, and to establish a new version" that "has a new perspective or optic" (Chorba, 42). The plot of the story is very simple: a XIX century house (*Casa Espíritu*), located in the San Ángel neighborhood in Mexico City, tells us the tragic love story of Javier and María. This story is repeated cyclically and inevitably in the 1810s, 1910s, and 2010s. The couple loves each other during these different times against all adversities and, overall, against the will of their families, who belong to conflicting political/social factions. The presence of a collection of Mexican art is also important in the story, as it symbolizes Mexico through the times and the seizure of power by opposing factions during these centuries. Like Mexico throughout the centuries, this art collection changes ownership according to each historical moment.

This romantic drama underwent a winding journey before crystallizing as a novel. In its initial stages conceived as a script for a film of the same name. However, the author later recognized that the novel format better captured her cinematographic imaginary. As Carmen Boullosa stated when discussing her creative process, the story migrated across mediums – from initial script to novel, and back to script again. This non-linear writing process allowed her to create a story that took on a life of its own, independent of the intended medium.

> After writing the script, when pre-production began, I realized that the film was going to be something very in tune with the vision of its director and producers. I decided that I was going to make a novel based on that script. The process, as you can see, was a bit backwards. First, we worked on the script and then...I wrote the book...As [the film] was emerging, I realized that they were going the other way. Because that's how it is, that's the adventure of cinema, the film belongs to the director. Sensitivity is different. That is why I decided to sit at the desk again, but now...to write the novel, *Las Paredes Hablan*. This is how we have the

---

[1] All English translations are mine.

same story with two versions, one on the big screen and one on paper (Boullosa, 2014).

The written word helped unlock nuances of character and narrativity that the cinematic script alone could not contain. So, while intended for the screen, the story found a new form – its ultimate imaginative realization – within the pages of Boullosa's novel. The author acknowledges that her work is a tribute to an imaginary Mexico that is mixed with her own memories.

In these pages, we will focus on the novel in which, as a creature of the postmodern world, pastiche reigns. Boullosa "reaffirms the revival of history, the freedom and flexibility of the postmodern narrative voice, and the innumerable creative uses of hypotexts...fed by rich Mexican and Latin American literary traditions" (Chorba 311). *Las paredes hablan* proposes a new reading of the History of Mexico during its independence and revolution in correlation with contemporary times, 2010. Among many others, we find criminal, political, social, historical, allegorical, and ideological references woven into a tapestry of historical memories that are filtered through the lens of its own inconsistencies and contradictions. This literary strategy serves, primarily to break down the borders between cultural references and fuse them into particular moments of Mexican official history. The reader receives continuous winks from familiar characters, situations, and even expressions that are common places within Mexican culture. According to Boullosa, the novel reflects on the violence that Mexico is currently experiencing. She brings to light the bodies left behind by the atrocious and unprecedented violence that Mexico is currently experiencing. By working creatively with this material, and reimagining it in fiction, Boullosa went from a collective pain to one that she internalized: 32,600 dead bodies were the raw materials she worked with in writing this novel (Flores). However, as Alejandro Flores points out, she goes beyond mere blood and gore; her literature speaks not just of violent conflicts but of disrupted families and homes. Indeed, it gives voice to those who died, uncovering the hidden secrets of those who survived. In an interview with *El Economista*, Boullosa explained some of the diverse influences present in her multilayered novel:

Para la parte de 1810, saqué a Fernández de Lizardi; el título es una referencia literaria a Juan Ruiz de Alarcón, saqué cosas de Sor Juana o me iba luego al círculo de bohemia de Othón. Los usaba. Para mí son seres tan queridos como mi abuela. Ese es mi mundo privado y al que entro y del cual robo según me guste, luego lo traigo, lo reelaboro y finalmente armo algo nuevo. A Payno yo me iba para sacar la descripción de San Ángel. Todo el tiempo estaba yo volteando a nuestros clásicos para

ver cómo veían a nuestro México. El resultado de la novela presenta un
México literario, no un México real (Flores).[2]

Las paredes hablan begins with the brief *Nota de la piedra* (*A note from the
stone*) where, in *Casa Espíritu* (Spirit House), emerges the awareness of the act
of remembrance. If for Juan Ruiz de Alarcon the walls listen (*Las paredes oyen*,
1617) for Boullosa, *Casa Espíritu* will speak. The stone has a voice, a female one,
which allows the reader to know that, once again, life has begun in her womb.
Drawing from the primordial history of Genesis, Boullosa's narration adopts a
poetic stream-of-consciousness style, weaving visual and auditory imagery
that brings to life the inner world of a sentient stone. Through this distinctive
feminine narrative voice, Boullosa creates an alternative historical record and
mythology. *Casa Espíritu's* story is reduced to the limits of the house and of the
memories of what was learned within its walls: "sé quién soy. Sé quiénes eran y
son los que aquí han vivido. Yo soy la piedra que se levanta de la inercia, sale de
la muerte, escapa al tiempo. Soy Casa Espíritu" (14).[3] The stone's impressions
of its surroundings, its conceptualization of time and space, and its
meandering associations of memories allow the reader to experience events
outside linear chronology and perceive the Bakhtinian interlinking of
temporality and spatiality. Past, present and possibility blend together as
sequences respond to an internal poetic logic rather than causal progression.
By using rich sensory details and eschewing objective realities, Boullosa
establishes the stone as the source of a subjective historical memory and
mythology unbounded by conventional ideas of time and space. The house will
affirm: "I have to give myself life with words, in a necessary language" (14). The
stream-of-consciousness style immerses the reader in the beginnings of the
stone's world, where timelines converge and diverge according to an internal
causality in the associations of ideas.

A few critics have mentioned the influence of Mexican writer, Elena Garro,
and her novel *Los recuerdos del Porvenir* (1963). Garro employs the fictional
town of Ixtepec as the collective narrator to relate her magical realist story.

---

[2] "For the 1810 part, I used Fernández de Lizardi; the title is a literary reference to Juan
Ruiz de Alarcón, I borrowed things from Sor Juana or I would later go to the bohemian
group of Othón. I used all of them. For me, all of them are as dear as my grandmother.
That's my private world, one that I go to and from which I steal as I like, then I bring it
back, I rework it, and, at the end, I create something new. I went to Payno to get the
description of San Ángel. All the time, I was going back to our classics to see how they
portrayed our Mexico. As a result, the novel presents a literary Mexico, not a real Mexico."
[3] I know who I am. I know who they were and who were the ones who lived here. I am the
stone who raises from dormancy, the one who leaves death behind and runs away from
time. I am Casa Espíritu.

Similarly, in *Las paredes hablan*, we are immersed in a mythical era outside the normal flow of history, delineated not through standard temporal demarcations but rather through the memories of *Casa Espíritu*. Furthermore, the mythical causality presented in both works is not founded on the standard relationship between cause and effect. Rather, it is based on a more symbolic linking of imagery and emotional resonance between different narrative elements. However, Boullosa makes this mode of storytelling distinctly her own through the richness of detail and layers of political and cultural commentary that she builds upon her story. For her, Mexico was existing in a nightmare, the novel serving as an exploration into the catalysts behind the nation's transformation – what produced the dissolution of an obsession with and aspiration for a Mexican homeland (2014).

Through Boullosa's narration, the city is portrayed as a metaphorical space which helps us to decipher the many different layers of a literary Mexico. Once a regular part of the country's daily life, that imagery has long vanished, preserved only in the recollections of *Casa Espíritu*. As the South Korean writer Jeon Sugntae has remarked in his writings, when memories are confronted with silence and rigidity, they rise higher in definition against the motionless backdrop. This resource allows Boullosa to present snapshots of ways of life that have gradually faded from Mexico City.

Memories of the past and the cyclical nature of time

Casa Espíritu's first memories let us know that we are in the year 2010, during the *Temporada del muérdago* (Season of the mistletoe) and that there is another house –*Casa Santo* (Holy House) – built in 1910 in its likeness. Like a parasite, the purpose of Casa *Santo's* existence is none other than to be a contradictory ostentatious twin to *Casa Espíritu*. The symbolism behind both names is important, the "*Espíritu Santo*" (Holy Spirit) has wisdom as its main gift. The Oxford dictionary defines wisdom as "the ability to use your knowledge and experience to make good decisions and judgments." From its beginning, the owners of both houses have always been on opposing spectrums of the Mexican political arena with those living in *Casa Santo* using violence and corruption to control those around them. To reinforce the symbolism of *Casa Espíritu*, "Casa Santo había nacido muerta; sus piedras mismas estaban muertas; en ella entraba la muerte incluso donde no puede penetrar, porque su esencia era la muerte" (171). Since the moment it was finalized, "Casa Santo was erected as a night of silence" (171). It is through the narrative voice that we can fully understand current events in Mexico.

The cyclical nature of time in *Las paredes hablan* is manifested through the repetition of events. The story commences in 2010, with *Casa Espíritu* transporting us to the moment in which the protagonist's fate is determined –

a destiny that will recur over the centuries. Each repetition entails a return to normality, a return to the state of things as they were before as if nothing had happened. In other words, it presents the characters an opportunity for a new beginning. Unfortunately, this is not the case, as each succeeding generation is fated to relive the same mistakes. From the outset, the narrative voice establishes that although the novel is structured across three historical periods, the narration loops back in a circular fashion unfolding in "a perpetual present" (18). Despite the characters adopting new surnames over time, they remain the same: "General Goribar is now Mr. Gutiérrez, metamorphosed by a sudden passage of time. My memory brings me back to the present" (44). In this timeless realm, the past constitutes the present that has already occurred, while the future signifies the present soon to unfold.

The initial memories of *Casa Espíritu* do not focus on the characters but on the description of its own decline throughout the centuries, as well as the oppressive and unusual heat that has settled around it. This oppressive and dark atmosphere is mirrored within the daily lives not only of *Casa Santo* inhabitants where violence and corruption are rampant but also in the financial ruin that we observe in the Vértiz family, current owners of *Casa Espíritu*. It will be due to an unparalleled shining light that time will stop and allow "my memory entered freely, replaced the cruelty of the king of heaven with its own, perhaps less fierce, perhaps not even cruel, although painful" (39).

In discussing this novel, Boullosa has emphasized the importance of legend over history, grounding her work in the idea that no home likes to change its owner (2014). Commemorating the two hundred years since the beginning of Independence and one hundred years since the beginning of the Revolution, *Casa Espíritu* narrates her recollections without judgment or bias for as she herself says "you ask, I don't answer, I say what I want" (346). To provide the reader with the events of the story, *Casa Espíritu* will narrate her memories and state that "to follow the scorching thread of time [she needs] to go back, following [her] story from its beginning, searching [her] footsteps" (55). Beyond the mythic theme of the eternal return, other universal thematic axes appear in the novel. These include the quest for identity, the place of origin, the journey of initiation, the Edenic couple, life and death, restless souls, the seizure of power through violence, and, the impossible love. As *Casa Espíritu* reflects on the veracity and accuracy of her memories, such archetypes are personified through the different characters and situations across the novel.

As literary critic Milagros Ezquerro pointed out, numerous characters across the novel share identical names despite the different time periods: Maria, Javier, Julian, Luz, Toña e Inés. This represents a deliberate maneuver from Boullosa to underline repetitions and introduce stereotypical roles that are easily recognized: Maria, as the headstrong, self-sufficient, courageous, and beautiful daughter who falls in love with Javier, the charming prince, handsome, brave, and intelligent. These two will not fear to die for their love and will always fight the evil Julian (205). Centered on the central couple and their antagonist locked in this endless loop, the perpetual present in which the three narratives unfold conveys a romance tragedy… alla Romeo and Juliet. We encounter three incarnations of María over different eras of Mexican history, each enamored by her era's Javier. Likewise, the destructive force of Julian propels the drama toward its fateful conclusion in each instance. *Las paredes hablan* is organized around this love story because it only exists in the recurring narration provided by the stone, whose memories are linked through the centuries to the female protagonist, Maria.

The characterization of the female characters follows the typical schemes of Boullosa's work, each one of the Marías walks through her century with a transgressive air. Inés Ferrero Cándenas noted how they are rebellious, creative, and too modern for their times, but they are also capable of living a love without limits. After realizing that everyone has died during the attack of the colonial army and setting *Casa Espíritu* on fire, the María of 1810, bastard daughter of Father Acosta, "conforma un batallón selecto con mujeres y arrojados indios, acumula victorias, concierta alianzas, ocupa un lugar sobresaliente en las luchas insurgentes y, llegado su tiempo, participa de la miel de la historia independentista"(116).[4] The María of 1910 is a revolutionary photographer, daughter of the Porfirian general Goribar, of whom some think that "perhaps she was not a woman, if she travels alone, if she dresses like that, God only knows what she was born with in between her legs" (198). The María of 2010, is the daughter of Mr. Gutiérrez, a violent drug trafficker who sexually abused her during her childhood. Therefore, although María was born in Mexico, at the age of twelve she moved to Spain where she spent her life and studied art history specializing in colonial Mexican art. In 2010, María returned to Mexico after the death of her grandmother who had declared her as her sole heir against the expectations of Maria's father. Maria doesn't decide *Casa Espíritu*'s future, but she is condemned to repeat her past during each historical period. Therefore, we know from the very beginning that, in 2010, the protagonist Maria dies in *Casa Santo*.

As in many other Boullosa's novels, the relationship between the central female characters and their mothers is nonexistent, full of silence and emptiness. For the Maria of 1810, her mother lost her mind after the betrayal of Father Acosta who was sleeping with other women and was unable to give her

---

[4] She forms a select battalion with women and courageous Indians, accumulates victories, makes alliances, occupies an outstanding place in the insurgent struggles and, when her time comes, participates in the glory of the independence history (116).

a place in his life or a position in society. In both 1910 and 2010, the Marias suffered the premature loss of their mothers. This lack of a maternal figure leaves the protagonists vulnerable to the desires of the male characters in their respective families –desires rooted in the patriarchal values of the Catholic church. The Marias will be despised, marginalized, and eventually killed at the hands of those expected to protect them. Through the narration, the female body becomes part of Mexico's history assuming a focal position across all three storylines. The victimization of this female body presents a possibility for empowerment by ultimately claiming ownership over their own stories. Though adopting a peripheral or safe space, which will endlessly return to its origin in each new cycle of the narration, the Marias move toward taking control of their fates.

As the house acknowledges, when evoking the past, she lacks control over what comes to her mind (60). Her recollections transport us to 1810, the dawn of Mexican independence, as *Casa Espíritu* is being built by Father Acosta, a revolutionary priest, who has the idea of establishing a house where all are welcomed, everything has an economic purpose and novel ideas can flourish. It is the time in Mexican History to build the dreams of independence and self-government (63). *Casa Espíritu* is the stone that remembers (346), yet is simultaneously alive and present (60). Within her walls, history is (re)imagined, and legends preserved, reflecting all idiosyncrasies of the Mexican people. Following the ideals of Father Hidalgo, *Casa Espíritu* symbolizes, for its 1810s inhabitants the creation of a Mexican homeland. However, these auspicious beginnings will soon be crushed by the colonial army with the help of Julian, the antagonist common to all three historical periods. During this time of new beginnings and opportunities, the art collection that Federico, a friend and confidant of Father Acosta, is establishing in one of the rooms of *Casa Espíritu* serves as a visual memory of this new independent Mexico that is emerging.

From here, we move on to revolutionary Mexico, in 1910, when on an increased scale *Casa Santo* was built at its left in the image and likeness of *Casa Espíritu*. As priorly noted, the latter will be mute, since she was born dead. During this time, *Casa Espíritu* is inhabited by the Serrans, a family of farmers who have acquired richness, and the new *Casa Santo* by the Goribars, a porfirista General, as well as his family. The coexistence between the two houses and their inhabitants will be the theme of the second story. This period in Mexican history is characterized by many economic, technological, social, and cultural changes that were executed through a policy of order and progress imposed by violent force if necessary. The failure of these policies was the seed for the Mexican revolution. A revolution that is already foreseen in the dynamics between families, In *Casa Espíritu* Javier Serrán, a famous painter, and his sister, Esperanza, a believer in progressive ideals, are befriended by

Maria Goribar one of the first professional photographers during this time. Javier and Maria will fall in love. Maria's brother, Julian, an evil villain, opposes this relationship and becomes the catalyst of the tragedy in which he ends up killing the two lovers while his father, the general Goribar will commit suicide due to the pictures taken by Maria and published by Esperanza.

Both houses continue to be inhabited in 2010 when the third story in Mexico takes place. Replete with cinematic stereotypes that unfortunately have become a reality in areas of modern Mexico; this vignette portrays a corrupt Mexico, full of violence, firearms, narcotrafficking, and femicides, among other themes. During this time, the dead *Casa Santo* is inhabited by Mr. Gutiérrez, a nouveau riche, who is a corrupt mafia-esque figure for whom power and control mean everything. His depravity as well as lack of taste and culture are described through the detailed narration of *Casa Santo*'s gaudy interior decor.

> Los muebles parecen Último Imperio extraidos de la bodega de un museo provinciano. Oro, trofeos de safaris, mármol, dos columnas de las ruinas de quién sabe qué palacete de quién sabe cuál ciudad centroeuropea. Lujo. Barroco. Una única pintura…un hombre semidesnudo en atuendo de Tarzán…El patio [con] una palmera artificial con cocos de cerámica, una jirafa disecada (real), una fuente de mármol negro (247-248).[5]

His daughter Maria's arrival in Mexico is a nuisance to him; one that he tries to control and which he will not hesitate to kill in order to maintain his corrupt empire. On the other hand, Casa Espíritu is the home for the Vértizs, an old family coming to less. The father, Javier Vértiz, contemplates selling part of the house's art collection to be able to pay his many debts. His son, Javier, later becomes hopelessly infatuated with Maria – much to his father's distress. Catalyzing the violence and destruction is another incarnation of Julian - this time, a corrupt lawyer obediently carrying out Mr. Gutiérrez's orders without questioning them.

Conclusion

Through the centuries, the art collection at the heart of *Casa Espíritu* has served as a rich metaphor for Mexican history and identity. As various inhabitants

---

[5] The furniture looks like Second Empire pieces extracted from the warehouse of a provincial museum. Gold, safari trophies, marble, two columns from the ruins of who knows what palace from who knows what Central European city. Luxury. Baroque. A single painting…a half-naked man in a Tarzan outfit…The courtyard [with] an artificial palm tree with ceramic coconuts, a stuffed (real) giraffe, a black marble fountain.

have added to it over time, the collection encapsulates layers of meaning that reach across eras. These artistic pieces encapsulate not merely the past but also the construction of modern Mexico. As General Goribar tells his daughter, Maria, "This, Maria, my child, this is Mexico. It is in my hands to save it, to take care of it, to protect it" (178). In 1810, we learn that Federico sold many of his paintings to Father Acosta, who started the collection, to financially support Ana and her daughter Maria (Father Acosta's daughter). In 1910 the collection moved to *Casa Santo*, only to return in 2010 to its original location (*Casa Espíritu*). This palimpsest of cultural material memory is experienced through different episodic glimpses rather than a linear timeline.

In her memories, the house distances itself from the paintings, explaining: "The paintings that honor me are not me; for the moment they are here, but they have not always been with me, and they may leave me, like the one in the bathroom of *Casa Santo*" (60). Therefore, the collection acquires layers of meaning, and its symbolism goes beyond the hegemonic historical narrative, encompassing the memories of specific events that brought particular works of art into it. For example, we learn how a bullet hole in one of the three hearts of Father Acosta's favorite painting, *La Divina Trinidad*, led to Federico's acquisition of the colonial-era casta painting *El Saltapatrás*. Thus, as a metaphor for Mexico, the memories of *Casa Espíritu* manifest an enduring tension with the outside world, the macrocosm surrounding her.

Throughout the narration, it is conveyed that the current owners, the Vértiz family, struggle to maintain not only *Casa Espíritu* but its priceless art collection even as they sell off paintings one by one. As the cycles of violence continue through the centuries, the art accrues bullet holes and bloodstains while families grieve those lost. Ultimately, by telling the collection's backstories, Boullosa insists that cultural legacy and national identity do not reside in images or objects alone. Rather, they find expression through memories, choices, and sacrifices – the shifting mosaic of Mexican life itself, embodied by Casa Espíritu's inhabitants over the centuries. Just as the narrator declares the paintings transient whereas the house endures, Boullosa implies that Mexico's true essence persists not through artifacts in need of protection but in the continuity of collective memory connecting one era to the next even amidst unrelenting change. If *Casa Espíritu* symbolizes Mexico and its history, the paintings on its walls also become a tangible metaphor for the formation of Mexico as a nation.

Throughout the novel, the tension between telling and narrating appears, sometimes dissipating due to the features of orality in the discourse of memory, but in the end, being resolved in favor of an omnipresent narrative voice. *Las paredes hablan* is a critical novel of what Mexico has become to be in present times. The passing of the existence of its inhabitants appears filtered through the words of *Casa Espíritu*, so effectively that it suggests a solipsism in which the entire outside world dissolves in her memories. There is no real progression of action, rather unfolding moments in the life of *Casa Espíritu*. Furthermore, when her memory turns on, something makes her associate a new memory. As a reader, we look forward to those associations, mirrors, and similarities because as the protagonist herself tells us: "Memory is a puzzle in three dimensions" (59). *Casa Espíritu* becomes through its memories a metaphor for Mexico, one in which violence in its different forms is rampant and a common theme throughout its history. Since according to the author, these memories are the legend of how an independent country was established; then we need to consider the novel as a totalization of life. Therefore, we can only think that Boullosa's work appears to us clearly responding to the desire to enclose Mexico's History in the microcosm of *Casa Espíritu* through three key periods in its history (1810, 1910, 2010).

Works Cited

Bachelard, Gaston. *The Poetics of Space*. Translated by Maria Jolas. Beacon Press, 1994.

Baktin, M. M. *The dialogic imagination: four essays*. Editor Michael Holquist. Translated by Caryl Emerson and Michael Holquist. U of Texas P, 1981.

Boullosa, Carmen. Personal communication conducted by Maria Matz at the 44th annual conference of the Northeast Modern Language Association (NeMLA), Harrisburg, Pennsylvania; April, 2014.

—. *Las paredes hablan*. Siruela, 2010.

Chorba, Carrie C. "The Actualization of a Distant Past: Carmen Boullosa's Historiographic Metafiction" *Inti: Revista de literatura hispánica*. Otoño 1995. No.42, Article 37. P. 301-314.

Ferrero Cándenas, Inés. "Review of *Las paredes hablan* by Carmen Boullosa." *Letras Femeninas*, Invierno 2011. 37(2), Pp. 269-270.

Flores, Alejandro. "Fui de nuestros muertos a mis propios demonios: Boullosa." *El economista*. March 7, 2011. https://www.eleconomista.com.mx/art eseideas/Fui-de-nuestros-muertos-a-mis-propios-demonios-Boullosa-20110 307-0038.html.

Garro, Elena. *Los recuerdos del porvenir*. Planeta Publishing, 2007.

Ezquerro, Milagros. "Géneros y gender en Las paredes hablan" In *Pensar en activo. Carmen Boullosa, entre memoria e imaginación*. Coord. By Assia Mohssine. Universidad Autónoma de Nuevo León. 2019: 197-208.

Ortega, Julio. "La identidad literaria de Carmen Boullosa." *Texto Crítico. Nueva época*, enero-junio 2002, no. 10, p. 139-144.

Chapter 6

The Scar of Writing Pleasure in *El Libro de Ana*

María Inés Canto

Colorado State University Fort Collins, CO

Abstract: Canto focuses on Ana Karenina's creative writing depicted in *El libro de Ana/Ana's Book* (2016), one of Boullosa's most recent novels. Her analysis explores two thematic axes: Women's writing and pleasure. Canto notes how intellectual and sensual pleasures function as small cracks in a social and economic structure sustained by silence, women's labor, and domestic exploitation. She uses *La ética del placer* (2003) by Mexican philosopher Graciela Hierro, who elaborates a series of principles for women to live and reflect on enjoyment, as a methodological framework. Canto also incorporates the concepts of family and evil developed by Kate Millet in *Sexual Politics* (1970), as well as the critical essay by Audre Lorde, "Uses of the Erotic. The erotic as Power" (1978). Thus, writing and pleasure are revolutionary acts that sustain the intriguing structure of Boullosa's book.

Keywords: Boullosa, Graciela Hierro, Audre Lorde, Kate Millet, Leo Tolstoy, Ana Karenina, Feminism, Writing, Pleasure, Ethic, Mexican, Female Writers, Women History, Patriarchy, Orgasm, Masturbation, Fairy Tale, Myth

***

One night, Claudia opens Pandora's box and finds the manuscripts that her mother-in-law, Ana Karenina, has left among her belongings. *El libro de Ana* (2016) by Carmen Boullosa reveals the creative writing of Tolstoy's famous protagonist, who decides to break up her marriage and bet on another way of life, one that society does not forgive. Evil associated with women and their sex is not new, neither in the Russian novelist nor in the Bible. As described by Millet in her book *Sexual Politics* (1970), Pandora is the representation of an ancient Mediterranean goddess associated with fertility and represented with "a wreath of flowers and a sculptured diadem in which are carved all the creatures of land and sea" (Kindle Ed). According to Hesiod in *Theogony*, she is guilty of introducing sexuality and ending the golden age of men who lived free from evil and danger. "Pandora was the origin of 'the damnable race of women— a plague that men must live with" (Kindle Ed.).

From this perspective, Ana and Pandora are the same characters. Boullosa designs a novel that explodes into many literary themes; for example, addressing Tolstoy as a writer now turned into a character, the structure of the fairy tale, and the theme of authorship. In an inverse sense, the novel promises, from the beginning, the implosion of the figure of Ana:

> Tolstoy wrote that Anna Karenina was the author of a book "of the highest quality...remarkable." Vordkief, the publisher, wanted to publish it (as Levin testifies the day he meets Karenina), she does not give it to him; she considers it to be only a draft, something in her story leaves her unsatisfied.
>
> ...
>
> Ana left, then, two books, the one that her contemporaries knew and the one that was her companion until the end of her —the night before her fall, she still wrote a few words.
>
> Here is the account of how the Karenina folios came out of oblivion, in 1905, in Saint Petersburg. The story is detailed where there are reports. Inserted in it, Ana's second manuscript is reproduced... (6)[1]

This quote marks the course of the novel in terms of its objective. However, in Boullosa's literature, the fabric begins to get complicated when the question is the search for a voice, as in *Llanto: novelas imposibles* (1992), *El médico de los piratas: bucaneros y filibusteros* (1992), *La novela perfecta* (2006) y *El libro de Eva* (2020), among others.

My essay analyzes *El libro de Ana* by using two thematic axes: Women's writing and pleasure. Intellectual and sensual pleasures function as small cracks in a social and economic structure sustained by silence, women's labor, and domestic exploitation. These thematic nuclei have in common the negation gestated in the literary myth of the women who ended up dead when their agency challenges the patriarchal structure: *Madame Bovary* (1856) by Gustave Flaubert, *Naná* (1880) by Émile Zolá, *Ana Karenina* (1878) by León Tolstoy, and *Santa* (1903) by Federico Gamboa.

---

[1] All English translations of *El libro de Ana*, "Mis cadáveres," "La destrucción de la escritura" and *La ética del placer* are mine.

My methodological analysis framework is the feminist theory of the Mexican philosopher Hierro, who elaborates in her book *La ética del placer* (2003) a series of principles for women to live and reflect on enjoyment. "The proposed ethics of female personal interest in a hedonistic approach are based on two considerations: the objective of moral action is pleasure, and in patriarchal societies the social group controlled based on their pleasure is women. Being free and moral means, for us, appropriating our body and choosing our desire and measure" (15). Hierro's book would not have been possible without the thought of Millet and Audre Lorde, which is why I will resort to certain concepts when appropriate.

The academic study of Carmen Boullosa's work in the United States began in the late 1990s. Emily Hind (2019a and b, 2010) puts the writing of Garro, Amparo Dávila, Boullosa, and Guadalupe Amor into perspective to make visible the patriarchal canon that operated in the Mexican literary circle well into the twentieth century. For her part, Sara Potter (2013) makes a similar exploration of the Mexican avant-garde. Assia Mohssine (2018) describes Boullosa's postcolonial gaze by discussing it with Mignolo and Quijano, the philosophers of Latin American transmodernity. In *Strategic Occidentalism* (2018), Ignacio Sánchez Prado analyzes the dynamics of the literary market from the 1960s to the present to place Mexican and Latin American writing in the context of global literature. Sánchez Prado highlights the exceptionality of the female authors on the literary map of Mexico in the mid-twentieth century: Campobello, Garro, and Inés Arredondo. So, if the exceptional was overcome, then the pigeonholing of authors in romantic themes, Ángeles Mastreta is an example of the above. The market strategy began to change at the end of the last century and already in the twenty-first century. The narrative stories of the authors begin to position themselves from a language that challenges the big literary story and the power relations between the historical and the fictional: Rivera Garza, García Bergua, and Carmen Boullosa.

In this context, I develop the two axes that motivate this feminist reflection and that, in turn, suggest these questions: if writing is the key to approaching Ana's character, why does the author choose the world of fairies to frame her voice? Is this literary structure corrupted or rewritten? Furthermore, if it is rewritten, to what end? Pleasure, for its part, takes center stage on Claudia's character, the wife of Ana's son and future reader of her mother-in-law's manuscripts. Thus, pleasure runs through the mundane points of the senses, aesthetic enjoyment, and the orgasm that underlines the questioning of the limits of pleasure and its objective: is Ana's erotic pleasure the transgressive motor of the monogamous family structure? Or was the lack of reason what motivated her tragedy? Moreover, would pleasure have been the central theme of Ana's motivations, why are guilt and rejection intrinsically part of her story?

To prove my point, I divide the essay into two sections: Women's writing and pleasure. Likewise, I dialogue with other texts by the author that suggest relevant contrasts for this work: "Mis cadáveres" (2003) and "La destrucción de la escritura" (1995).

Women's Writing

Writing and woman are two nouns in Spanish and many other dominant languages that until a few centuries ago were mutually exclusive or appeared together as an exception: Santa Teresa de Ávila (1515-1588), Sor Juana Inés de la Cruz (1648-1695), and Catalina de Erauso (1592-1650), with her controversial autobiography considered apocryphal by many. In Latin America, the nineteenth century gave rise to numerous women's/feminist newspapers that began to make cracks in the editorial market dominated, for the most part, by political writers – Domingo Faustino Sarmiento, Ignacio Manuel Altamirano, and Manuel Gutiérrez Nájera, among others. Following the European political and philosophical model, women's groups began to build and imagine the different national identities of the newly independent Spanish colonies (Rosado Avilés, 2019, González Rey, 2015 Goswitz, 2009). However, in Latin America, that model functioned as a stage set since the colonial structure of exploitation founded on the idea of race, gender, and servility has remained present to date (Quijano, 2003).

Accordingly, not only were women excluded from higher educational settings, created and directed by the church until well into the nineteenth century, but the moral dynamics of catholic societies in America promoted strict teaching of gender roles. Although the colonial period had temporarily passed, the educational model for women was still very present. These were some of the recommended titles for women's reading during the colonial period: *Tratado sobre la demasía en vestir y calzar, comer y beber* (1477) *Instrucciones de la mujer cristiana* (1524), *El jardín de nobles doncellas* (1550) y *La perfecta casada* (1583), *todos los textos de autoría masculina* (Guardia, 2005). An exceptional example is the famous *Carta Atenagórica* (1690) by Sor Juana. Her philosophical reflection led her into an arduous controversy with the Holy Inquisition and the archbishoprics of Puebla and Mexico City.

Developing a woman's writing in this context was a revolutionary act. Solid but not expansive networks were created between groups of friends and women from higher classes since literacy was a privilege in urban areas. For example, in the Southeast of Mexico, *La Siempreviva* project in Merida, Yucatan, headed by Rita Cetina, Cristina Farfán, and Gertrudis Tenorio Zavala, created the first magazine edited only by women in the country, as well as a public school for girls (Rosado Avilés, 2019). Manuela Sanz de Santa María organized literary gatherings in Colombia (González Rey, 2015) and the

Argentinian Juana Manuela Gorriti wrote nonstop and organized newspapers and literary evenings in Buenos Aires and Lima, Peru (Goswitz, 2009). Regarding indigenous traditions, the knowledge of the original peoples was profoundly undervalued since their ancestral writing or wisdom systems occurred in an "atypical" form from the Western point of view. Mayans wrote on stone — women were also excluded since the male scribes were in charge of carving history in stone—or the mnemonic formulas of ritual and scientific knowledge transmitted orally.

In this historical framework, there is a dissociation between writing and women, and simultaneously, physical and moral rejection of women who work outside the patriarchal and religious framework. Walking outside the pattern challenges the hierarchy of power in social institutions, such as marriage and family (Millet, Kindle Edition).

Boullosa is responsible for representing this double knot that encircled Ana's character in Tolstoy's novel. With a strategy that keeps the reader's different questions in suspense: What happened to Ana? What happened to her writing? Without redeeming Ana's suicide and choices, nor presenting her as the hidden literary figure of the moment, Boullosa constructs the context *a posteriori* of the fiction from the fiction and, consequently, from the margin. These characteristics provide experimental freedom to the narrative voice that allows her to jump from one genre to another, subvert expectations, and create a three-dimensionality in her characters that gives the reader an ironic text, full of knots and revealing folds. The aesthetic scaffolding is woven into several threads, along with the metafictional. There is the intertextuality with Russian literature, the linguistic twists typical of nineteenth-century literature built in installments and suspense. Nevertheless, it is not the formal or metaliterary analysis that governs my reflection, but the parallelism of Ana's writing and the women who revolve around her name.

The book consists of 43 chapters divided into four parts. Three parts are located in a specific time and space: St. Petersburg, 1905; the third section is reserved for Ana's book.

So, discovering her manuscript is surrounded by another story Tolstoy did not see, perhaps because of his privileged place in the hierarchy. If Tolstoy showed the brilliance and elegance of lace on Karenina's dresses, Boullosa presents the hands of the seamstresses, the very long days of 14 and a half hours, and their revolution. Thus, the book opens and closes with the figure of Clementine, an orphan and anarchist worker who has been working since she was twelve years old to support her grandmother and her siblings:

> She is a seamstress by profession (and one of the best in Petersburg), with an activist heart and her unemployed situation. She was "released"

from the workshop for participating in a strike; she was confined to confinement. However, for a short time, they did not measure her role in organizing the workers because of seeing her as a beautiful woman. They ignored the only informant who knew about it, convinced that he was allowing them to hide the big fish. Clementine is the big fish. She is cautious and furious as she only knows how to be a whale. She is now a radical… she left the needle for the sword and, this is saying because she changed the thread and scissors for homemade bombs (18-19).

Thus, the novel is written from the hem of Ana's skirt, that is, from the margin. By the margin, I understand the following concepts: individual and collective care actions–material work, but invisible to the patriarch– and women's reflection, synonymous with action and thought. Clementine is a strategist of the most radical labor movement. She makes bombs and plans violent acts to demonstrate the rage worthy of her class and gender. She is, in this sense, Ana's opposite mirror in terms of class, but both have chosen to challenge the patriarchy that oppresses them at different points.

If writing is reflection and agency, Clementine and Ana are two extremes of the conception that Boullosa raises in her essay "La destrucción de la escritura" (1995). For her, literature has an instinct for destruction, which manifests itself in 3 dimensions. Firstly, words must be stripped of their usual meaning to be reconfigured in poetry. In fiction, according to Boullosa, one must "wait for the words to jellify" to disarm the readers' expectations and put them at risk, forcing them to ask questions and surrender to a structure that vanishes. "The novelist cannot be the scavenger or the builder. The novelist must be the destroyer" (217). The second dimension refers to the characters, which must be "forced to rethink themselves, to refract, to remake themselves." (218). Finally, the dimension of reality evaporates and is "in question." From this theory of literary writing, Boullosa creates a mechanism in constant motion and without absolute truth; achieving an atypical artifact that does not build worlds but exploits them so that the reader questions and remakes them from destruction.

These approaches are present in *El libro de Ana*. The directions change course to show the cruel superficiality of that golden age longed for by Hesiod in his *Theogony* and destroyed by Pandora, just as Clementine embodies the theory of writing as destruction. In this context, Alexandra's character is another vital name. This name multiplied by three illustrates those tangential but essential women dedicated to caring for others to exist. When could one write or create if the basic needs are not covered?

Alexandra's name is repeated 26 times in the novel. The first Alexandra is Annie's maid, Ana Karenina's daughter with Vronsky, he lover. It is relevant that the center of Boullosa's novel is not Annie either, physically very similar to her mother and, therefore, rejected by Sergio, her half-brother, but her maid "Aleksandra, the Naryshkina lady of the queen" (26). We enter the precarious world of domestic workers through her, who seem not to have an alternative life to that of their bosses. This Alexandra is fully involved in the march that workers are organizing.

Alexandra Kollontai, the second in this trilogy, is a speaker committed to the ideology of Father Gapon, the spiritual and political head of the workers. This Alexandra inspires because she knows. Bolshevik workers and other communists know her as "the teacher of Marxism;" she is an important figure, but she cannot vote in the revolutionary organization because she is a woman. She represents an opposite line to Clementine, the anarchist since she is subject to Pope Gapon in his corporatist hierarchy, which Segato talks about in her book *The War Against Women* (2016). This hierarchical division of patriarchy gestated in the traditional family, was proposed before by Millet in 1970: "Marriages are financial alliances, and each household operates as an economic entity much like a corporation" (Kindle Edition).

In Chapter 23 it is announced: "We have three Alejandras on our hands, and we have only introduced two. Her names have a slight spelling alteration, they are Aleksandra, Alexandra and Alexandra" (91). Boullosa distracts us with the spelling difference of their names, but the last two words belie the narrator, right here is where the game of the destruction of the characters stated above manifests itself. Here the differences between these poor women of the most oppressed class are marked. The third Alexandra, "Sasha was stolen by the Pope from the orphanage when she was thirteen years old, she became a woman next to the force of nature that is Gapon. She has matured from her neck to her knees, but the rest of her person hasn't gotten out of her thirteen" (92). Boullosa does not need to delve further into descriptions to situate the sexual violence that Sasha and one in four women in the world go through. Sasha depends on her sexual aggressor, she has not been able to choose another life when she has been economically and socially dependent since childhood on a pederast national hero, Father/ Pope Gapon. Perhaps for the readers of Jean Austen in the nineteenth century, this data could seem "normal." Of course, this type of violence was normalized, and reading that George fell in love with Emma when she was 13 years old and he, 29, was usual in 1815. Luckily, *El libro de Ana* was written in 2016 and here the question could be: How is the agency of a body enslaved in trauma since childhood recovered? How and what to write?

This multidimensional Alexandra reveals the power of women outside of writing, but not of knowledge, agency, and survival. Through these characters, a variety of nuances and combinations are ensured that do not intend to build pathetic or mythological heroines but to make visible the violent and systematic network from where they live. This would be the first knot that distances the words 'woman' and 'writing.' And the second?

The second knot appears when it is possible to overcome the first due to class privilege in most cases, so women can access writing and time for reading, and imagination. Anna Karenina belongs to this core and explores it: Anna writes, but Tolstoy never reveals her interests or her creative dimension. In the nineteenth century, writing was a class attribute, not a professional option for women, therefore their writing was secondary unless it was linked to education. In any case, it was a private activity, or "being for others" from the pedagogical point of view.

In Boullosa, Ana's voice takes shape within the fairy tale framework. The fairy tale is a European folk tale that acquired this name at the end of the seventeenth century when Madame d'Aulnoy shared her stories collected on different trips through Europe in the Paris literary salon. In 1697 she published one of two books attributing the title "Fairy Tale" to a group of stories involving magic, and mythological beings such as fairies, dragons, elves, mermaids, and talking animals. This magical world of enchantments provides a mobile and flexible environment for the plot since the actions do not seek to create verisimilitude, but rather to frame a chain of adventures with infinite potential. Originally, fairy tales were stories for adults, and it was not until the 19th and 20th centuries that they began to be associated with children's literature.

Nor is it my intention to discuss the characteristics of the fairy tale, whose theoretical framework is deep and extensive. Among the authors who have devoted themselves to its study are Antti Aerne (1867-1925), Stith Thompson (186-1976), Vladimir Propp (1895-1970), and, more recently, the German folklorist Hans-Jörg Uther (1944). In his *Morphology of the Tale* (1928), Propp studied Russian folk stories and determined that fairy tales were distinguished by a primary function in intrigue: the search. However, this feature is not exclusive to this sort of story, just as talking animals are not exclusive to fables with a moral imperative.

In the "Relato de hadas bañado en opio: El libro de Ana por Ana Karenina," elements correspond to this literary form, mixed with mythical and biblical characteristics. For example, animals with human characteristics, a Lady of Light woman who could correspond to a fairy or the Virgin Mary, palaces, princes, tests, and temptations symbolically represent original sin, guilt, fear, the oppression of patriarchy, and writing. Ana is the main character, and her trajectory from a poor girl without privileges happens miraculously to life with all the luxuries, dresses, comforts, and riches that in fantasy are painted as an ideal. The truth is that Ana is trapped in either of these two extremes. In the beginning, her childhood in extreme poverty threatened her existence due to lack of food; when she becomes a woman, the Lady of Light women's palace rules fence her off and expel her from paradise by exploring the limits of her curiosity. In this transition, Ana changes her name and becomes the Girl of the Forest, Cinderella the Mop, and, finally, The Queen, just like the hero of a chivalric novel.

The prohibition in this story has no explanation or foundation, just like the prohibition of the apple in the biblical paradise. The Lady of Light woman goes on a trip and leaves three keys in possession of the Girl of the Forest:

> There are only three locks, and here I am giving you the three keys that open them. The first is the one to the door that connects this part of the palace with my private room, the second is the lock on the room where I keep my jewelry, and the third is not to be used, for any reason. You can go through it and touch everything, except this last room, you will distinguish it because it is at the bottom and because the door is purple. This is the key, unmistakable. I will also leave her in your custody. I repeat: do not use it, at the risk of losing everything (142).

Of course, the third door becomes Ana's object of desire. It is the door of curiosity, fear, and guilt. What is relevant in this story is the intertwining of desire, punishment, and fear which means "the loss of everything" regardless of the name, class, or social function; the female character resembles a prisoner. However, the ending returns us to the origin of fairy tales: the power of the voice in oral transmission: "As she was alone, Ana, the girl of the Forrest, Cinderella, the Queen tried to speak. A scratchy sound came out first, but the throat cleared, and words came out like a torrent. What you just read was what she said" (170). That is what we just read. In this sense, Ana is not the bland character who goes from adventure to adventure or from failure to failure, but rather an author, a link in that power of knowledge that does not need printed books or institutional records, since History is lodged in its living memory. In addition to being metaliterary, this ending is an anti-colonial stance to recover ancestral knowledge that was made invisible or assigned to the rank of the demonic in western ideology.

Pleasure

According to the Real Academia Española (RAE), the verb pleasure in Spanish comes from the Latin placēre, which means "to please or give pleasure." As a noun, pleasure is "1. Enjoyment or physical or spiritual enjoyment produced by the performance or perception of something that is liked or considered good; 2. Fun, entertainment; 3. Will, consent, approval" and also means a "Sandbank or idea at the bottom of the sea, flat and quite extensive" (online).

In any of these meanings, pleasure denotes a particular expansion associated with positive emotions or expressions such as happiness, enjoyment, and fun.

Philosophical reflection on pleasure has traditionally been masculine. In classical philosophy, Aristotle associates it with an ethical dimension and a sense of perfection and wisdom. Plato distinguished between bodily and mental pleasures, preferring the latter. In the opposite sense, Epicurus, the philosopher of the garden, indicates that pleasure comes from necessity (Herrera Bastardo, 2016). In this same line, the hedonistic philosophy comes from Hedoné, the goddess of enjoyment or pleasure. As the daughter of Eros, she was more associated with physical pleasure. So, it is theorized in ethical (normative), axiological, psychological, and aesthetic terms. In modernity, Freud dedicated part of his psychoanalytic theory to this term, associating it with psychic energy that seeks the fulfillment of a specific objective. In this context, *La ética del placer* (2003) by Hierro is a revolutionary proposal, as it conceptualizes pleasure based on a feminist methodology. Her reflection is preceded by reading the *History of Sexuality* (1976) by Michel Foucault.

For Hierro, the ethics of pleasure must be aligned with "an ethics of freedom and maturity because it means the possibility of achieving the right to pleasure, desire and the expression of eroticism, lost in the ups and downs of apples and prohibitions" (21). Her thought examines the superimposition of pleasure, eroticism, desire, sexuality, and freedom, since, as Hierro points out, echoing Foucault, "morality from the nineteenth century focuses on sexual behavior: gradually it focuses on in the sexual field, and a strict regulation is formulated for each gender" (38). Therefore, the patriarchal system has reinforced the sexual double standard for each gender in the religious, political, and cultural spheres. Therefore, exploring the situation of women in the world is an act of freedom and maturity; understanding by maturity the knowledge and reflection that allows directing energies towards tasks that pursue the search or the realization of pleasure.

Although Audre Lorde's thought is not directly quoted in Hierro's theoretical framework, her essay "Uses of the Erotic. The Erotic as Power," originally presented at a conference in 1978, proposes a very revealing definition of the erotic that has points in common with that proposed by Hierro:

> The erotic is a measure between the beginnings of our sense of self and the chaos of our feelings. It is an internal sense of satisfaction to which, once we have experienced it, we know we can aspire. For having experienced the fullness of this depth of feeling and recognizing its power, in honor and self-respect we can require no less of ourselves (54).

Lorde argues that the erotic reduced as a pure "sensation" or a superficiality has also been interpreted as a sign of female inferiority. Likewise, the erotic has been confused with the psychotic or sinful; therefore, the exploration of the erotic has not been freely available, and less has been considered as a source of power (54): Pandora, Eva, María Egipciaca, Sapho, and Ana Karenina, among many other names. In addition, it has been associated with pornography, and, according to Lorde, there is nothing further from the erotic.

Just as Hierro proposes a "maturity and knowledge" to embody the erotic, Lorde explains that "this recognition" of the power of the erotic is also a conscious and directed process. Both agree that the erotic goes through the body because that is the medium to experience the world. However, the erotic is related to sexual pleasure and the pleasure and sense of satisfaction that an intentional action produces in each area of our lives. These areas simultaneously involve the physical, emotional, and spiritual components: touching a texture, listening to music, reading, writing, spending time with friends, communicating knowledge, experiencing emotions, and being an active part of a cause. All of the above and many others are erotic actions under these terms.

Following this premise, intentional creative or reflective writing is an erotic and pleasurable act. I return to *El libro de Ana* to examine pleasure in two characters, Claudia and Sergio, and the fairy tale written by Ana. We read *El libro de Ana* through Claudia's eyes as she discovers her mother-in-law's manuscripts kept in a blue box protected by a ribbon. This meeting between the author and reader is the flame finding the fuse that will make the bomb explode to destroy the text itself.

Claudia is a traveler, the daughter of a Russian diplomat born in Spain who knows how to get along in the high class of St. Petersburg deftly. She is married to Sergio, Ana Karenina's eldest son. From her eyes, we access the fear and social pressure that her husband experiences when he receives a note from the Tsar requesting the portrait of her mother for the Hermitage collection. Here the contrast between "the duty to be" and feminine curiosity and intelligence is marked. The contrast is clear between a man ashamed of his origin and a woman who pulls the strings between the palace and the family home so that Sergio approves the evaluation of the portrait, on the condition that Claudia is in charge of the bureaucratic processes since he does not want contact with the canvas:

> The idea of giving her mother's portrait to the public eye disgusts Sergio because of the scandal, the affront of seeing her exposed, the gossip around her. Exposing the paint will cause an intolerable environment. The suicide, the adulteress, the lost woman will be on everyone's lips.

And Sergio, again, will only be her son, that poor woman, if one can call her that... (54)

This list of adjectives hiding behind Tolstoy's copious novel prevents the patriarchal vision from reading Ana from another angle. The narrative voice, taking advantage of this friction between the mandatory and the metafictional, takes the opportunity also to imagine the death of Vronsky, Ana's lover, in the tragicomedy that the official discourse represents: "He was killed by the bullet of a KRNK model 1867 that escaped a man from his own squad, just as Vronsky dropped his hat and bent down to pick it up. A reckless bullet, good for nothing, that required the cooperation of its victim..." (58). Boullosa's novel does not seek to create another moralizing scheme but to reveal the cracks and contradictions of characters that embody the reproduction of traditional values. For this reason, the use of a realistic portrait as a source of Sergio's annoyance is a very suggestive mirror to illustrate the prison that patriarchy also means for men.

When Claudia searches the attic for the canvas, she also comes across a blue cloth-lined box containing the leather-bound manuscript mentioned by Tolstoy, along with other loose folios, cards, and letters. In a note, Ana Karenina specifies: "I wrote this novel twice" (133), which indicates that writing was not an accessory activity, but an intentional and conscious practice. After this chapter, the "Fourth part (Without place or date)" opens, and we read only Ana's voice. The title "Relato de hada bañado en opio: *El libro de Ana* por Ana Karenina" faces speculation on Ana's death, which her poor judgment may have caused by her opium addiction. This is not relevant either, since, as demonstrated in the previous section, the purpose of the text is to show the character as author and agent, something that in the nineteenth century could well be a delirium caused by opium. I return to the fairy tale to analyze what happens after Ana decides to open the third door. Before, she decides to take a nap, and places next to her, on her bed, the keys that the Lady of Light woman gave her:

As she begins to dream, the leather-covered key, the one to the purple door of the forbidden room, shifts, pulling on the chain, and settles between her legs. There, she curls up and finds a way, nestles past her groin. The Girl of the Forest feels her in her dreams, and without exerting her will, she sways her hips, as if she were walking. The key sticks closer to her feminine body. The Girl feels a pleasure that she does not know. She had never felt that... she did not wake up until the following day. She is amazed to find the key chain looped around her bare legs. She disgustedly separates her from her body and jumps off her bed. She keeps the keys in a drawer. She promises herself never to cross into the rooms of the Lady of Light again (144-145).

The curiosity of that third room precedes this scene. So that key-shaped dildo opens another register in the bodily sensations of The Girl from the Forest. Interestingly, this character's pleasure comes in the privacy of her intimacy, without the need for another body to validate or guide her pleasure and movement. Although pleasure appears and moves freely, the closing of this scene is loaded with disgust that can only be explained by the imposed moral fences and a pang of guilt that materializes with the promise not to explore that territory again. However, the transition to the third room happens. The adventures *ad infinitum* are connected, concluding with the voice of the author-character presented in the previous section.

From this point of view, pleasure is a practice. A path that goes against the current and that the story's author does not finish placing or understanding. However, as Lorde mentions in her definition, a door has been opened from which one cannot return because the body has experienced erotic depth and expansion. From my perspective, this experience that does not end up being placed in the fairy tale as a liberating affirmation represents the conflict that the individual affirmation has meant for Ana Karenina. A conflict that did not have much room for interpretation in the nineteenth century. Twenty-first-century readers fly by this scene, predicting how liberating it could be for her first reader, Claudia, who also accesses a more intimate letter addressed to Vronsky, in which she describes the impact of their physical encounter:

You opened a window in me that I was unaware of. I must tell you about this window. Unlike any building, instead of opening to outer space, it opens to me. Without that window, you showed me when you touched me —and that you taught me to touch in myself. That window that sees through touch (not through the eyes, you say yes, that the eyes give you pleasure: my greatest delight has arrived with closed eyelids, even more so when there is nothing to radiate light at night), I did not know about a continent in myself. It is not that I am someone else: the difference is that now I understand what my margins are. I understand firsthand that my limits are not here, where my skin is, but somewhere else, much further away. Traveling through me is crossing vast territories that... (173).

We read Ana's pleasure, her pleasure that transgresses the known and that is in charge of affirming her difference in solitude with her eyelids closed. The impression of this reading on Claudia appears in a dream that she does not remember in the morning. She recognizes the impact that her mother-in-law's novel could have on her husband, so she decides to attach the blue box to the portrait, with one condition, "that the manuscript be kept in strict reserve for fifty years (180)." However, what has been read cannot be forgotten, which is why Boullosa stores this information in the territory of dreams' subconscious.

Emily Hind analyzes "Mis cadáveres" in the context of autobiography and highlights the absence of masturbation scenes in literature written by women in Mexico. In 1959, Guadalupe Amor published the *Galería de títeres*, which included "La solitaria," the story of a woman who spends her time alone pleasuring herself. "This writing marks the first published mention of female masturbation by a Mexican woman (Hind 2019b, 15)." Taking this reference date and the deeply patriarchal Mexican literary context until a few decades ago, Boullosa's "Mis cadáveres" represents a fundamental piece in the Mexican literary imaginary. After describing her first encounter with water, she typifies her "genital pleasure" at a very young age, she adds:

> I sat on my foot to make myself taller and managed to recline my body at times on the table, but I also sat on my foot to feel pretty. I already knew that feeling; it accompanied me often and without any anxiety about it... My skin erased me from others. It forced me to an adventure within myself, to territories that I had no desire to conquer at the age of four (30-32).

Boullosa describes the encounter with his body as a real learning experience such as breathing or eating and does not centralize her experience of the world, but it does amplify it. This description is very similar to Ana's description in her letter, where orgasm is a window to the inside. A form of self-knowledge. Ana's book is, therefore, a search that explodes inward, literally. The end of this book finds us with a bomb that targets the luxury car carrying Ana's portrait and the blue box with her manuscripts. Of course, Clementine is the author and manager of planting the bomb. She shows up at the attack wearing one of the dresses that Karenina's "semi-mother-in-law" donated to hospices after her death. Thus, the pleasure of fiction is built, savored, and extinguished, as in the wave of orgasm.

Final Considerations

In this novel, Carmen Boullosa conjures up her deep literary knowledge and her theory about writing and pleasure, pointing to an integral vision of the world from Ana's character. The marginal characters open a window to the diverse experiences of "being a woman" in a Russia agitated and revolutionary. This contrast creates a balance in the novel since it is not limited to the private prison of Ana Karenina. However, the focus incorporates the hardest working and poorest women of St. Petersburg. Thinking of Ana's writing without looking at these many other realities would return to the train tracks. The novel changes these parallel lines' direction: joining the tracks, and narrating two or more realities, to create a bridge or a scar. This trace could well be the metaphor of female sex or a box that opens and reveals the complexity and power of enjoyment.

Boullosa will continue investigating the mythical or literary figures, penetrating deep into that historical scar to tell us the other version of those feminine symbols that populate our collective imagination. In *El libro de Ana*, Boullosa recovers the eroticism of the body, not only from her sexual register but from the creative potential that is gestated inside that window open inward. *El Libro de Eva* (2020) is the next stop on this topic.

Works Cited

Boullosa, Carmen. *El libro de Ana*. Alfaguara, 2016.

—. "Mis cadáveres." *Debate Feminista* 28, 2003, pp. 23–50.

—. "La destrucción en la escritura." *Inti* 42, 1995, pp. 215-220.

González Rey, Diana Crucelly. "La educación de las mujeres en Colombia a finales del siglo XIX: Santander y el proyecto educativo de la Regeneración." *Revista Historia de la educación latinoamericana* vol. 17, no.24, 2015, pp. 243-258.

Goswitz, María Nelly. "De pizarras y pupitres a borrones y bosquejos: el rol de las veladas literarias en la escritura femenina peruana del siglo XIX." *Escritoras del siglo XIX en América Latina*, 2009, pp. 77-85.

Guardia, Sara Beatriz. "Historia de las mujeres: un derecho conquistado." *Escritura de la historia de las mujeres en América Latina El retorno de las diosas* 13, 2005, pp. 13-27.

Guidotti, Marina Liliana. "Juana Manuela Gorriti, una periodista argentina del siglo XIX." *Caracol* 2, 2011, pp. 42-71.

Herrera Bastardo, Yolimar. "El placer: escenario estético-vitalizador de la educación." *SABER. Revista Multidisciplinaria del Consejo de Investigación de la Universidad de Oriente*, vol. 28, no.2, 2016, pp. 338-350.

Hierro, Graciela. *La ética del placer*. Universidad Nacional Autónoma de México, 2003.

Hind, Emily. *Dude Lit: Mexican Men Writing and Performing Competence, 1955–2012*. Arizona UP, 2019.

—. "Contemplation as Resistance to Ageism, and its Historical Context: Mexican Writers Carmen Boullosa, Guadalupe Nettel, and María Rivera." *Life Writing* vol 16, no.1, 2019b, pp. 11-24.

—. *Femmenism and the Mexican Woman Intellectual from Sor Juana to Poniatowska: Boob Lit*. Springer, 2010.

Lorde, Audre. "Uses of the Erotic. The Erotic as Power." *Sister Outsider: Essays and Speeches*. Crossing Press, 2012, pp. 53-59.

Millett, Kate. *Sexual Politics*. E-book, Booksurge, 2000. Kindle Edition.

Mohssine, Assia. "La opción descolonial en *Llanto: novelas imposibles* de Carmen Boullosa." *Cuadernos americanos* vol.4, no.166, 2018, pp. 133-153.

Placer, N. Real Academia Española, España, 2021, https://dle.rae.es/placer

Potter, Sara Anne. Disturbing Muses: Gender, Technology and Resistance in Mexican Avant-Garde Cultures. 2013.Washington University in St. Louis, PhD dissertation.

Prado, Ignacio M. Sánchez. *Strategic Occidentalism: On Mexican Fiction, the Neoliberal Book Market, and the Question of World Literature*. Northwestern UP, 2018.

Quijano, Aníbal. "La colonialidad del poder, eurocentrismo y América Latina." *La colonialidad del saber: eurocentrismo y ciencias sociales*, edited by E. Lander, Consejo Latinoamericano de Ciencias Sociales, CLACSO, 2003, pp. 201-242.

Rosado Avilés, Celia Esperanza. "Fomento y censura en el periodismo literario para mujeres en el Yucatán del siglo XIX (1860-1870)." *Telar: Revista del Instituto Interdisciplinario de Estudios Latinoamericanos* vol. 14, no.22, 2019, pp. 101-119.

Segato, Rita Laura. *La guerra contra las mujeres*. Traficantes de sueños, 2016.

Vázquez, Lilia Granillo. "La escritura de la historia como gestión de la identidad: perspectiva de género1." *Escritura de la historia de las mujeres en América Latina El retorno de las diosas* 13, 2005, pp. 29-43.

Chapter 7

Una mirada caleidoscópica al mundo de Carmen Boullosa. Entrevista con la autora /A Kaleidoscopic Look at the World of Carmen Boullosa

Interview with the Author. November 2021

María del Mar López Cabrales
Colorado State University Fort Collins, CO

María R. Matz
University Massachusetts, Lowell

Abstract: The following interview was done in Spanish via email during Fall 2021, eliciting reflections on the craft of writing, stylistic approach, recurring motifs, and other insights from the author herself. For Boullosa, Spanish represents the language of her upbringing - each word steeped not only in emotion but memory, even those terms encountered for the first time. Therefore, in deference to her deep connection with the lyrical and sensorial qualities of her native language, the original Spanish transcript has been retained to best preserve Boullosa's unique voice and expression.

The English translation aspires to capture the essence of her speech like cherry blossoms, transient yet vividly capturing her perspective for those unable to access the initial Spanish interview. Just as subtle fragrances linger despite the delicate blooms fading away, echoes of Boullosa's voice persist through this translated intermediary that strives to transport readers to her ideas' source.

Keywords: Magali Lara, literary evolution, *El libro de Eva*, Writing process, corporeal writing, female perspective in history, Casa Refugio Citlaltépetl, *Let's Talk about Your Wall*

***

Introduction to the interview

Mexico is my privilege. That other Mexico that others are trying to demolish.
It is my sadness, my deep melancholy (Boullosa).

Talking to Boullosa about literature is like creating another work of literature within the interview; it is to enter dark spaces from which we will never be able to remove ourselves because this writer's reflections on her work reveal themselves to us as an unfathomable universe. Strange things happen as we read her responses. Our descriptive but awkward questions served as a starting point from which the Mexican writer shares with us deep thoughts on topics such as creation versus voice, the multigeneric condition of human beings, cooking, her notebooks, her penchant for poetry, La Casa Refugio Citlaltépetl, her mission as a Mexican in New York, the night, melancholy, the mushrooms of mutilated trees, the cherries, the corporeality of writing, and the intimacy and collectivity of language, among many other topics. We would not want to repeat what has been said by the writer so we leave you to read both in Spanish and in English, this handful of ideas and reflections. We would have liked to keep asking Carmen Boullosa questions, pulling on the endless thread, to somehow never stop listening to her.

This interview took place in Spanish via email in November 2021.

Una mirada caleidoscópica al mundo de Carmen Boullosa. Entrevista con la autora.[1]

1. **Para comenzar, ¿cómo dirías que ha evolucionado tu obra? ¿Consideras que hay un tipo de temática presente desde tus primeros textos publicados no solo novelas, sino cuentos, ensayos, poemas y obras teatrales hasta este último (*El libro de Eva*)?**

Son décadas de por medio. Sé cómo escribí mi primera novela, también preciso cómo la segunda novela. Tengo claro en qué contexto (el personal, el político, el ambiente literario), y sé que, ni yo vivo en esa misma condición sentimental (la certeza de haber perdido a mi papá, aunque él viviera, la muerte de mamá, la expulsión abrupta del colchón de protección "infantil" que los dos me daban, más la furia y la preocupación por la situación de mis hermanos pequeños), escribir mi primera novela fue para mí una necesidad - como el poema-, un acto necesario que una vez ejecutado (aunque fuera doloroso), me habilitaba para no zozobrar hasta el completo ahogo. Mientras escribía hubo desesperación, la violencia en distintas formas y también, aun antes de acabarla, estuvo presente la bondad generosa de un medio literario opulento

---

[1] Original versión in Spanish

(de opulencia literaria) que, juguetón, nos abría puertas y nos invitaba a conversar, a dialogar, a entenderle, a estar con él, e incluso contra él. La posibilidad de tropezar con autores admiradísimos en una librería, de asistir a una exposición y ver a Octavio Paz, viendo como lo hacía uno, con curiosidad, una pintura... eso enriquecía. Los ejemplos de esa experiencia abundan. Eso no existe ya, en parte porque el papel de las ciudades, de los barrios de las ciudades, ya no es el mismo. Alimentada por esos años, ha crecido mi curiosidad por entender, explorar, tanto asuntos personales como históricos colectivos. Obviamente, mi obra ha ido pasando por fases y rumbos, guiada por la brújula única de la curiosidad. Amo esa brújula: no indica dónde está el Norte, dónde el Sur, sino dónde hay que colocar la curiosidad, que debe estar afocada. No sé si la red juegue el mismo papel. Me temo que no.

La lengua, que es siempre íntima y que siempre es colectiva, también ha quedado tocada, alterada por el tiempo. Ya sé que es en nuestra naturaleza permanente. También sé que no se me ha roto la pluma, pero, confieso, escribo ahora literalmente con cuatro plumas fuentes diferentes, cuatro ligeras con tintas de colores distintos. Yo escribía solo con una pluma fuente, una que era mi tesoro. Pasé de una, a cuatro: valga la metáfora. De tinta oscura a clara, de punto ancho a delgado: requiero esa variedad, la necesito para avanzar en el libro en el que trabajo. Ahora, en lugar de reverencia una pluma única, tomo decidida la que tiene el lomo (el cuerpo) amarillo, o escojo la del gris, o la del morado o la del blanco. Y están los frascos de tinta frente a mí. Así me veo a mí misma décadas después: echando mano de diferentes tintas: pero el mismo puño, el mismo, aunque ahora menos aplomado. Más lento, no sé, tal vez más lento que entonces. Eso no lo puedo afirmar, es una duda. No es el tiempo invertido: es la actitud ante el objeto mismo que es *la transmisión* del cuerpo al papel.

2. **Tu obra poética *El Tierro, la Caos, la Espeja* fue la obra ganadora con el XIX Premio Casa de América de Poesía. ¿Puedes hablarnos de esta experiencia y de esta obra?**

Tenía poemas escritos en varios años, dispersos entre mis libretas. Todos, por cierto, con la misma tinta, y con la misma pluma (una de lomo negro). Por capricho, o por instinto, un día los recopilé, descarté un buen número, limpié los que restaban y era posible leer reunidos. Como me gusta el juego de azar (no que lo practique, pero me deleita tentar la probabilidad, como se pueda - esa sensación de aventura, de no tener los cabos en la mano, ese navegar sin controlarle la vena al viento-) siempre juego en mi imaginación a que apuesto: busco con quién apuesto, rarísima vez encuentro, - y no sabría qué hacer si entrase a una casa de juego, pero esa es la idea: tentar la suerte-. En hipotético, jugar, en ese sentido, me atrae. Rarísima vez lo hago con lo que escribo, pero viendo la naturaleza extraña de los poemas *desbarrancados*, tuve el deseo de enviar ese libro, el que iba yo generando, a ser candidato de un premio que respeto. Ese libro en proceso de selección, aún no tenía título. Eso es extraño para mí: por lo regular, el título nace al tiempo que un libro. Pero esta recopilación de poemas no había salido de un parto, sino de partos dispersos, eran mis poemas bastardos, bastardos de su propia madre, poemas desmadrados que, un día, la madre recogía para arroparlos. La madre era yo, y encima de todo decidí echarlos a la ruleta. Se vencía la convocatoria, y no tenía yo aún ese título inherente. Inventé uno al azar, jugaba con el de uno de los poemas, e hilé una frase que lo contenía: "Lo Tierro." No la Tierra que genera vida, sino un Tierro cruel. Aún me gusta ese título, mucho. Y con ese collar impuesto - más que un título, un collar ceñido-, los envié. Ya obtenido el premio, deseé repensar qué título - sabía que había algo arbitrario en el que tenía-. Me enfadaba una resignación: pensé, en mexicano "ya me amolé, es el título" - no porque me molestara, pero era un collar ajeno-, y el editor preguntó cuál sería el título final, y yo ya entonces lo tenía impreso en mí, pero aun sin palabras, un título perdido. Era algo indeciso: una confesión de bastardía de los poemas. Así fue como *El Tierro, la Caos, la Espeja* pasó a ser *La aguja en el pajar.* Qué espanto: ser una aguja en el pajar. Con ese título se publicó. Dice uno de los poemas:

Aguja en el pajar

Vivir como la aguja en el pajar,
perdida entre pares frágiles,
sin el hilo, sin la tela.

Aunque este poema explica bien el espíritu del libro, la ceremonia del Premio fue todo lo contrario. Hablaron colegas, García Montero leyó un texto generoso - y de primera, como es él-: con este, regresé a aquellos primeros años de vida profesional donde el mundo profesional parecía recibir de brazos abiertos. Si la escritura - y lo que produjo esa escritura- de los poemas roza el dolor, el festejo rozaba la sed de vida, y la fiesta, que es siempre compañera de lo dicho.

3. **Volviendo a tus inicios como escritora, ¿cómo explicarías tus primeras obras? ¿Cómo dirías que nació tu inclinación a la escritura? ¿Considerarías que hubo "un natural impulso que Dios puso en mí," en palabras de Sor Juana? ¿Cómo recuerdas que nació este impulso?**

No diría que fue un "natural impulso." Fue a la muerte de mi mamá. Yo me moría con ella. No había espacio para mí aquí, entre los vivos: debía irme entre los muertos para poder vivir. Escribir fue el oxígeno vital. Me fue dando vida, me dio espacio, me dio columna vertebral: con eso pasé de ser niña huérfana y sin casa, a ser mujer en el mundo. Lo sigue haciendo. Como es de palabras este oficio, si no sigo escribiéndolas me veré obligada a irme donde el único espacio "natural," donde mi "natural impulso" me llevaría: a la tumba. Las últimas semanas he releído obsesiva a *Hamlet*: le pasó lo contrario que a mí. A él, la muerte de su papá, pero sobre todo las palabras del padre, lo dejaron sin vida posible. No era posible ya más su vida. A mí, la muerte de mi mamá pareció dejarme sin vida, pero las palabras que yo formulé *sin escucharla*, me hicieron posible. Ese personaje, Hamlet, me parece un buen punto para centrar obras y vocaciones literarias. En el caso de la mía, el silencio de mi mamá me dio vida, más que la muerte. Hay autores que escuchan al fantasma de sus muertos y los siguen al dedillo. Yo no la escuché. La oí caminar en las noches. Intenté escribir esa otra novela (la llamé Dulces afectos, fue para la que pedí mi primera beca - que sí obtuve- de escritora, la Salvador Novo. Pero tuve que borrar esa voz: yo vivo de su silencio, de su muerte. Es tremendo, también).

4. **Has dicho en varias entrevistas que para ti la escritura es corpórea y que el cuerpo es el "invitado de piedra" ¿podrías hablarnos sobre este concepto?**

Escribí esto siendo joven: creía que el cuerpo era el invitado de piedra. Ahora pienso que no: mientras esté viva, yo soy la invitada del cuerpo, y solo habito en él, por eso la escritura es corpórea. Se escribe, en mi caso, como se huele, como se ve, la piel percibe y como el cerebro elabora, por lo tanto, se escribe con el cuerpo. Ya dije que con la pluma y la tinta: hechuras, extensiones corpóreas que, de manera absoluta, vuelven a hacer cuerpo al cuerpo en el papel. Hay escrituras que son de piedra, de hierro, vestido entero, o piedra. La mía, definitivo, no. Cuerpo, cuerpa, cuerpa.

5. **Muchas de tus obras son traducidas a otros idiomas. ¿Puedes hablarnos sobre el proceso de la traducción en tu obra y cómo te sientes cuando ésta es realizada en idiomas que no hablas de manera fluida?**

Punto de conflicto: detesto regresar al libro ya escrito, al que ya queda atrás. La peor de las pesadillas para un novelista sería verse confinado a revivir persecula-seculorum (por los siglos de los siglos) una trama que ya inventó. Estar vivo es saber que puede ocurrir lo inesperado. Lo que aún no está ahí. Nos parecemos más a los hongos que crecen de los troncos de los árboles, inesperados, de formas inexactas, únicas, que a los cerezos, tan bien diseñados, como las naranjas de Valencia, que reproducen, de contar con las condiciones y el cuidado, su forma y sabor. La escritura no: más se parece a esas especies de improvisaciones naturales: porque el tiempo cambia, la forma cambia. El trabajo arduo y valiosísimo de la traducción es similar a los cerezos: deben reproducir, en otra lengua, lo original. Claro que las cerezas saben distinto si nacidas en Culiacán, diferentes a las de Kyoto: pero son cerezas, identificables como tales. Los hongos, esas formaciones inéditas en los troncos de los árboles mutilados, son lo que hacemos los escritores.

6. **Se ha dicho que tu estilo es denso, sesudo y a veces incluso un poco teórico, ¿hay alguna relación entre tus textos y tu experiencia personal? ¿Podrías marcar tu trayectoria vida-obra? Igualmente, si tuvieras que elegir un momento de tu vida que ha marcado tu escritura, ¿cuál sería?**

Ay, ay. Yo no soy teórica: soy la salvaje. Soy mucho más bestia que intelectual, a mis ojos. Me atribula ese decir. Pero también es cierto que comprender a la Bestia siempre tiene algo arduo. Muy arduo.

De la otra parte de su pregunta: el momento que marca mi escritura es la noche. O mejor sería decir dos noches: la noche nocturna, la que se ilumina - o desilumina- cuando se va el sol. Y esa otra noche temible que es la melancolía. Esa segunda me persigue con mayor eficacia que la primera. No creo eso sea sesudo... ¿O sí, y no entiendo nada?

Lo que sí sé absoluto es que "teórico" no puedo ser. No es lo mío. Detesto las fórmulas y las teorías. Como las detestan los hongos de los árboles. Dije que así era la escritura: no sé si toda, pero sí la mía, sin duda.

7. **¿Piensas que algunas mujeres narramos de manera distinta? ¿Puedes explicar cómo y por qué?**

Es difícil de contestar. Cada persona es un mundo. Y no hay dos géneros: habemos un montón. Más todavía: yo soy de otro género sexual del que fui de jovencita, tan llena de bocas en todo el cuerpo, tan ávida de penetraciones diversas. Ya no tengo ese género. Ya escribo y vivo distinto. Soy mujer - una categoría amplísima donde cabemos de neutras a no, de Marietta de Veintimilla a Sor Juana, de Carson McCullers a Anaín Nin a Virginia Woolf. ¿Un género? Pensar eso, ¡sería un pecado! Somos plurigenéricas. Los varones suelen estar más encasillados, pero como no son mi especialidad, no digo.

8. **Tus dos últimas novelas (*El libro de Ana* y *El libro de Eva*) parecen recordarnos a un diario escrito por las protagonistas. En muchas entrevistas hablas de cómo tú misma mantienes libretas. Si hacemos una extrapolación, estas novelas son las libretas de Ana y de Eva, un diario escrito por una mujer que reescribe la historia oficial o del padre para dar voz a lo femenino. ¿Qué nos puedes decir de la reescritura de la historia desde el punto de vista de la mujer?**

Es inválida la extrapolación. Mis libretas siempre han estado ahí, desde que escribía una novela donde solo había protagonistas varones - y una mujer por error-, *Son vacas, somos puercos*. El espacio más íntimo no es el de la Voz: es el de la Creación. La Voz es para proyectarse, para dirigirse a otros. La Creación es otro territorio. En *El libro de Ana* uso el narrador que ve a distancia, y uso la Voz de Ana Karenina escondida en el resultado de su Creación. En *El Libro de Eva...*

Es su espacio verbal, su voz (con minúscula) contando la historia que por no ser en mayúscula (la Voz) es rebatible por los que la escuchan: esos son los papeles de Eva. Es un problema: ¿debe la libreta del autor ser visible en su obra? Es un problema insoluble: si no aparece al final, la obra es sin su voz íntima. Si aparece demasiado, la Voz se come a la Creación. Espero haberme sabido explicar: es una combinación complicada.

9. **Muchas de tus obras se centran en personajes femeninos, igualmente en muchas de tus entrevistas y ensayos hablas del papel de la mujer a lo largo de la historia y de cómo ésta ha sido ignorada ¿Cuándo decidiste dedicar tu obra a los personajes femeninos que se ubican fuera del sistema patriarcal o que luchan contra éste?**

Por deseo, por amor, por capricho, y porque somos hijos de nuestro tiempo. Aunque yo sea una autora a contrapelo, soy un ser literario: estoy en lo que es hoy. Siempre se lee el presente en la obra literaria: hablamos aunque no queramos del presente. Y es el subsuelo hoy, es lo que mantiene viva la vibración contemporánea, la voz de las autoras pasadas (ignoradas) o presentes. Estoy aquí: no quiero y no puedo evitarlo.

Ha sido también curiosidad. Por saber cómo y qué era esa Cleopatra que yo de jovencita desprecié (*De un salto descabalga la reina*), esa artista no estridente que fue Sofonisba Anguissola (*La virgen y el violín*), ese concierto de autoras marginadas aunque a veces muy famosas, pero como tales marginadas (*El complot de los Románticos*, donde aparece una novela "borrada" de una autora decimonónica borrada)... En *La otra mano de Lepanto*, donde retomo a Cervantes y a su mundo, vuelvo a dar vida a su Gitanilla, ella es la guía, y cuenta su historia como debió de ser. Podría seguir. Pero también tomo varones aquí y allá: el mundo me interesa, completo.

10. **En *La novela perfecta* (2006) desarrollas la relación entre la tecnología y la narración, nos interesa la relación entre distintos discursos artísticos. ¿Cómo fue tu experiencia al hacer y escribir *Las paredes hablan* o incluso en la colaboración para *Mejor desaparece* con Magali Lara y sus ilustraciones?**

Fueron experiencias muy diferentes. Con Magali tuve la suerte de colaborar desde 1980. Desde adolescente había coqueteado torpemente con la idea de hacer de mis poemas lo que yo no sabía se llamaban "libros de artista," dibujando, pintando, haciendo cosillas con la tinta y las crayolas, y con el papel y el hilo. Primero aún más rudo, con las hojas perforadas de la carpeta que usaba para mis trabajos en la prepa, y los plumones de colores que había a mano, las hojas ya con rayas azulitas pálidas, o con cuadrícula (me encantaban, aunque no me permitieran ser: ¿amor de esclava?). Intentarlo me llamaba. No conocía, no sabía de ningún libro de poeta, pero sí de los poemas visuales de

Tablada y Apollinaire y otros. Los visuapoemas, por llamarles así. Pero no era un afán de copiar: era un afán de decir, de estar en mí en lo que yo escribía: cuerpo, forma visual, no cerebral, presente. Eso era la apariencia visual.

Después, para mi suerte, apareció Magali. Primero ella les dio vida visual a unos poemas cortos míos, y muy descarnados y violentos, *Lealtad*. Yo imprimí su versión (la versión visual de Magali Lara, que respeta cada palabra, pero que les da una forma visual: no es ilustrar, es darles cuerpo) en el Taller Martín Pescador en 1980: primer encuentro con alguna técnica, en este caso, la técnica tradicional del impresor que hacía honor a su nombre: quedaba en el papel lo que se "imprimía" literal, presionando el papel. Juan Pascoe, muy generoso, me guio, y trabajé en su taller como mano de obra, junto con Gilberto Gutiérrez. Cortamos el papel, lo humedecimos, llevé los originales a reproducir en fotograbados; en la prensa de pedal de Juan Pascoe, conseguimos las preproducciones, hojita por hojita. Una gran experiencia. Después, secado del papel, doblado, compaginar, doblar, coser... No creo seguir el orden, han pasado demasiados años. Fue una experiencia práctica, y para tener contacto con una tradición de impresores. Al mismo tiempo, yo dialogaba con Magali para las siguientes. Esa aventura con ella ha sido, y sigue siendo, perdurable y larga.

Lo de La novela perfecta...

Apenas ayer leí a Malva Flores, ensayista y crítica literaria finísima, decir que desearía su pensamiento quedase en palabra automático... Es lo que ocurre en La novela perfecta. No sé si es más que una aventura "tecnológica," un ansia humana: aterrizar como un hecho lo que aún no está hecho: imponer el reino de la imaginación en el territorio cotidiano del habla.

Como digo: son aventuras distintas, y diría divergentes: las colaboraciones con Magali, y las que seguí conmigo en mis propias prensas, con la colaboración de Georgina Quintana, Laura González Durán, Katya Ontañón, y algunas más en casa, con imágenes de Rowina Morales, y poemas de Verónica Volkow (a quien debo me haya llevado a Juan Pascoe), Kyra Galván, Enriqueta Ochoa, Gloria Gervitz, y otras poetas, todo eso fue sucediendo como un hacer colectivo. Fue maravilloso. Mujeres poetas, hombres también, poetos y de otras facciones como artistas plásticos: Marcos Límenes, el Fisgón, Marcos Kurtycs, Juan Manuel de Rosa, Alejandro Aura (claro, no podía faltar, vivíamos juntos), y Mónica Mayer, y Maris Bustamante (que es también maravillosa). También el libro que hicimos conjunto con otra "técnica" en La Flor de Otro Día, Marieliana Montaner, y siempre presente en otras teatrales y libros CHAC... Me faltan nombres. Más de un libro debiera escribirse de esta aventura comunitaria. ¿Qué puedo decir? Que esa aventura pre-tecnológica fue muy fértil. Mientras que el autor que no puede escribir su siguiente bodrio vendimiable, su nuevo *besteller*, requiere de "tecnología" para hacerlo posible. Pero no tengo nada en contra de nuevas tecnologías. Hace un par de meses terminamos nuevas versiones de Lealtad, una mía comentada, bajo la batuta de Magali Lara otra - todo coordinado gracias a "nuevas tecnologías"- No somos separables los escritores de las "nuevas tecnologías," y menos aún los artistas que trabajan más con objetos que nosotros.

11. En *El libro de Eva* hablas del origen de la gastronomía. ¿Qué importancia tiene la cocina en tu obra?

Cero presencia. Fui décadas, todas las de mi vida profesional, una cocinera y amante y hacedora de la buena cocina, pero fui una cocinera de clóset. No quise enseñar esa pasión mía a nadie, la guardé como si fuese un error o un pecado inconfesable: una mujer creadora no debía ser un ente de la cocina. Yo lo soy, como lo fue mi abuela materna, que era verdaderamente genial cocinera. Mi mamá opinaba que la cocina era algo inferior, que debíamos estar en el pensamiento abstracto, a distancia con esas labores "femeninas." No yo. Pero guardé distancia con mi persona y mi obra... Siempre pretendí que no era lo mío hasta que me harté de pretender y salí (poquito, a medias, a penas) del clóset ... Cuando planeaba mi primera novela (allá en 1973 o 74), la cocina jugaba un papel importante, la mesa que la abuela nutría con sus joyas culinarias... Deseché todas esas páginas. Pensé que no era presentable. Veo lo que hice ahora con desprecio: no supe sobreponerme a los prejuicios. Pero había algo más: "mi ansia de escapar de todo modelo de mujer." Yo no quería ser eso. Creo que la batalla campal ya acabó para mí.

Ese desprecio mío me enseña lo poco que vale ese valuarse al escritor como un ente admirable. Yo no soy admirable: lo que importan son mis obras, que tienen su valor, y que lo han acumulado por cuatro décadas y un pilón. No sé cuánto perdí por cuidarme del fogón: tal vez aún lo pierdo.

12. En 1999 se funda en la ciudad de México la Casa Refugio Citlaltépetl contigo como uno de sus miembros fundadores. ¿Nos puedes hablar de esta experiencia?

La Casa Citlaltépetl fue idea mía, y fue un azar. Me invitaron a participar en una actividad contra el entonces candidato a dirigir la Francia, Le Pen. En una mesa redonda memorable, participamos Rushdie, Soyinka, Breytenbach, entre otros. De ahí la idea de Christian Salmon (promotor de este movimiento), de hacer ciudades refugio. Cuauhtémoc Cárdenas, que es un ser de primera, fue elegido poco después a la alcaldía de la ciudad de México. Le llevé el proyecto. Lo acogió, y lo hizo posible. Salman Rushdie vino a apoyarlo, como Coetzee y otros. Fue un proyecto colectivo, como todo lo que vale la pena. Después - casi inmediato- Alejandro Aura, que era mi compañero de vida- fue invitado por Cárdenas a dirigir la Secretaría de Cultura, y yo tuve que hacerme a un lado de esa Casa Refugio, me duele hasta hoy, pero era lo prudente. Es pues esto una experiencia agridulce. Dulce primero, luego ya no tanto, aunque generosos amigos que la acogieron me han, de nuevo algunas veces, recibido en su mesa directiva, Villoro, Vicente Rojo, Mutis, Monterroso. A los más, yo los había invitado antes de hacerme a un lado, pero eso no importa: sino su generosidad en el tiempo invertido, y la voluntad. La Casa Refugio Citlaltépetl sí funcionó como refugio algunos años. La historia que sigue es más difícil. Por el momento, María Cortina le ha dado un giro afortunado: recuperar un espacio para periodistas amenazados por su oficio en México. Javier Valdés tiene su memoria ahí, su biblioteca. Es un proceso en marcha.

13. **Para ti es muy importante la pervivencia del idioma español y la cultura hispana en los Estados Unidos. ¿Cómo describirías proyectos como *Café Nueva York* (2007) o el programa de televisión de CUNY TV *Nueva York* con Patricio Lerzundi dentro del contexto político actual de los Estados Unidos? Vives a caballo entre Brooklyn, New York y la ciudad de México, siendo Coyoacán tu barrio, ¿te consideras desterrada, inmigrante, extranjera o tienes muy clara tu identidad?**

No tengo duda: soy de la ciudad de México. No vivo a caballo: vivo en la frontera siempre. Estar en Nueva York me da la posibilidad de usar sus bibliotecas, sus universidades, su diseño urbano, para concentrarme en mi trabajo como escritora. Pero paso larga parte del año en Coyoacán, que no es donde yo crecí - eso fue en Santa María la Ribera, mayormente-. Por otra parte: identidad es una palabra muy fuerte. No hay duda de que no soy brooklineta ni neoyorkina - no soy de aquí, soy de allá-.

14. **Relacionado con la pregunta anterior, nos puedes hablar de tu última colaboración con Alberto Quintero *Let's talk about your Wall*.**

Fue idea de mi agente literaria, Jennifer Lyons, y del editor de The New Press, y se las agradezco. Como es el caso de mi programa de televisión (Nueva York, se llama, en TV pública de Nueva York, y por el que he ganado seis NY-EMMYs) es posible por una voluntad política: para que no quede invisible nuestra lengua y presencia en el norte del continente. Ellos se llaman "América:" nosotros somos parte constitutiva de este continente. Quiero nuestra presencia viva. Mi pequeña contribución a las decenas de millones de mexicanos en Estados Unidos, al 30 por ciento de hispanos en Nueva York: nosotros no somos "inmigrantes:" esta tierra es nuestra también. Un día, el sueño fue el "sueño mexicano." Y recuperarlo también exige un trabajo diplomático, en el exterior.

15. **Para terminar, una palabra: México.**

México: mi herida. Mi fuerza. Mi dolor. Mi ansia. Mi origen. Mi matria. Mi ser. Vivo allá, trabajo acá. Tuve la suerte de crecer en un estadío de un México que ofrecía florecimiento, futuro, alegría, capital cultural. Fui dichosa. Usé huaraches de suela de euzkadi, viví en una casitita de techos corrugados, no tuve un céntimo, pero fui riquísima gracias a los que estaban a mi alcance. Estaba yo afuera del círculo de privilegio que me hubiera quedado cerca si yo no fuera el ser monstruoso que requería la escritura: no me hacía falta, para nada. México es mi privilegio. Aquel otro México, que otros intentan terminar de demoler. Es mi tristeza, mi profunda melancolía.

A Kaleidoscopic Look at the World of Carmen Boullosa. Interview with the Author[2]

1. **To start, in what ways would you say your work has evolved over time? Do you believe there are themes present in your early novels, essays, stories, poems, and theatrical productions that have stayed consistent throughout your body of work, and are present in *El Libro de Eva*?**

Entire decades have passed. I know how I came to write my first novel, also precisely how I came to write my second. To me, the context of this first novel is clear (personal, political, artistic), and I understand that I do not live in that same context nowadays (the certainty of having lost my father regardless of whether he was dead or alive, death of my mother, abrupt expulsion from the infantile protection the two offered me; more so, anger and worry tied to the situation my younger siblings had been put it). From my perspective, writing that first novel was a necessity - similar to the poem - a necessary act that once complete, would allow me to not keel over towards complete suffocation. While I wrote I was surrounded by desperation, and violence of all kinds, but also the kindness and generosity of an opulent literary medium that, playfully, opened doors and initiated conversations, dialogues, and understandings. The possibility of stumbling upon admired authors in a library, of serving as an assistant for an exposition for Octavio Paz, of seeing how individuals created art, with curiosity...that was my enrichment. The examples of that experience are abundant; but that context, place in time, only exists in the past, in part because the foundation of cities, and neighborhoods is forever changed. Fed by my early years, my curiosity to understand, and explore, personal issues, as much as societal and historical issues, has done nothing but grow. Obviously, my work has gone through phases, different courses guided by the compass of my own curiosity, one which must stay focused; I don't know if the internet plays the same role; I fear not. Language, always simultaneously intimate and collective, has also been touched and altered by time; I now know it forms part

---

[2] Translation into English by Nicolás Kulisheck-López

of our permanent nature. I also know that my pen was never broken, though, I must admit I now make use of four different fountain pens each with a differently colored ink. In the beginning, I only had one fountain pen, and it was my treasure. I moved from one to four: which serves as a metaphor. From dark ink to light ink, from a thick tip to one more precise one: I require variety, I need it to advance in the book on which I work. Now, in place of absolute reverence towards a single fountain pen, I opt for the one with a yellow body, or I pick the gray one, or the purple one, or white, and the clear vials filled with ink sit in front of me. This is how I see myself after all this time; making use of different inks; but writing with the same hand, though nowadays less plumb. Do I write slower? That I cannot tell, it is a doubt. Time is not inverted; it is the attitude towards the object itself that makes way for a connection between body, pen, and paper.

2. **Your poetic work *El Tierro, la Caos, la Espeja*, won the XIX Premio Casa de America de Poesia. Could you talk about the writing process and the work as a whole?**

I had various poems written across various years, dispersed across various notebooks. All, in fact, with the same ink, and the same pen (one with a black body); going off a whim, or my instinct, one day, I recompiled them. I discarded a majority of them, but I polished those that remained, and they read well together. I am interested in the game of chance, (not to say I gamble, but it delights me to test luck in any way possible - that feeling of adventure, of sailing without being in control of the boat, without trying to harness or control the will of the wind - I always make bets with my imagination: I look for someone to bet on, I rarely find anyone, - and I would not know what to do if I entered a casino, but that is the idea, of tempting luck.) Hypothetically, gambling, in that sense, entices me. I rarely gable with my work, but seeing the strange nature of *desbarrancados* poems, I wished to send this book, one which I was still in the midst of creating, into consideration for an award I deeply respect. The book, while in the awards selection process, remained untitled; this was strange to me, because usually a book's title is born with the book, but this compilation of poems hadn't been birthed just once, it was the product of multiple separate births that spread across decades, they were my bastard poems, runaway poems that, one day, would be collected and clothed by their mother. I was that mother and on top of all of that, I chose to send them to the roulette. The announcement of the award was imminent, and I still had not come up with a title inherent to the work. I created one randomly, playing with one of the poems I threaded a sentence that contained "Lo Tierro," not La Tierra, mother earth, that generates life, instead a cruel Tierro; to this day I am still very fond of this title. That imposed collar, more so than a title, was what I submitted for the award. Once I received the award, I wished to rethink the title; it felt arbitrary. It frustrated me and I thought in Mexican "ya me amolé, es el título" - not because it bothered me so to speak, but because it was a migrant title. The editor asked me what the final title would be and at that time I felt it was so imprinted in my soul that I was not able to put it into words; a lost title. The title was indecisive: a confession regarding the bastardy of the poems; that is how *El Tierro, la Caos, la Espeja* came to be *La agua en el pajar*. What a horrible predicament: being the water in a haystack. With this title, the book was published. One of the poems reads as follows:

Aguja en el pajar

Vivir como la aguja en el pajar,
perdida entre pares frágiles,
sin el hilo, sin la tela.

Although this poem does a good job of portraying the soul of the book, the award ceremony is the opposite. My colleagues spoke, Garcia Montero read a generous text - as he too is a generous person - with this, I returned to those early years of my career where the professional world seemed to welcome all with open arms. If the act of writing - and what came from it - the poems bordered on pain, the fanfare it received bordered on thirst for life, and the feast that came with it.

3. **Going back to your start as a writer, how would you describe your early works? How would you say your literary inclination was born? Do you believe there was a "natural impulse god put in you," in the words of Sor Juana? How do you remember this impulse?**

I would not say there was a "natural impulse." It was the death of my mother; I felt I died with her; I felt there was no room for me in the land of the living, and that I could only live in the land of the dead. To me, writing became vital oxygen. It gave me life, gave me space, it became my backbone: that is how I transitioned from a homeless orphaned girl to a woman of the world. And writing still serves that purpose in my life to this day. Since I work through words, if I don't continue writing them, I'll see myself forced to the only "natural" place where my "natural impulse" would take me: to the grave. In the past weeks I have reread *Hamlet*: what happened to him was the opposite of what happened to me; to him, the death of his father, but mostly the words of his father, made the continuance of his life impossible; to me, the death of my mother seemed to leave me without life, but the words I formulated *without hearing her*, made my existence possible. Hamlet, to me, seems a good focal point for all literary works and forms of employment. In my case, my mother's silence gave me life, more so than her death. There are authors that try and listen for the ghosts of the people they have lost and they follow them to a tee. I did not hear her. I heard her footsteps at night. I tried writing that second novel (I called it *Dulces afectos*, and with it, I asked for my first grant - which I was given - as a writer, it was called the *Salvador Novo* grant. But I had to erase my mother's voice; I live off her silence, her death).

4. **You have said in various interviews that, in your opinion, writing is corporeal, and that the body is the "stone guest." Could you speak on this concept?**

I wrote this when I was young; I believed that the body was the "stone guest." I now don't believe this: while I live, I am the body's guest, my body is my habitat, and that is why writing is a corporal act. I write the same way I smell, the same way I see, the same way I touch, and the same way the brain thinks, because of this, I write with my body. I already spoke on the pen and the ink: construances and corporal extensions through which, in an absolute manner, reconstrue the body and soul onto paper. There is writing on stone, on iron, fully cloaked, or of stone; but not mine, definitely not. *Cuerpo, cuerpa, cuerpa.*

5. **Many of your works are translated into other languages. Would you speak on that translation process in your work and how you feel when you encounter words written in languages you do not speak fluently?**

Point of conflict: I hate returning to books I already wrote, it is in the past. The worst nightmare a writer can endure would be to see themselves forced to relive, per-secula-seculorum (forever and ever), plots, and storylines that they already created. To be alive is to understand that improbable does not mean impossible. What does not yet exist? We look more like the fungi that grow on tree trunks, unexpected, of ambiguous shape and form, unique, as opposed to cherry blossoms, so perfectly shaped, like Valencian oranges, that reproduce its form and flavor. This is not the case for writing: writing is more like a type of natural improvisation; because as time passes, form is inevitably changed. The arduous and invaluable work that is translation is similar to the cherry blossoms; they must reproduce, in another language, the original form. Of course, the individual cherries will taste different if they are grown in Culiacan instead of Tokyo; but in the end, they are cherries, and identifiable as such. The fungi on the trunks of mutilated trees are what we writers create.

6. **It has been said that your style is dense, cerebral, and, at times, even a little bit theoretical, is there any relationship between your work and your personal experiences? Could you talk about your life story in relation to the art you created? Similarly, if you had to select one moment in your life that has deeply marked your writing, which would it be?**

Ay, ay, my writing is not theoretical: I am untamed. I am much more of an animal than an intellectual, in my eyes. It is also true that understanding the beast is an arduous process., Very arduous. To answer another part of your question, the moment that marked my writing was the night. Two nights to be specific; the nocturnal night, that which becomes illuminated when the sun is gone; and the other horrible night, that is melancholy. The second night follows me with greater efficiency than the first; I don't think that is so cerebral... Or maybe it is and I don't understand anything?

7. **Do you believe, as women, we narrate differently? Can you explain how and why?**

That is hard to say. Each person is a different world, and there are not two genders; we are each our own gender. Furthermore, I am of another sexual gender than I was when I was young, covered by different mouths across my body, so avidly prone to the diversity of penetrations. I am no longer that gender. I write and I live differently. I am a woman - a vast category where we all fit in, from Marietta de Veintimilla to Sor Juana, from Carson McCullers to Anin Nin to Virginia Wolf. One gender? To think that would be a sin! We are multigeneric. Men tend to be more typecast, but as they are not my area of expertise, disregard that.

8. **Your last two novels (*El libro de Ana*, and *El libro de Eva*) seem reminiscent of a written diary from the two protagonists. In many interviews, you speak on how you, yourself, keep diaries. If we extrapolate, these novels are the diaries of Ana and Eva, a diary written by a woman who rewrites official history or of the father in order to give voice to what is feminine. What can you say about the rewriting of history from a female point of view?**

Your extrapolation is invalid. My diaries have always been there, even when I would write novels with only male protagonists - and one woman by mistake - *Son vacas, somos puercos*. The most intimate space is not reached through one's Voice (capitalized); it is reached through the act of Creation. Voice exists to protect oneself, and to refer to others. Creation is a different territory. In *El libro de Ana* I make use of a narrator that watches at a distance, and I use the voice of Ana Karenina, hidden in the outcome of her creation. In *El libro de Eva*...lays her verbal space, her voice (lower-case), telling a story that is retractable by those who hear it because it is not capitalized. There lies the dilemma; does an artist's personal life and writings have to be apparent in their work? If the two are completely separate, in the end, the novel lacks an intimate voice. If an author's personal life becomes too apparent, their voice eats up their own creation. I hope that made sense; it is a complicated conceptual combination.

9. **Much of your work is centered around female characters, similarly, in many of your interviews and essays you speak on the role of women throughout history, and how that history has been ignored. When did you decide to dedicate your work to female characters that exist separate from the patriarchy or that fight against it?**

Due to desire, due to love, due to my own fancy, and because we are all children of our own time. Though, as a writer, I go against the grain, I am a literary person: I exist in the moment, in the present. The present always reads in literary works; we speak even if we do not love the present. The present is the subsoil of today, what keeps the contemporary buzz alive, the forgotten voice of past female authors, and the voice of those in the present. I am here; I cannot and do not want to avoid it. It has also been due to curiosity. Curiosity to know how and what was Cleopatra, who I despised as a young adult (*De un salto descabalga la reina*), the soft-spoken artist that was Sofonisba Anguissola (*La virgen y el violín*), the concert of marginalized female authors that, though, at times very famous, stayed marginalized (*El complot de los Románticos* where we see an "erased" novel belonging to a nineteenth century erased female author)...in *La otra mano de Lepanto*, where I retake Cervantes and his world, I give life to his Gitanilla, she is the guide, and i retell his story as it should have been told. I could go on. But I also take men here and there; the world interests me, period.

10. **In *La novela perfecta* (2006) you develop the relationship between technology and narration, we are interested in the relationship between different artistic discourses. How was your experience of creating and writing *Las paredes hablan* or even in the collaboration of *Mejor desaparece* with Magali Lara and her illustrations?**

They were two very different experiences. I have had the luck of collaborating with Magali since 1980. Since adolescence I had clumsily flirted with the idea of taking my poems and creating what I did not know were called "artist's books," drawing, painting, and doing things with ink, crayola, paper, and string. Before that, even more rudely, with perforated sheets of paper that I used for my high school assignments, and the colored lungs that were at hand, the sheets of paper with the pale blue lines, or with a grid pattern (I loved them even though they wouldn't let me be: a slave's love?) To try is what called me. I didn't know of any "poet's book," but I did know of the visual poems created by Tablada, Apollinaire, and others; the *visuapoemas*, to give them a name. But it wasn't an eagerness to copy; it was eagerness to speak, to take my words from within me: body, a visual form, not cerebral, but present. That was the visual appearance. After that, to my luck, Magali appeared. At first, she gave life to some very raw and violent short poems of mine, *Lealtad*. I printed her version (the version with Magali's visuals, each word treated with respect, but giving them visual form: that is not to illustrate, it is the act of giving words a body) in the Taller Martin Percador in 1980. It was my first encounter with this technique, the traditional technique of a printer that honors his name; left on the paper laid what was printed, literally, by pressing the paper. Juan Pascoe, very generously, gilded me. I worked in his workshop as a laborer, with Gilberto Gutierrez. We cut paper, we dampened it. I took the originals to be replicated through photograving. In the pedal press belonging to Juan Pascoe. We obtained the pre-productions, page by page. It was a great experience. Later, once the paper had dried, been folded, collated, folded, sowed...I don't think that was the right order, too many years have passed. It was a practical experience that taught me about contact with the printing tradition. At the same time, I held dialogues with Magali regarding the ones that followed. That adventure with her has been, and continues to be, long-lasting. That of The Perfect Novel. Just yesterday, I read something by Malva Flores, essayist and critic of very fine literature. In other words, I wish her thoughts stayed on automatic words...that is what happens in The Perfect Novel. I do not know if it is more than a "technological" adventure, a human angst; to convey as fact, what is yet to become fact; to impose the reign of one's imagination in the day-to-day area of speech. As I say: they are distant adventures, and divergent at that. My collaboration with Magali, and those which I created at my own print, the help from Georgina Quintana, Laura Gonzalez Duran, Katya Ontañón, and others at home, with the images of Roina Morales, the poems of Veronica Volkow (to whom I owe being introduced to Juan Pascoe), Kyra Galvan, Enriqueta Ochoa, Gloria Gervits, and other poets, everything was a collective feat. It was marvelous. Female poets, men too, (of course, I must add, we lived together), and Monica Mayer, Maris Bustamante, who is also marvelous, and the book that we are creating together, using a different "technique" in La Flor de Otro Dia, Marieliana Montaner, ever present in other theatrical productions and books made by CHAC...I know I'm forgetting some names. More than one book should be written about that communal adventure. What can I say? That pre-technological adventure was very fruitful. While the author that cannot write, creates their next harvestable mess of words, their new bestseller, they require "technology" to make it possible. But I have nothing against technological advancements. A couple of months ago we finished new versions of *Lealtad* under the supervision of Magali Lara - all made possible by "new technologies" - As writers, we are inseparable from "new technologies," and, more so, authors that work with objects more than we do.

11. In *El libro de Eva* you speak on the origin of cuisine. What is the importance of food and cooking in your work?

Zero presence. I went decades, all of which spanned my professional life, working as a cook, lover, and maker of a good kitchen, but I was a closeted cook. I wouldn't want to show my passion to anyone. I kept it as if it were an error or unspeakable sin; a female creator shouldn't also be fond of the kitchen; however, I am, as was my maternal grandmother, who was genuinely a great cook. My mom was of the opinion that the kitchen was an inferior place, that we should exist in abstract thought, at a comfortable distance from homely, feminine duties. I disagree, but I kept space between my person and my work…I always pretended that I wasn't until I got tired of pretending and came out (a little bit, halfway, and barely) of the closet…when I planned my first novel (1973 or 74), the kitchen played an important role: the table on which the grandmother nurtured her culinary jewels…I threw out all of those pages. I thought they weren't presentable. I now look back on that act with disdain; I wasn't able to get over societal prejudices. But there was more: my angst to escape the mold of what a "woman was meant to be." I didn't want to be that type of woman. I think the battle is over for me. That disdain teaches me how little worth the act of treating a writer as an admirable entity, actually has. I am not admirable; what matters is my work, they have worth, and that worth has been accumulated across four decades. I don't know how much I missed out on due to my protection from the fire; I still miss out to this day.

12. In 1999 the Casa Refugio Citlaltepetl was founded in Mexico City, with you as one of its founding members. Can you speak on that experience?

The Casa Citlaltépetl was my idea, it was random. I was invited to participate in an activity against the then-candidate to lead France, Le Pen. In a memorable roundtable, I participated alongside Rushdie, Soyinka, and Breytenbach, among others. From there came Christian Salmon's idea (promoter of the movement), of creating refuge cities. Cuauhtémoc Cárdenas, the first-class person, was chosen shortly after to be mayor of Mexico City. I brought the project to him; he took it in and made it possible. Salman Rushdie came to support the program, as did Coetzee and others. It was a collective effort, as is anything worth time. After that - almost immediately - Alejandro Aura, who was my life partner, was invited by Cardenas, to lead the Secretaria de Cultura, and I had to separate myself from the Casa Refugio, it hurts me to this day, but it was the right thing to do. Because of this, it was a bittersweet experience. Sweet, at first, not as much anymore, even though my generous friends have welcomed me in their directive roundtables, Villoro, Vicente Rojo, Mutis, Monterroso. The rest, I had invited before moving away from the project, but that doesn't matter; what matters is their generosity, time, and volition. The Casa Refugio Citlaltepetl was functional as a refuge for some years. Its present state and story are more difficult. At the moment, Maria Cortina has given it a fortunate twist; it has become a space for threatened journalists in Mexico. Javier Valdes has his memorial there, in his library. It is still a work in progress.

13. Clearly, the survival of Hispanic culture and language in the United States is very important. How would you describe projects such as *Cafe Nueva York*

(2007) or the television show, by CUNY TV, *Nueva York* with Patricio Lerzundi, contextualized with the current political climate in the United States? You live across Brooklyn, NY, and Mexico City, Coyacan being your neighborhood. Do you consider yourself banished, an immigrant, or a stranger, or do you have a very clear picture of your identity?

I have no doubt, that I am from Mexico City. I don't live in constant motion; I live on a constant border. Being in New York opens the possibility of using its libraries, universities, and urban design to focus on my work as a writer. But I spend extended periods in Coyacan, which is not where I grew up - that happened in Santa Maria la Ribera, primarily - Identity is a very strong word. I have no doubt I am not a Brooklynite or New Yorker - I'm not from here, I'm from there.

14. Relating to the last question, could you speak on your last collaboration with Alberto Quintero *Let's talk about your Wall*.

It was the idea of my literary agent, Jennifer Lyons, and the editors of The New Press, to whom I am thankful. As is the case in my television show (*New York*, aired on New York public television, and recipient of six NY-EMMYs) it is possible to give political motivation; that is, that our language and presence in the north of the continent won't become invisible. They call themselves "America," but the South is an integral part of that word. I want our live presence. My small contribution to the tens of millions of Mexican Americans, to the 30% of Latinos in New York: we are not "immigrants" this land is ours as well, there was a day when the dream was the "Mexican Dream" and the act of recovering it requires external diplomatic work.

15. To finish the interview, one word: Mexico.

Mexico: my wound, my strength, my pain, my angst, my origin, my motherland, my self. I live there, I work here. I had the luck to grow in Mexico a state that offered flourishment, future, happiness, and cultural capital. I was in a state of bliss. I wore huaraches with Euzkadi soles, I lived in a house with corrugated ceilings, and I didn't have a cent, but I became more than rich thanks to what was within my reach. I was outside the circle of privilege that would remain close if I wasn't the monster that literature required; I didn't miss it, at all. Mexico is my privilege. That other Mexico, that others try to demolish, is my sadness, my profound melancholy.

Chapter 8
Épica mía/ My Epic[1]

Carmen Boullosa

"Being a woman and crossing the territory of our language is euthanasia."

Abstract: In "My Epic," Carmen Boullosa explores the gendered authorship of *The Odyssey*, challenging the traditionally attributed male authorship and proposing that a Sicilian poet, possibly a woman, penned the epic. Drawing inspiration from Samuel Butler's speculations, Boullosa delves into the construction of her epic, envisioning a narrative that centers on diverse female figures throughout history. From Teresa of Ávila to Clorinda Matto de Turner and beyond, Boullosa weaves a tapestry of heroines who challenge societal norms, confront collective demons, and reshape the literary and historical landscape. The essay reflects on the literary achievements, societal contributions, and personal battles of these women, presenting an alternative epic that redefines the canon and celebrates the untold stories of female authors.

Keywords: Authorship, gender identity, narrative, female heroes, literary canon, societal challenges, alternative history

***

Introduction

My Epic, commissioned by Professor Mohssine, a contributor to this volume, was previously published in Spanish as part of the text *El heroísmo épico en clave de mujer* (Guadalajara, Mexico). In this essay, Carmen Boullosa gives an explanation of what would be her own particular epic: a tour of the heroines and the writers who, like the supposed Sicilian female author of the *Odyssey*, were silenced. Boullosa, with painstaking mastery, names each and every one of these women who stood out in the history of Spanish language literature, from its origins because, according to her, she is a writer in the present time,

---

[1] Carmen Boullosa, "Épica mía," commissioned by Professor Mohssine, appeared published in Spanish in Assia Mohssine (coord.) *El heroísmo épico en clave de mujer.* Guadalajara, México, Editorial Universidad de Guadalajara (con el apoyo del CELIS, Cátedra Fernando del Paso y Biblioteca Iberoamericana Octavio Paz), 2019, p. 43-55.

and now, she dreams of twisting the swan's neck and showing a historiography of literature that unearths all these women who, like warriors, fought their literary battles and fought for their place in the intellectual world, one that was forbidden to them while. At the same time, they made sure they did not burn their onions, a metaphor that reminds us of the words of Juana de Asbaje and/or Teresa de Avila. Boullosa's goal in this text is to have all her heroines of high literary level in chorus, and together, battle against any social inequality whether it be race, gender, or income, with their pens. All of these women have wanted to fight against the violence that has plagued them and continues to plague them on a daily basis. Boullosa comments that Mexico is a country where seven women die every day in the domestic sphere which is an uncommonly high number and women are here to denounce it. We leave you this gem of Carmen Boullosa's writing so that these heroines are not forgotten. We hope you like it.

My Epic by Carmen Boullosa[2]

At the end of the nineteenth century, Samuel Butler, grandson of the celebrated writer of the same name (1835-1902), to whom Aldous Huxley recognizes that he owes part of his *Brave New World* for the satire and utopia *Erewhon: or, Over the Range*, who was, in addition to novelist and traveler, the translator of the canonical English prose version of *The Iliad* and *The Odyssey*, conjectured in his book *The Authoress of the Odyssey*, subtitled, *"Where and When she Wrote, who she was, the use she Made of the Iliad, and how the Poem Grew Under her Hands,"* that the version we know of *The Odyssey* is written in the hand of a woman – a Sicilian poet (1050 – 1000 BC), a real person, whose tomb exists in Sicily with the appropriate epitaph.

Samuel Butler's version does not deny the most widely accepted version – which was used by Ismail Kadare (1936, Albania) in his Spanish-translated novel, *The File on H.–. The Odyssey* and *The Iliad* are of popular creation, collective making, a song of bards, passing from speech and music to the written word, a decided leap that, according to Samuel Butler, was undertaken, understood, and assumed by the Sicilian poet (and according to Kadare was still being sung in the 1930s, in the Balkans, in its original format). There is one more point to note about the novel by Ismail Kadare: the attribution of authorship of *The Iliad* and *The Odyssey* is a hot topic for neighboring nations, in this lies its legitimacy and true existence. Kadare's novel is in fact based on a real event from the 1930s, in Albania, two academics study *in situ* the singing of popular bards.

---

[2] Translated into English from the original Spanish text by Abbey Ervin

Samuel Butler explains that his book arose from a question that struck him when he was studying *The Iliad* and *The Odyssey*, facing the astute perception of the dialogues between women, the skills in the stroke of the female characters, and "*the territories by female tradition*," while the "*masculine*" characters, their dialogues, works and "*territories*" seem vague and imprecise. He then suspected the gender of the author: *could the author of these books actually be a male?*

In the book in which he tried to answer his question, Butler allows us to follow the construction of his thesis. First, he suspects that the author was a servant, without access to the proximity of their masters. He immediately discards this first argument because, if it had been the case, the said servant author would have blurred the princesses, and it is not the case, the women rise from pearls, regardless of their social class, not like the men, nor their world. Butler proceeds to weigh the possibility that the authorship was from a person affected by blindness but found the explanation insufficient as it clashed with the abundance of "visual" skills. After discarding other explanations, Butler notes errors in the text that he thinks had been made by a woman:

> Furthermore, there are many errors in *The Odyssey* that a young woman would easily make, and in which a male would hardly have fallen, such as making the wind whistle on the waves at the end of the second book, thinking that a lamb could survive drinking twice from a sheep that would have already been milked [...] to believe that a ship had a rudder at both ends [...] to think that well-aged wood could be cut from a growing tree [...] to make a falcon destroy its prey while it is still carrying it on its wing, which no falcon could do (Butler 240, 244-245, 308-309, 483, 527 and 540).

Butler abounds in examples of the author's unfamiliarity with tools and weapons (for example, an axe), objects (for example, a boat), or horses, and in these faults he finds the evidence to conclude that the author of this classic work of the universal epic – as the title of his book anticipates – could not have been a man, but a woman.

Anticipating a "*major*" objection to his ruling, Butler rebuts:

> I would be refuted on the grounds that it is far too unlikely that any woman, whoever she is, whatever her age, would have the ability to write a masterpiece such as *The Odyssey*. But the same applies, regardless of the male. In the hundreds of years since *The Odyssey* was written, no male has ever written anything comparable to it. It is extremely unlikely that the son of a Stratford cloth merchant could have

written *Hamlet* of that a Beforshire tinsmith could produce a masterpiece such *as The Pilgrim's Progress from This World, to That Which Is to Come* by John Bunyan. An admirable work requires an admirable worker, but there are admirable women as well as admirable men (*ibidem*).

Let us presume (for today's purpose) Samuel Butler's conjecture – that the author of the epic was not such as Homer, but a Sicilian poet – and, instead of making a novel out of it – as Robert Graves did in *Homer's Daughter* (1955) –, let's take it and set it as a background, or rather as a landscape, because the landscape, which has a life of its own – changes second to second –, will not be our protagonist, but that which the landscape gives: environment and a form of governance of the mood.

The central concept of our study today is the reworking or rewinding of a reel distinct from the epic, other further pressure, and its necessary protagonist: *the heroine*. It will not be the domestic Penelope embroidering, although we will not discard this, it remains in our story because she also has a bard's voice – like those who were reciting the adventures of Hector and Achilles –, a narrator's voice – like the Scheherezade –, she has a needle and quill in hand, and she writes the adventures of those who fight for Troy.

Let us focus on women who live the adventure firsthand and among them the classics, and, for me, very dear ones, the Amazon women or the Antianiras from *The Iliad*. Not to the Penelopes, but to the Penthesileas.

Another Brush Stroke to the Landscape

The one I called the preface, then, has become the landscape –the Sicilian authoress and her protagonists, the heroic men. On this, I will draw, in short, the epic of which I would like to be the authoress: the text that has a plot, a focus, a motto, a tone, the lives and works of the authoresses of our language. Known, famous or not, read or forgotten, they will be my heroines, with their personalities and their battles. They will run the adventures, they will confront the collective demons, they will prepare to vanquish the tyrants –and sometimes to take their place–, they will want to displace power, change the laws; they will lay siege to the city, and its customs.

Before starting the plot, the sketch of my story, I attach a brush stroke to the landscape, emerging from the immediate plot that I am about to tell. Just as it happens to the color of the sky at a distance, which depends on the immediate tone of the sea surface: the brush stroke to the landscape is given by María Enriqueta Camarillo (Mexican authoress of the nineteenth century) in the short novel *The Owl's Advice*. A young orphan is the center of the story, he is the "hero," the one who carries the collective history on his back. He will go from the province to the capital, where he will learn and inherit a trade. A meaningful trade. He will be a tailor, the one who gives the appearance of civility to the gentlemen.[3]

While the hero of María Enriqueta Camarillo's novel conquers the big city, makes a fortune, and earns money, he forgets his provincial life and with it, his dearest friend, the woman –smiling and pure–, like good Penelope, she waits and waits... until suddenly, called perhaps by the anxiety of marriage (this is how the association can be read in the text), the hero returns home, returns for his first love, whom he presumes dead several times on the way. She is his home and will be the one who narrates his story, that is: she is the one who gives meaning to the garment maker.

Let us keep María Enriqueta Camarillo there, next to the Sicilian authoress of *The Odyssey*, an addition to our landscape.

The City

The landscape is in the distance, hidden behind constructions, cables, and other elements of urban space, in order to get closer to what is ours: the epic that I would like for myself would consist of narrating the frenetic plot of our authoresses, their works and lives, going from one generation to the next – perhaps skipping a few – going from the very well-known, like Teresa of Ávila and Juana of Asbaje, to unknown but great authoresses. I would write, having them as heroines, a founding epic, History, and legend, or perhaps more legend than History, as an epic should be.

The legend has relative authorization from History, it counts on the popular vote, it moves by word of mouth –from ship to poet, from poet to novelist, today perhaps from novelist to filmmaker or screenwriter, and from the latter to the community, to the village.

The plot of the adventure that I would like to write would include the works and lives of these authoresses. Narrating them as if they were beyond, more expandable than History: our origins, the Hectors, and the Aquilases. In a collective voice, which was also personal. To give it, Dr. Mohssine would say, another return to the epic, a different meaning to the collective legend, in a new way, in another direction. To resize these authoresses would be to change the historical and literary body –the literary canon–, not just the proportions.

---

[3] Notice one detail: the tailor will make the clothes for the gentleman, the seamstress for the lady, and the common woman will make her own. Tailors are, for Cervantes, an example of the transaction, of corruption; Cervantes associates the masculine suit with lies; but that, although related to ours, is another issue.

Each one of the women would be listed with and for their heroism, their battle, their triumph, and their defeat. Each one of them would challenge a tyrant, the unjust laws –such as the death penalty–, customs, prejudices (against women, against the indigenous), demons, certain ideas, and some also the Good because they are undoubtedly wicked heroes –it is the greatest charm of the Batmans or the Supermans: they go on destroying while they fight against evil, always conflicting and psychologically unstable.

Others of the authoresses, their characters, and their plots, would defend a theological point, a theoretical possibility, or, more importantly, the fantasy, imagination, that resource that must be nurtured with education and rigor in order to find the exits at the difficult social or ecological crossroads or to defend freedom of thought.

I would start my adventure with Teresa of Ávila. From a family of Spanish Jews (her grandfather and father were identified by the Inquisition for Judaizing practices), nailed to her phobias, tormented by bulimia (she suffered persistent vomiting due to being bulimic), in the midst of the Counter-Reformation, she will challenge the ecclesiastic order –the same order which prejudicially discredits her due to her blood and gender. She, a woman, of "unclean" blood (if that exists), founds her own religious order. She knows how to make money from nothing – like a good banker. She conquers the modern literary territory of memorials, and –if the above does not serve to thrust authority onto her feet– she experiments with mystical abductions which free her to be swept off her feet. Defeated, she will go unpunished when she surrenders herself to the maddening visions, in delusions which have their pair in that which she most seemed to fear: erotic delusion.

We will say that Teresa of Ávila wins the titles of modernity one by one and uses them to her benefit: mystical and with a banker's vein (making money from nothing), she founds the religious order, is an entrepreneur, a memorialist, and is erotically free, she surrenders openly to the arrow of her chosen beloved: the divine being. Her triumphs and victories consist of beating the reigning power, which tries to close the doors and take them to achieve their victories.

Upon her death, the defeat will continue in episodes: they lock up her corpse so that no one steals it; even so, weeks later, her confessor half dismembered her uncorrupted body (he took out her heart, cut off an arm, hand, little finger), they turned her into a capital value against heretics, and over the years, into a saint (As for the little finger: it will fall into the hands of French pirates, and ransom will be paid to recover it). The caricature of her defeat belongs to Francisco Franco, who always slept next to the relic of the saint's hand, choosing her as the talisman that protected him from his enemies. Her victories have also continued: her readers, the permanence of the Teresian order.

In my epic narrative, after the divine Teresa would come the courageous María de Zayas. They pass the torch because by then Teresa has been used by her enemies and requires revenge. María de Zayas develops her own literary personality, not following in the footsteps of the narrative of Cervantes –in the short novel– or of Lope –in *La Dorotea* (*Dorothy*)– (it could be argued with which she felt greater affinity), but those of the translator of Cervantes into French, freely using true crime stories to feed his plots of violence and arouse reader interest. In this manner, not only did he obtain a huge number of readers, but, with violence in hand, he set out to defeat misogynistic structures that today are, in the best of cases, glass ceilings, as they have been throughout the centuries tombstones. María de Zayas says it with all her words: they give us "spinning wheels for swords, and pincushions for books."

De Zayas made a sharp sword from her spinning wheel-quill with which she insisted on defending women's rights, and from her pincushion-book, the throne that crowned her as the best-selling author of the sixteenth century. In the Golden Age, it was the one who earned the most silver.

She did not seek heroines but rather criminals –someone like Batman or Superman –, she did not try to write History giving a leading role to women, but her use of the plot, fiercely feminist is elsewhere – in her short novel *La fuerza del amor/ The Strength of Love*, she says: "because souls are neither men nor women, what reason is there for them to be wise and presume that we cannot be?" (De Zayas).

She was only a tragic heroine postmortem when she disappeared from us. It was everything; upon dying they did nothing to her.[4]

Juana de Asbaje bursts into my epic. So many things can always be said about her, such as that she is the founder of the idea of a Mexican homeland, the idea of the best that Mexico is, multicultural and prosperous. But I will only dwell on one detail.

In her *Respuesta a Sor Filotea/ Reply to Sister Filotea* (March 1, 1691), there are some lines where she elaborates a genealogy of women, as Margo Glantz has pointed out, in order to gain legitimacy. I want to highlight the courage of this genealogy that does not omit either the Queen of Sheba or Queen Christina, considering above all that she is replying to a letter that condemns her "in such a way that she becomes dispirited by the despicable news of the earth" and does not "apply her understanding to the Monte Calvario (Mount Cavalry)"

---

[4] It is worth remembering here the landscape that we have in the background: the Sicilian poet and authoress of *The Odyssey* was erased, the cloud blow that inks heroes that leave women waiting, marginalized from the epic, adventure, action, government of her own destiny...

(Soriano Vallés). The incredibly wise Queen of Sheba, worldly and rich, traveled to put to the test, to give an exam, to King Solomon. The queen was impressed with Solomon's clothes, food, and architecture. In response, she gave him a generous tip: "she gave the king one hundred and twenty talents of gold [...] and a large quantity of aromatic spices and precious stones. Never again entered such an abundance of aromatic spices as those that the Queen of Sheba gave to King Solomon," (Song of Songs). Spices, aromas (sensory pleasures), jewels, money, and earthly wisdom, of a single woman, queen, and traveler.

As for "the great Cristina Alejandra, Queen of Sweden, as learned as she is courageous and magnanimous," although it is true that she had converted to Catholicism, it was *vox populi* that, like De Zayas, the queen-king, did things of Men, she wore manly clothes (as Juana wanted to do to go to study in Salamanca), she had erotic affections for women, without dismissing gentlemen in that area either. Her sexuality was free, and she exercised it guided by pleasure.

There is something else in Juana de Asbaje that I do not want to stop mentioning –the Sor Juana-esque cherry–, paraphrasing it: The dream will not make you men or women or idiots or very smart: it will make you free.

I Go on and Rush my Epic Story

The Ecuadorian Dolores Veintimilla (1829-1857) was born when her country was born, when the one founded by Simón Bolívar fractured, and became a conglomerate of three rival provinces. Dolores would live in the three capitals of these: Quito, Guayaquil, and Sucre, and would be the beneficiary and victim of the division of the Bolivarian country, since, it would be said, her quarters remained in Venezuela, the university in Colombia, and the convent in Ecuador. Her enemy, for daring to argue against the death penalty, and for defending the human rights of an indigenous person, would be a religious follower (signed as "Fray Escoba") who would attack her fiercely in Cuenca.

Dolores Veintimilla wrote poems that should be considered among the best of Latin American romantics. They insulted her body –the autopsy ordered to find out if she had a child, although her husband had left her long ago– they dragged her body through the streets, she was not buried in a Christian cemetery. They burned her papers, and less than a dozen formidable poems survived, like this one:

The Night and My Pain

The black cape that the gloomy night
Tends, invites the world to rest,
His body extends already in the cold earth

The poor man tired and his pain forgotten.
Also, the rich man in his soft bed
He sleeps greedily dreaming of his riches,
The warrior sleeps and in his dream he exclaims:
I am invincible and great are my feats.
The happy shepherd sleeps in his cottage
And the calm sailor in his ship;
To this the sea does not alter ambition nor cruelty
Of that the sea does not disturb the repose.
The beast sleeps in a gloomy thicket,
The bird sleeps in the sheltered branches,
The reptile sleeps in its impure dwelling,
Like the bug in its flowery mansion.
The wind sleeps… the breeze silent
Caressing the flowers, they barely moan;
All in the shadows at the same time rest,
Here sleeping beyond dreaming.
You, sweet friend, that maybe one day
When contemplating the mysterious moon,
You exalted your fervent fantasy
Shedding a loving tear.

(Veintimilla, Barrera Agarwal 63-70)

The romantics, like Dolores Veintimilla, wanted to change the world: the Cuban Gertrudis Gómez de Avellaneda (1814-1873), with the first –and the best– antislavery novel, *Sab*; the Galician and extraordinary narrator Emilia Pardo Bazán (1851-1921), who fought for Gertrudis to be incorporated into the Academy in Spain, failing because her candidate was a woman; the Argentinian Juana Manuela Gorriti (1818-1896), of celebrated social gatherings in Lima – which brought together several of the various women listed here–, is the first Argentinian authoress of fantastic stories, leader of fantasy and defender of the defenseless, including her spouse –with whom she had a bad marriage and who she already didn't live with–, Belzú, Bolivian president killed in office, whose memory she rescued.

The Mexican poet, essayist, storyteller, chronicler, novelist, pedagogue, and editor (like various of the other romantics mentioned), the long-lived Laura Méndez de Cuenca (1853-1928), of a long life. She spent nine years in San Francisco, where she founded a magazine that was good business (she used to keep company with William R. Hearst). She owed her first education (the most solid one) to the reforms of Benito Juárez, her professional development to the regime of Porfirio Díaz, her first broken heart to the popular poet Manuel Acuña

–she was his lover and the mother of his son, dead at three months, a little after the suicide of the poet–, and some of her best verses to the Revolution. There is no time here to cover the range of her work. Of Juarez, she wrote a biographical essay:

> With you, oh Juárez, the nation begins its autonomous life: the spirit of patriotism that you have left for the new generation promises to be everlasting. You gave us the example: we have followed (Méndez de Cuenca 301).

Of the *Carrancistas* she wrote:

> They are the yellow soldiers
> That they seek, and come, and approach,
> With his X of cartridge belts on his chest,
> With their boot knives in their greaves,
> With their belts gleaming with cartridges […]

> (Méndez de Cuenca 301)

In the epic story that I imagine writing with them as heroines, the challenge with Laura Méndez is superior: she knew to observe and represent the changes of a volatile and strong country at a time (for long-distance periods –from Berlin and in St. Louis, Missouri–, that which exacerbated her capacity of observation). She lived with another woman for a year who embroidered very well, Aurora, her accomplice, her partner, her ally in the almost impossible task of having a daughter.

Another Ecuadorian is her contemporary, the very distinct, Marietta de Veintemilla (1855-1907), the first lady of her country –on the arm of a coup, her uncle–, who, before the threat of another coup d'état against him, named himself general of the armed forces of his nation, because of this, the soldiers nicknamed her "The Little General." She is an authoress, amongst other things, of an exceptional book written in exile, published in 1898, *Pages of Ecuador*, a delicacy of the epic narrative, legitimization of her homeland, vindication of women, and interpretation of Latin America. Years before she would write about Madame Roland:

> This notable figure of the French Revolution will always rise as evidence of the spirit that doesn't conform to the constituencies of the topic, and that in order to rise very high she doesn't need the strong muscles that a man boasts. One's self is, however, of the masculine vanity, to absolutely deny women of certain qualities, and there are men who

believe of good faith superior to that of Roland, to that of Staël, or to that of Gertrudis Gómez de Avellaneda, only because he lifts the weight of two hundred pounds or is ready to let himself be killed in any quarrel (De Veintemilla 63).

A little before her death, already on her way back to her country, while the allies congregated in order to stage a coup d'état and maintain spiritualist sessions, she wrote a treatise on modern psychology in which she argues that all universal philosophy has been a study of the human psychology.

In that story which I dream to write one day, the Peruvian Clorinda Matto de Turner (1852-1909) would burst in with her fight. In her novel *Birds Without a Nest,* she denounces the abuses of the town's priest –it was another woman who went against Samson with a kick–, they fired her from the job (she was the editor-in-chief of *El Perú Ilustrado (Peru Illustrated))* and her house was attacked by the mob. Clorinda overcoming her problems, converted to a rich mill owner thanks to her practical and managerial abilities, and she would continue her profession as a writer.

I would incorporate in my story one revolutionary: Dolores Jiménez y Muro. Although her verses do not reach the height of the other heroines, I would take the license of including her for having been Colonel Zapata's wife (Uprisings call her "Zapata's beloved"), for having been a writer at the service of the cause, for coining manifests, phrases, slogans ("The earth is from who works it"), for being the only face of a woman in the photography that we know of Zapata and Villa in the presidential seat –all the others present, very diverse, are male– and for having been the economic support of her sister, who was married to Díaz Mirón.

I end with hasty jumps: Nellie Campobello and Alaíde Foppa could not be absent. Those who sang their verses were Violeta Parra and Chabuca Granda. The editors and authoresses of the magazine *Rueca/The Spinning Wheel,* the Costa Ricans in Mexican flight Yolanda Oreamuro, and Eunice Odio. And what to say of Delmira Agustini, Gabriela Mistral, Teresa de la Parra, Alfonsina Storni (her voluntary heroic death is also an epic), Rosario Castellanos, Inés Arredondo, Victoria Ocampo and Silvina Ocampo.

Can all my heroines appear incorporated in the same story? They are so diverse. They were in the war against codes of behavior that asphyxiated great sectors of the population, and yes they opened, in their texts, space for women, for indigenous peoples; they liberated slaves, they refused to have the death penalty, they asked for the right to divorce; they gave fullness to the odds and ends, to imagination without no other sign than itself, to pleasure, to joy, and to their rivals. To the sense that the native gives to the folly. And outside of their own room in which they work, and of the house where they made a commotion, the same "journey" that I verbally drew at the beginning of these pages, I would have to be present. I would give a tone to and induce an atmosphere. And this would appear as real life, as the world in which we dwell. By altering that phrase of Ambrose Bierce, someone would say: "To be a woman –crossing into the territory of our language– is euthanasia."[5]

My heroines, narrating at the highest literary level, fiercely criticizing social concerns for race, gender, and income, wanting with her sword to win territory from violence, in the landscape that claims, only in Mexico, seven women's lives a day in domestic settings.

The epic story would have to have echoes from time to time. One that would be able to come near the end would be a literary link –not spiritual– between Teresa de Ávila and Silvina Ocampo, who wrote four centuries after the other the story "Sibila's boyfriend," where the feminine character says:

> When I was a girl, I fell gravely ill. I lived in the mountains. I was paralyzed. In order to heal me they put me in an icy river; they gave me snake soup and after, upon seeing that nothing cured me, my parents called a healer. He came on horseback from far away. He said that I had to eat three fleas from his horse. When he knew that they had bathed me in an icy river and that I had drank snake soup, he felt pity, and said that he would eat the fleas. It was the same. He ate the three fleas that were already prepared in the hollow of his hand, and within a few hours I improved. [...] I thought that the sirens existed because they appeared in the dictionaries (Ocampo 225-226).

Here I Close

I spoke about them, my heroines, instead of writing what Dr. Mohssine asked me, which was to observe in my published work the point that interests her and that has been her study's interest. Yes, it is true that in my novel *Lepanto's other hand* I take the word from Cervantes and give it to one of his characters, *The little gypsy*, while the prose moves on after the legend of his century, the expulsion of the Moorish and Lepanto's war; which in another work, *Sleep*, the woman dressed as a man is able to run the world with a sword in hand; which in *The virgin and the violin*, I bring to life Sofonisba Anguissola, the painter of the court of Felipe II who had no place in history but to whom I opened the door in legend, balancing her life with that of the luthier from her home Cremona, her lover in search of the most perfect violin, with, of course, the company of the devil. In *Texas, The Great Theft*, with a hero feminized by the

---

[5] Ambrose Bierce's phrase was: "To be a gringo and cross the Bravo river is euthanasia."

dispossession of Mexican territory and his own lands, and with him riding I epically rewrite the novel, the loss of that territory. In *Cleopatra Dismounts* I revive the Amazonians and Cleopatra put together in the same adventure. In *They Are Cows, We Are Pigs* I describe the dream and violence of the pirate De la Costa brothers. In *The Book of Anna*, I give Anna Karenina the adventure that her author denied her in life: to make her the authoress of a published book. And, above all, it is true that in *The Romantics' Plot*, I make a biased epic of the authoresses of our language, three of those mentioned here on the fly, inserting them into a wild adventure.

It is also true that for the moment I am in what I have shared with you: dreaming of twisting the neck of a narrative so that, in a new way, it allows me to have these heroines in chorus, warriors fighting battles while caring for the well-cooked onion in their plates, and I, in turn, draw my weapons on my war front, which is against and with words, to get hold of a literary text that belongs to the reader.

Works Cited

Barrera Agarwal, Helena. *De ardiente inspiración: obras de Dolores Veintimilla.* Academia Nacional del Ecuador/Sur Editores, 2015, https://circulodepoesia .com/2016/02/dolores-veintimilla-la-noche-y-mi-dolor/.

Butler, Samuel. *The autoress of the Odyssey. When and where she wrote, who she was, the use she made of the Illiad, and how the poem grew under her hands.* E. P. Dutton & Company, 1922.

Ocampo, Silvina. *El novio de Sibila. Cuentos completos*, Vol. 21. 1961. Emecé, 1999. pp. 225-226.

Graves, Robert. *Homer´s daughter.* Doubleday & Company, 1955.

Soriano Vallés, Alejandro. *Sor Filotea y sor Juana. Cartas del obispo de Puebla a sor Juana Inés de la Cruz.* Fondo Editorial Estado de México-Secretaría de Educación del Estado de México, 2014.

Méndez de Cuenca, Laura. *Impresiones de una mujer sola. Una antología general.* Preliminary study by Pablo Mora. FCE, 2006, pp. 301-306.

Veintemilla, Marietta de. Mme. Roland. In Ana María Goetschel (cf.), *Orígenes del feminismo en el Ecuador. Antología.*1904. Consejo Nacional de las Mujeres/ Flacso Ecuador/Comisión de Género y Equidad Social-Secretaría de Desarrollo y Equidad Social del MDMQ/Fondo de Desarrollo de las Naciones Unidas para la Mujer Región Andina, 2006, pp. 63-70.

Zayas y Sotomayor, María de. *Novelas amorosas y ejemplares.* 1638. Enrique Suárez Figueredo ed. *Lemir*, No. 16. Text 357. 2012, https://parnaseo.uv.es/Le mir/Revista/Revista16/Textos/04_Z.

Contributors

Co-editors

María Del Mar López-Cabrales. Professor of Spanish and Latin American Literature. Department of Languages, Literatures and Cultures. Colorado State University. Fort Collins, Colorado. Professor López-Cabrales teaches Latin American and Spanish culture and literature. Her research focuses on the intersection of literature and culture in Latin America and Spain and Women and Gender Studies. Dr López-Cabrales has been the Editor of *Confluencia* since Fall 2018. She is particularly interested in women's writing as a "space" in which women create social discourses and communicate with each other. Her publications include the books *Marinera en tierra adentro. Edicion anotada de la obra narrativa de Pilar Paz Pasamar*, (Ediciones Alcor, 2013), a book of interviews with contemporary Cuban female writers titled *Arenas Calidas en alta mar. Entrevistas a escritoras contemporaneas en Cuba* in Cuarto Propio, Chile with a Prologue by Catherine Davies (University of Nottingham), in 2006, *Una Isla con cara de mujer. Prominentes mujeres de la cultura de Cuba* in Ediciones Nuevo Espacio, New Jersey, in 2007 and *Rompiendo las olas durante el periodo especial. Creacion literaria y artistica de mujeres en Cuba* in Corregidor, Buenos Aires with a Prologue by Mary Berg (Brandeis Univ., Harvard Extension), in 2008, *La pluma y la represion: Ecritoras contemporaneas argentinas* (New York: Peter Lang, 2000), and *Palabras de mujeres. Escritoras españolas contemporáneas* (Madrid: Narcea, 2000), as well as articles and interviews in *Letras Femeninas, Revista Iberoamericana, Bulletin of Hispanic Studies, Especulo. Revista de Estudios Literarios, Confluencia, A Contracorriente*, and other scholarly journals and edited volumes in Spain and Latin America.

Professor López-Cabrales served a two-year term as Secretary of the Asociacion Internacional de Literatura y Cultura Femenina Hispanica. She has been a visiting professor at the Universidad de Cadiz, Spain (Summer 1999) and on the Semester at Sea program (Fall 2000, Fall 2017).

In 2019-2020 Professor López-Cabrales received the John N. Stern Distinguished Professor Award in the College of Liberal Arts and in the Spring of 2020 the Center for Women's and Gender Studies recognized her with the Hazaleus Award as a role model for other women on campus

María R. Matz is an associate professor of Latin American Studies and Culture and chair in the Department of World Languages and Cultures at UMass Lowell. From 2013 until 2016, she served at NeMLA as the Spanish and Portuguese Board Director, from 2018-2021, she served at NeMLA as the Cultural Studies and Media Studies Director and she is currently the Creative Writing, Publishing, Editing Director (2022-2025). From an interdisciplinary approach, her current research and scholarship reflect an interest in transnational literature and human rights, feminist theatre and performance in the Americas, as well as film studies. Among her publications are the book *Definiendo a la mujer: Cristina Escofet y su teatro* (Puerto Rico: Penelope Academic Press, 2012) and a co-edited bilingual (English and Spanish) volume *How the Films of Pedro Almodóvar Draw upon and Influence Spanish Society* (New York: Edwin Mellen Press, 2012), as well as several publications in peer-reviewed journals.

Contributors

Michael Paul Abeyta (Ph.D. University of California, Davis) is an Associate Professor of Spanish American Literature at the University of Colorado Denver where he teaches and does research on contemporary Mexican literature, Contemporary Spanish American Novel, Mexican Women Writers, critical theory, and transatlantic studies including Mexican colonial and Golden Age literature. He is the author of *Fuentes,* Terra Nostra *and the Reconfiguration of Latin American Culture* (The University of Missouri Press 2006), and has written on other contemporary Mexican authors as well: Elena Poniatowska, Alberto Ruy Sánchez, Ignacio Solares, Roger Bartra, David Toscana, Margo Glantz, and Juvenal Acosta. He has also written on Arab orientalism in Spanish and Spanish American fiction and poetry. Recently his research has focused on Mexican film and the reception of Georges Bataille's thoughts and writings in Mexico.

Emily Hind is a Fulbright scholar and Professor of Spanish at the University of Florida, where she received a University of Florida Term Professorship for a distinguished record of research and scholarship, 2016-2019. She was voted Professor of the Year 2016-2017, 2018-2019, 2021-2022, and 2022-2023 by the graduate students in the Hispanic literature program. Hind is the author of *Dude Lit: Mexican Men Writing and Performing Competence, 1955-2012* (University of Arizona, 2019), which received an honorable mention for Best Book in the Humanities 2019 from the Mexico Section of Latin American Studies. She has also published *Femmenism and the Mexican Woman Intellectual from Sor Juana to Poniatowska: Boob Lit* (Palgrave Macmillan, 2010). Her third book of interviews, *Literatura infantil y juvenil: Entrevistas* (Peter Lang 2020) gathers 22 conversations with writers and editors of children's and young adult literature in Mexico. She is currently working on a book about plants and oil in Mexican literature and film.

Assia Mohssine is currently a professor-researcher of Latin American literature at Clermont Auvergne University. She has coordinated the research project "Descentramientos" and the research program "Gender, Colonialities, Modernities. From Postcolonial Studies to the Decolonial Turn"(with Chloé

Chaudet and Anne Garrait) at the Center for Research on Literature and Sociopoetics (CELIS) of the Clermont Auvergne University.

Her main areas of interest are Mexican literature of the 19th, 20th and 21st centuries, Cultural Studies, Gender Studies and Sociocriticism. She has published the collective books: *Sociocritique et tournant décolonial*, Bern, Peter Lang, 2023, *Figuraciones del mal en las creadoras hispánicas contemporáneas* (Sevilla, Alfar, 2023), *Pensar en activo. Carmen Boullosa entre memoria e imaginación* (Nuevo León, UANL, 2019), *Genres littéraires et gender dans les Amériques* (Clermont-Ferrand, PUBP, 2019), *Heroísmo épico en clave de mujer* (Guadalajara, Editorial Universidad de Guadalajara, Academic Excellence collection, 2019), *De l´héroïne mythique à l´héroïne en haillons. Métamorphoses du genre épique dans l´écriture des femmes des Amériques et de l´aire Ibérique* (CIMEEP / Federal University of Sergipe, 2017), *Récits de voyages et gender dans les Amériques (1830-1950). Une esthétique de l´ambigüité* (University of Granada, 2014), *Dissidences génériques et gender dans les Amériques* (Tours, 2012). Her individual publications include more than 40 book chapters in academic publications in France, Spain, Portugal, Poland, Mexico, Argentina, Brazil and Morocco.

Dr. Ericka H. Parra Téllez is a Professor at Valdosta State University, Georgia, United States. She teaches Spanish & Hispanic Women Writers at the Modern and Classical Languages Department. She did her undergraduate and Master studies at *Universidad Nacional Autónoma de México* (UNAM). She also holds a Master of Arts degree from Illinois State University and a PhD from Florida University. She writes, serves the community, teaches, and researches about women's representations of violence, exploring the role of women in different literary genres. She has published book chapters and academic articles about Latin-American women writers, teaching culture and global competences on titles such as *Descifrando Latinoamérica: Género, violencia y testimonio, Encuentros, Istmo, Brujula, Olhar,* and *The Latinamericanist.* She is the author of the Spanish manuscript *Beyond the Narrative Boundaries: Cuban Women Writers and their deterritorialization* where she discusses how women writers apply literary techniques to represent the feminine subject and her deterritorialization due to the economic crises in different narratives such as testimonies, historical novel, fantastic story, and detective novel. She is currently working on a book project on Women and Different Forms of Violence in Literature and several projects on Care-Based Pedagogy.

María Inés Canto is an Assistant Professor of Spanish on Mexican Literature in the Department of Languages, Literatures, and Cultures at Colorado State University. She is a feminist from the Yucatan Peninsula, Mexico, and has published articles on Latin American Literature. Currently, her research project focuses on incest in the narrative of contemporary female Mexican writers.

Index

E

El complot de los Románticos/The Plot of the Romantics, xv, 19, 20, 30, 31, 117, 126
El Cuervo, 67
El Hijo del Cuervo, 21, 37
El libro de Ana/Ana's Book, x, xvi, 95, 96, 100, 101, 105, 106, 109, 116, 125
  Alexandra, 95
El libro de Eva/ The Book of Eve, x, xii, 96, 111, 112, 116, 119, 125, 127
El médico de los piratas: bucaneros y filibusteros, 96
El muerto vivo
  obra de teatro en cuatro cuadros, 68
El tour de corazón/The Heart Tour, 68
Energency, 19, 35
Energetic *gratitude*, xv
Energopolitical, xv, 19, 23, 24, 25, 26, 29, 33, 34, 35
Energopolitics, 19, 22, 23, 27, 32, 34, 36
Energopower, 19, 21, 22, 25, 31
Energo-tude, xv, 19, 35
Energy, xv, 19, 20, 21, 22, 23, 24, 25, 26, 27, 29, 30, 32, 33, 35, 36, 104
Epic, xvii, xviii, 44, 131, 133, 134, 135, 137, 138, 140, 141, 142, 143
Épica mía/My Epic, xii, xvii
Erauso, Catalina de, 98
Erotic, xvii, 76, 95, 97, 104, 105, 107, 136, 138
Ethic, 95
Exemplary Novels, 1
Experimental theater, xvi, 65, 66, 68, 73, 81

F

Fairy tale, x, 69, 95, 96, 102, 103, 105, 106, 107
Female heroes, 131
Female perspective, 111
Female Writers, 95
Feminism, 95
Fossil-fuel-reliant, xiv, 19, 28
Fragmentation, xi, 47

G

Garro, Elena, xvi, xix, 83, 86, 93, 97
Gender, x, xi, xiii, 4, 24, 25, 41, 43, 44, 66, 69, 74, 75, 77, 78, 79, 80, 98, 100, 104, 125, 132, 133, 136, 142
Genesis, xii, 86
Gómez de Avellaneda, Gertrudis, 139, 141
Gorriti, Juana Manuela, 99, 139
Granada, 1, 4, 6, 7, 8, 9, 10
Gratitude, 19

H

Hamartia (o Hacha), ix
Hierro, Graciela, xvii, 95, 97, 104, 105
Hind, Emily, xii, xiv, 71, 97, 108
Historia general de las cosas de Nueva España, 45, 54, 62
History, x, xi, xii, xvi, xviii, 45, 60, 83, 85, 90, 93, 103, 104, 135, 137
  Women History, 95
Homeland, 26, 59, 61, 87, 90, 137, 140

I

Identity, x, xi, xiii, 4, 6, 8, 9, 33, 50, 51, 56, 59, 88, 91, 92, 129, 131

Intertextuality, xi, 14, 44, 99

J

José Emilio Pacheco Excellence in Literature Award, ix

K

Karenina, Ana, xii, xvi, 95, 96, 99, 100, 102, 105, 106, 107, 108, 116, 125, 143
Kristeva, Julia, 66

L

La aguja en el pajar, ix, 114
La ética del placer/The Ethics of Pleasure, xvii
La gitanilla, xiv, 1, 2, 9, 15
La memoria vacía/Empty Memory, ix
La Milagrosa, 19
La novela perfecta/The Perfect Novel, xiii, 19, 96, 117, 118, 126
La otra mano de Lepanto/Lepanto's Other Hand, xiv, 1, 2, 4, 5, 8, 15, 16, 117, 126
Lara, Magali, x, 111, 117, 118, 119, 126, 127
Las paredes hablan/The Walls Speak, xii, xvi, 83, 84, 85, 86, 87, 89, 92, 117, 126
Let's Talk about Your Wall, 111
Literary canon, xii, xviii, 131, 135
Literary corpus, ix, xi, xii
Literary evolution, 111
Llanto novelas imposibles/Crying, Impossible Novels, xv, 19, 20, 30, 31, 39, 40, 44, 45, 46, 48,

49, 50, 51, 52, 53, 55, 57, 58, 59, 60, 61, 96
Lorde, Audre, xvii, 95, 97, 104, 105, 107
Los totoles, 67, 71, 72

M

Masturbation, 95
Maternal figure, 90
Matto de Turner, Clorinda, 131, 141
Memory, vii, xii, xvi, 13, 14, 15, 25, 44, 48, 50, 51, 56, 59, 60, 61, 83, 86, 88, 90, 92, 93, 103, 111, 139
Méndez de Cuenca, Laura, 139, 140
Mexican, ix, x, xvi, xvii, 3, 5, 10, 12, 19, 21, 22, 23, 27, 35, 36, 37, 42, 50, 51, 54, 56, 59, 66, 67, 68, 69, 71, 76, 77, 80, 83, 84, 85, 86, 87, 89, 90, 91, 92, 95, 97, 108, 112, 123, 129, 134, 137, 139, 141, 143
Mexico, ix, xi, xiii, xvi, 1, 3, 11, 20, 21, 22, 23, 25, 31, 32, 35, 36, 37, 45, 48, 50, 51, 53, 67, 76, 83, 84, 85, 86, 87, 89, 90, 91, 92, 97, 98, 108, 112, 128, 129, 131, 137, 142
Mignolo, Walter, xiv, xv, 1, 2, 4, 5, 9, 16, 39, 40, 41, 42, 43, 45, 59, 60, 62, 63, 97
Millet, Kate, xvii, 95, 97, 99, 101
Moctezuma, xv, 30, 31, 32, 39, 44, 45, 46, 47, 48, 49, 50, 51, 52, 53, 54, 55, 56, 57, 58, 59, 60, 61, 62
Motecuzoma, 45
Mohssine, Assia, vii, xii, xv, 39, 97, 131, 135, 142
Moriscos, xiv, 1, 2, 3, 4, 6, 9, 16
Motherhood, ix, 65, 67, 74, 79
Myth, 82, 95
Mythical causality, 87

Milton Keynes UK
Ingram Content Group UK Ltd.
UKHW021925201124
451474UK00013B/944

9 798881 901486